PENGUIN BOOKS

THE HIROSHIMA MAIDENS

Rodney Barker has been an editor, an investigative reporter, and a feature writer for a wide variety of regional and national magazines. In 1979 he was one of three American journalists awarded travel grants to Japan to write about Hiroshima; his resulting reportage, which was published in the *Denver Post*, reawakened his involvement with the Hiroshima Maidens, two of whom had stayed with his family when he was a child.

THE HIROSHIMA MAIDENS

A Story of Courage,
Compassion, and Survival

Rodney Barker

PENGUIN BOOKS

PENGUIN BOOKS

Viking Penguin Inc., 40 West 23rd Street,
New York, New York 10010, U.S.A.
Penguin Books Ltd, Harmondsworth,
Middlesex, England
Penguin Books Australia Ltd, Ringwood,
Victoria, Australia
Penguin Books Canada Limited, 2801 John Street,
Markham, Ontario, Canada L3R 1B4
Penguin Books (N.Z.) Ltd, 182–190 Wairau Road,
Auckland 10, New Zealand

First published in the United States of America
by Viking Penguin Inc. 1985
Published in Penguin Books 1986

The author is grateful to Ralph Edwards for
permission to draw on material contained in
"This Is Your Life . . . Reverend Kiyoshi Tanimoto."

LIBRARY OF CONGRESS CATALOGING IN PUBLICATION DATA
Barker, Rodney.
Hiroshima maidens.
Bibliography: p.
1. Atomic bomb victims—Japan—Hiroshima-shi—Biography.
2. Hiroshima-shi (Japan)—Biography.
3. Hiroshima-shi (Japan)—History—Bombardment, 1945—
Personal narratives. 4. Atomic bomb—Physiological effect.
5. Atomic bomb victims—Medical care—United States.
I. Title.
D767.25.H6B37 1986   940.54'25   86-806
ISBN 0 14 00.8352 9

Printed in the United States of America by
R. R. Donnelley & Sons Company, Harrisonburg, Virginia
Set in Avanta

To

TADAKO EMORI · YOSHIE ENOKAWA

TAKAKO HARADA · YOSHIE HARADA

HIDEKO HIRATA · SUZUE HIYAMA

MISAKO KANNABE · TERUE KAWAMURA

KEIKO KAWASAKI · CHIEKO KIMURA

SAYOKO KOMATSU · MITSUKO KURAMOTO

TOYOKO MORITA · TOMOKO NAKABAYASHI

SHIGEKO NIIMOTO · MICHIKO SAKO

TAZUKO SHIBATA · HIDEKO SUMIMURA

EMIKO TAKEMOTO · HIROKO TASAKA

MASAKO WADA · ATSUKO YAMAMOTO

MICHIKO YAMAOKA · MOTOKO YAMASHITA

MICHIYO ZOMEN

FOREWORD

In 1955, ten years after World War II, a group of twenty-five young Japanese women crippled and disfigured in the atomic bombing of Hiroshima were brought to America for reconstructive surgery. The operations were performed at Mount Sinai Hospital in New York City, and Quaker families in the surrounding area provided home care, which is how two of the "Hiroshima Maidens," as they were called by the press, came to stay with my family. I was nine years old at the time.

Looking back now, almost thirty years later, it is difficult to pinpoint the significance of that experience or say how it affected me. I suppose I was too young for the feelings of awe or terror that one might expect. Our two visitors lived with us in an intimate everyday way; they seem more like a fact of my early life than a formative event. And there were competing first impressions: I had never come into contact with Orientals before; I was the oldest of three boys, and one might say these were my first and only sisters.

My memories of the Hiroshima Maidens are the fare of

family life. Because they did not speak English, they seemed to
be more comfortable and natural around children than adults.
We engaged in activities with a shared spirit of innocence and
wonder that made them easy to be with. It's true they could be
terribly unsure of themselves, but often that shyness would lead
to a new experience. They liked to swim, for instance, but were
too self-conscious to appear on a public beach in bathing suits, so
on warm summer evenings when my father came home from
work, he would drive us all to a private cove where we would wade
into Long Island Sound under cover of night.

My contact with the Maidens taught me something valuable
and lasting. They were people who in their own quiet way continued to be a lasting part of my consciousness. At an impression-
able age I learned that war leaves a legacy of human suffering that
does not end with peace. From then on I understood that at any
given moment the world I knew could come to an end. To have
learned that at an early age is no small thing, although I am not
sure how much more differently inclined it made me than others
who grew up in the fifties.

Twenty-five years passed before the memory of the Maidens
came around in such a way that I thought of it as a subject to be
written about. At the time I was a free-lance journalist writing for
a number of magazines, so the idea of doing a follow-up on the
Hiroshima Maidens was framed as an article in my mind. But
when my research revealed that there had been no books written
about them in either English or Japanese, and that the several
magazine attempts at updates were superficial and incomplete, it
struck me that here was an unwritten story not only of great
personal interest but timely and important. In the process of
writing that story, I felt I would discover the meaning of the
experience.

Every writing assignment bristles with its own set of difficulties, and the complexities involved in researching this story were
daunting. While there was a considerable amount of press coverage of the Maidens during their stay in America, for all intents

and purposes they had dissolved as a group once they returned to Japan. No one knew what had happened to them individually, or, for that matter, how many of them were still alive.

Over the next few months I tracked down a dozen or so American families who had hosted the Maidens, and I visited them in their homes, probing their memories and leafing through scrapbooks retrieved from their attics. Next I located and interviewed the key figures involved in organizing the project that brought the Maidens to America, including the surgeons who performed their operations. Thanks to a grant from a foundation in Japan willing to pay my way over and back in exchange for a series of articles about my impressions of Hiroshima, I was able to depart for Japan in the summer of 1979.

The day I arrived in Hiroshima, I was made aware that the relationship between atomic bomb survivors and the press in that city had become an exceedingly difficult one. The news editor of a major daily newspaper met me at the train station; after escorting me to the newspaper's main office building and leading me through a ceremonious round of civilities with department heads, he casually suggested that we pay a visit to Suzue Hiyama, one of the Hiroshima Maidens who had stayed with my family. I had half-expected this to come up—it made a good reunion story— but not so abruptly nor in this manner. I replied that I preferred to wait; etiquette alone dictated that I should talk with Suzue first and clear such a meeting.

My hesitation seemed to take him by surprise. Surely, as a fellow journalist, I could see the value of an immediate visit, an experience captured live?

It was assumed, I think, that we would have roughly the same aggressive attitude toward news. And, as I later learned, the idea of a detailed follow-up story on the Hiroshima Maidens had tantalized and frustrated Japanese journalists for years; the women either could not be found or reached, or flatly refused to be interviewed. It took some doing to convince my editor friend that I intended to handle this my way, and I was deliberately vague about giving assurances I would keep him informed of my plans so he could arrange for his paper's sister broadcasting company to have a television crew standing by.

Later that evening, with the assistance of a young Japanese woman I met at an international boarding house, I telephoned Suzue Hiyama. She was expecting my call. Reporters had been phoning her for weeks. I apologized for the inconvenience my coming had caused her and assured her that when we got together I would be alone except for an interpreter. We arranged to meet the following evening.

On the phone she had said she lived in an apartment above her place of business, and when the taxi pulled up in front of a beauty parlor named after my home town in Connecticut and her home in the States—the Darien Beauty Shop—Suzue was waiting outside. She bowed, I nodded, and as she eyed me inquiringly, I appraised her. Her face still showed signs that it had something very much wrong with it; the flap of skin grafted to her left cheek was too smooth and had not wrinkled the way one would expect it to with age. But while that might have attracted the notice of a stranger seeing her for the first time, it corresponded with the mental picture that I had carried for twenty-five years. After all, scarred was the only way I had known her. She seemed more unsure of me, which was understandable enough considering the fact that she remembered an energetic, freckle-faced nine-year-old. Smiling down at her (she came barely up to my chest), I produced an old photograph taken the night she and her roommate dressed me up in a young girl's kimono. Her embarrassed little smile let me know I had passed the test.

We spent the next few hours catching up on the previous twenty-five years. I told her what had happened to my family, and she introduced me to hers. Her husband shook my hand and thanked me for the hospitality my parents had extended to his wife. Her two teenage daughters grinned sheepishly. Her grandchild burst into tears.

I had already decided that at some point in the evening I would bring up the matter of why I had come to Hiroshima. So when we seemed to run out of questions for each other and it was clear she was relaxed with me, I told her my primary reason for coming was to research a book about the Hiroshima Maidens. She looked down in apparent distress. She said she had cooperated with the making of a film about them several years earlier, as a way of showing people she was doing well, and she was not happy with the way the film had turned out.

Before coming to Hiroshima I had seen that film. It was titled *The Scars of Hiroshima.* Suzue had not granted an interview, but she had allowed herself to be filmed at work, styling a patron's hair. The camera angles and close-ups took every advantage of the irony of her work as a beautician to highlight the horror of her past: zooming in on fingers she was still unable to straighten or spread, filling the screen with the side of her face scarred most severely. I had wondered what it must be like seeing one's disfigurement displayed with such artless sentimentality. Apparently it had been mortifying.

The presumption behind my objective was beginning to cause me considerable discomfort. I had come in hopes of gaining access to the inner minds of the people around whom this story revolved. Now I saw that, if being a man and a foreigner trying to tap into the thoughts and feelings of women from a culture where expressions were almost always veiled and who had known great tragedy in their personal lives was not barrier enough, these were people already traumatized by hit-and-run journalists.

Speaking slowly so all the nuances were clearly communicated in the translation, I told her I was aware of the challenges involved in this undertaking but hoped that in the months ahead I would be able to convince her and the other Maidens that I was a person who would keep in mind a proper respect for their feelings and interests while writing about them.

Suzue's reaction, I could see, was ambivalent. Sensing this was not the time to press the matter, I chose to remark on the media interest my visit had generated. I said I wanted her to know that, apart from everything, my primary loyalty lay with the Maidens. I did not want my presence to hurt or embarrass them, and as far as I was concerned, all my conversations and interactions would be considered a private affair.

Although I had declared my intentions, I had done so in a way that did not require an immediate answer but left the matter open to future discussion. I felt at the time that if I were sensitive to her feelings and prepared to move slowly, then things would happen. And they did. I had been in Hiroshima less than a month when I received a phone call from Suzue checking in on me and inviting me to a dinner party that was being given in my behalf by the Maidens.

It was held at a tempura restaurant in a private room behind sliding paper doors. Only the Maidens and I were present. The tables were arranged in a rectangle, with a setting at the head table designated as mine. Suzue sat beside me, and to my right was a woman whose command of English was proficient enough for her to serve as interpreter. Looking around, I thought to myself that these women were more matronly than maidenly now, and that they could have passed for a group of club women were it not for certain facial peculiarities—uneven or slightly smeared features, all heavily covered with make-up—that marked each of them like members of some secret society.

The protocol was natural, forthright, friendly. Each woman introduced herself while I did my best to memorize each face and name. Then I presented them with letters and tape-recorded messages I had brought from friends in America. It was obvious that their ties to America were still strong, which created an opening for explaining my purpose in coming. Trying to be both precise and brief, I said that many of the people who had had the privilege of meeting them twenty-five years ago considered the Hiroshima Maidens the leading ladies in an epic of international goodwill that had been all but lost in history. I said I had come to Hiroshima in hopes of rescuing their story for those people and generations who had not known nor heard of them. How successfully this could be done depended on them, on whether they agreed theirs was an experience worth preserving and if they chose to cooperate with my research.

The ensuing discussion, conducted in Japanese, was surprisingly short, leading me to conclude that my proposal had already been talked about in depth and that this meeting was the occasion for announcing their decision. The Maiden who knew English raised her glass and proposed a toast. "To your success." My eyes went around the room to confirm that she was speaking for the group. Humbled, I murmured the Japanese words for thank you. Another toast followed—"No more Hiroshimas"—and we all drank to that. Then there was an awkward moment of silence that was joyfully relieved when a Maiden at the far end of the table sang out, "Merry Christmas. Happy New Year."

Torn though they were about having public attention beamed on their private lives, the Maidens felt a sense of indebtedness to those Americans who had taken them into their homes and hearts, and saw in me an opportunity to repay them.

ACKNOWLEDGMENTS

M uch of the material contained in this book was collected
under conditions impossible to repeat, not the least because some of the principals are no longer living. Dr. Arthur
Barsky is gone, as are Dr. Sidney Kahn and the Reverend Marvin
Green; I am honored that they allowed me to be the custodian
of their final thoughts on the Hiroshima Maidens Project.

Essential to this effort was the trust and cooperation of
Norman Cousins and Helen Yokoyama. As two people who
figured prominently in the story, they could have sought to align
my perspective of the overall events with their own. But both fully
recognized that truths are best perceived after looking at all sides,
and for permitting me to distill and order the varying and sometimes conflicting impressions and viewpoints in the way I saw fit,
they have my respect and appreciation.

The skill and sensitivity with which an interpreter is able to
convey a spirit of compassion while probing for details and insights is crucial to the success of an inquiry into a delicate and
difficult subject. For their fine work I wish to express my admira-

tion and gratitude to my talented interpreters Naoko Naganuma, Keiko Ogura, and Toru Kinoshita.

For their assistance in arranging interviews and providing resources that facilitated a broad understanding of Hiroshima and its legacy, I must also acknowledge the valuable help of the Hiroshima daily newspaper *Chugoku Shinbun* and of the Hiroshima International Cultural Foundation, and in particular its Secretary-General, Mr. Koichiro Kanai.

Thanks must go to Ned Jaros, for without his friendship and backing I would not have been able to devote myself full-time to the research and writing of this book; and I am especially indebted to Star York, whose assistance took many forms, and without whom this work would have been longer in the making and minus much of its aesthetic grace.

CONTENTS

Photographs appear following page 118.

THE HIROSHIMA MAIDENS

PRELUDE

THIS IS YOUR LIFE

~

In 1955, Ralph Edwards's *This Is Your Life* on NBC ranked among the Top Ten in the television popularity ratings, reaching an estimated forty million viewers weekly. Much of the appeal of the half-hour live Wednesday night program was due to its provocative format: Edwards went to unorthodox lengths to trick outstanding personalities onto his stage, where they were informed their life story was about to be recreated before a coast-to-coast television audience. Edwards acted as narrator and a supporting cast of friends, relatives, and surprise guests were secretly assembled backstage and brought on to highlight events from the "star's" past.

On May 11, 1955, the show began as usual. An offstage orchestra struck up the catchy symphonic theme song, and an announcer took the cue: *"This Is Your Life,* America's most talked about program, brought to you by America's most talked about cosmetics: Hazel Bishop long-lasting lipstick, Hazel Bishop long-lasting nail polish, Hazel Bishop long-lasting complexion cream. And now, Mister *This Is Your Life* himself, Ralph Edwards."

Seated on a divan, the avuncular emcee smiled broadly at the camera. "Good evening, ladies and gentlemen, and welcome to *This Is Your Life*. The ticking you hear in the background is a clock counting off the seconds to 8:15 a.m., August 6, 1945. And seated here with me is a gentleman whose life was changed by the last tick of that clock as it reached 8:15. Good evening, sir. Would you tell us your name?"

The camera pulled back to reveal a short, compact Japanese man in a baggy blue suit, seated beside Edwards.

"Kiyoshi Tanimoto," the man replied in accented English.

"And what is your occupation?"

"I am a minister."

"And where is your home?"

"Hiroshima, Japan."

"And where were you on August 6, 1945, at 8:15 in the morning?"

The answer was drowned out by a deafening ticking sound. The camera cut to an enormous clock with hands set at 8:15. A photograph of an atomic bomb explosion flashed on the screen, accompanied by a blast from kettledrums.

Edwards spoke in a sobering voice. "This is Hiroshima, and in that fateful second on August 6, 1945, a new concept of life and death was given its baptism. And tonight's principal subject, you, Reverend Tanimoto, were an unsuspecting part of that concept. Reverend Tanimoto, when did you arrive in this country?"

"Two days ago."

"And have you ever heard of *This Is Your Life*?"

"No. This is the first time."

The audience packing the studio tittered and the Reverend threw a confused glance their way, as if he had missed something. His puzzled expression seemed to shrink his diminutive stature a size smaller.

Edwards showed his foreign guest a large album with his name inscribed on the cover. "We have been working for weeks with your friends Norman Cousins, editor of the *Saturday Review*, John Hersey, author of the best-selling book *Hiroshima,* and many others to bring you to our stage tonight so we could retell the story of your life. The facts are between the covers of this book. You will meet many people who have helped shape your destiny, and we hope that at the end of this half-hour you will have had some pleasant moments." Turning to the camera, Edwards added, "And that you, ladies and gentlemen, will have a better understanding of what it is to look into the face of atomic power—to survive and die. Now we will pick up the threads of your life in a moment, Reverend Tanimoto, after this word from Bob Warren, our announcer, who has something very special to tell the girls in our audience. Bob?"

Over the next sixty seconds, a dapper male of the fifties guided a vivacious blonde through the Metal Scouring Pad Test. After Hazel Bishop long-lasting nail polish proved it could take a scrubbing that raked dirt and grime off a filthy frying pan without scratching or chipping, the show resumed.

While an overhead shot of the map of Japan, in shadow, gradually brightened in a rising-sun effect, Edwards read from the album. "The morning is perfectly clear and as the warm summer sun rises above the mountains which run around three sides of the city, it awakens a sprawling community of 245,000 people. The time is 6:00 a.m. What were you doing at 6:00 a.m., Reverend Tanimoto?"

Tanimoto answered that a friend was helping him move furniture from his church in the city center to the safety of the suburbs.

"So at six in the morning a member of your parish is lending you a helping hand, when suddenly—"

Midsentence an air-raid siren began to wail, like the one that had warned the people of Hiroshima early that August morning that enemy planes were approaching the city. But following the lead of Edwards's questions, the Japanese clergyman admitted that the siren did not send him running for cover. At this late stage of the war the Japanese people were accustomed to seeing American planes buzzing through the skies, he explained, and weather reconnaissance planes passed frequently in the morning.

"So, as might happen even today in any typical American community, the sound of an air-raid siren, even at six in the morning, is not taken too seriously?"

At that moment an offstage voice boomed through a loudspeaker. "At zero six hundred on the morning of August 6, 1945, I was in a B-29 flying over the Pacific. Destination, Hiroshima."

The camera switched to a full-figured silhouette of a man standing behind a curtain, then zoomed in to a close-up of Tanimoto glancing around for the source of the voice. The business of special effects was part of the way Edwards packaged a story, but it was obviously new to the Japanese minister.

"A voice of a man whose life is destined to be woven up in the threads of your own, Reverend Tanimoto. We'll meet him later on in your story. Right now, it's after eight. The all-clear has sounded and you and your friend have reached your destination. Tired from climbing the hill, you pause to rest for a moment in the garden of Mr. Satow's house. Looking out, you can see Hiroshima lying before you, the silvery threads of the seven river branches which divide the city into six islands, the commercial and residential districts, the docks to the south, and the Inland Sea. You could be looking at Buffalo, New York; Boston, Massachusetts; St. Louis, Missouri; but this is Hiroshima, Japan, and the morning is quiet and very peaceful."

At the instant the hands on the ticking clock reached 8:15, footage from an authentic United States military film showing the city of Hiroshima disappearing in a puff was broadcast over the air, and forty million atomic bombs exploded on forty million television sets across America. The orchestra erupted in musical pandemonium. The camera switched to a tight head shot of the Reverend Tanimoto. A newspaper report the next morning would describe the look on his face: "Rarely have you ever seen such pain in a man's eyes."

The orchestra segued to a broad Japanese mood-theme as Edwards said, "The time has come—that split-second of eternity which comes in one way or another to every man in his lifetime. Will you tell us what you saw in your second, Reverend Tanimoto?"

In his own words Tanimoto told about a tremendous flash of light that traveled from east to west like a sheet of sun. Instinctively, he threw himself between two big rocks in the garden, certain that his friend's house had received a direct hit from a bomb.

Edwards stopped him at this point, leaving him tucked between two boulders, covered with bits of board and tile. "Lying there, your mind must have lived through a lifetime," he said, rolling the action back to present the Reverend's conversion to Christianity.

It was orchestrated to appear like memories passing before the mind's eye. To the musical accompaniment of a harp, a frail elderly lady, Miss Bertha Sparkey, the Methodist missionary who had been responsible for introducing the young Kiyoshi Tanimoto to Christianity, hobbled through the *This Is Your Life* Archway to relate the details of the tragic family break-up that occurred when he crossed faiths with his stern Buddhist father. A violent argument erupted that so upset his mother she suffered a fatal stroke. Kneeling beside her body, he vowed to carry his Christian faith throughout his life as a blessing on her death. The story moved to the United States with the introduction of a portly pastor of a New Jersey Methodist church who was a former classmate of Kiyoshi Tanimoto's at the Candler School of Theology at Emory University in Atlanta, Georgia, which Tanimoto attended on an international scholarship from the Methodist Mission Board. With folksy humor, the Reverend Marvin Green reminisced about the American education his Japanese friend received *outside* the classroom. "One of the boys told Tani that the phrase 'bats in your belfry' was a term of affection when speaking to lovely young ladies, so at the first opportunity he said just that to a coed and almost created an international incident." In 1940, Kiyoshi Tanimoto was ordained a Methodist minister and took a temporary ministry at a church for Japanese-

Americans in Hollywood, California. "Not far from where we are sitting right now," Edwards commented, and directed Tanimoto's attention to the studio audience where a group of his former congregation at the Hollywood Independent Church sat waving from seats in the front row.

Now Edwards switched time forward to December 7, 1941, Pearl Harbor Day, and found the Reverend serving as a minister on the island of Okinawa; to the pulpit of the Nagarekawa Methodist Church in Hiroshima, where he was transferred in 1943 as part of a general retreat from advancing Allied Forces; and at last back to "where we started your story, on August 6, 1945."

"Time is standing still as our earth shakes to an explosion never before equaled. In a daze, you pull yourself from your position between the two garden rocks. From your vantage point you again look out over the city. What did you see?"

A moment before, there had been nothing to distinguish Hiroshima from other cities of the world. An instant later, it seemed to blow apart from the center. Now Tanimoto had to force himself to look. He had not even heard a big bang, but something had struck from the sky. Smoke and flames were drawing the entire city into a monstrous black cloud that surged upward thousands of feet.

"Did you know Hiroshima had been the first city to feel the force of atomic power?" Edwards asked.

"I didn't know what happened," Tanimoto replied. What he did know was that he belonged with his wife and baby, his home, his church and parishoners, and all were down below. Calling on God to help him, he started running—the only person making his way *into* the city.

Back came the voice of the mystery guest who had spoken earlier: "And looking down from thousands of feet over Hiroshima, all I could think of was, 'My God, what have we done.'"

"The voice again of a man whose second of eternity was woven up with yours, Reverend Tanimoto. Now you have never met him, but he's here tonight to clasp your hand in friendship. Ladies and gentlemen, Captain Robert Lewis, United States Air

Force, who along with Paul Tibbetts piloted the plane from which the first atomic bomb was dropped on Hiroshima."

A tall, heavy-set man walked stiffly onto the stage and stood beside the Japanese clergyman. After an awkward hesitation, they shook hands. Edwards asked Lewis to move a step closer and tell about *his* experience on August 6, 1945. In a trembling voice, Lewis said he had taken off from the island of Tinian at 2:00 a.m. that morning, flying a B-29. He said there were three prospective targets: Hiroshima, Konkura, and Nagasaki. About an hour before they reached the coastline of Japan they were notified that the weather was clear in Hiroshima. "Therefore, Hiroshima was our target."

For a long, strange moment Lewis faltered. He closed his eyes and rubbed his forehead, more as if he were fighting back tears than as if he were trying to recall his lines. But a deep breath steadied him and he continued. "At 8:15 promptly the bomb was dropped. We turned to get out of the way. Shortly after, we turned back to see what happened . . . and in front of our eyes the city of Hiroshima had disappeared."

Tanimoto remained silent and very still, listening closely to the flyer, nodding his head from time to time. But nothing in his face showed a reaction, and when Lewis had finished he did not respond.

"Did you write something in your log at that time?" Edwards prompted.

"I wrote down the words, 'My God, what have we done.' "

"And so, Reverend Tanimoto, you on the ground, and you on your military mission, Captain Lewis, in the air, both appeal to a power greater than your own. Almost at the same moment you both utter the same words: *My God.* Thank you, Robert Lewis, now personnel manager at Henry Heide Incorporated (candymakers) in New York City."

As he walked to his place at one side of the stage, Lewis received a big hand from the audience. Edwards turned the page and read aloud. "In that split-second when one atom bomb exploded, one hundred thousand people were either killed or destined to die. One hundred thousand more were hurt. Were you hurt, Reverend Tanimoto?"

The Reverend said he was not, and confessed that indeed he was ashamed he was unhurt. As he ran into the city he apologized to the endless lines of gravely wounded people streaming out of the city.

When Edwards came to the part where Tanimoto doubted whether his wife could possibly have survived, he staged the entrance of Mrs. Tanimoto, flown all the way from Hiroshima just for this occasion, to coincide with the miraculous discovery that she had lived through the blast. With their wailing baby in her arms, she was wandering through the streets in a daze when she met her husband coming for her; and you could tell by the way his eyes rounded suddenly when his wife materialized in the *This Is Your Life* Archway that his surprise now was almost as great as it had been then. Costumed in a striped kimono, her features similar enough to her husband's to pass as his sister, Chisa Tanimoto pattered to his side, grinning shyly, her head slightly bowed. Edwards smiled over the reunited couple while the audience clapped.

Assured that his family was safe, Tanimoto began making himself useful to those not so fortunate. He brought water to the thirsty unable to move. He ferried wounded people across a river to safety. He read verses from a Japanese Bible over those he could do nothing else for.

"It's a week before news begins to leak out from official Japanese headquarters that the city had been destroyed by the energy released by the splitting of an atom. . . . Then Nagasaki feels the terror of the second bomb . . . and on August 15 the Emperor of Japan broadcasts to the nation that the war is over . . . and out of the carnage that was Hiroshima at 8:15 a.m. on August 6, 1945, the Japanese people have built a new city. . . . But ten years later all is not forgotten. There are still very visible reminders of what atomic power can do."

"Visible reminders" was Marvin Green's cue to step forward

and speak in behalf of the Reverend Tanimoto's crusading spirit to rebuild, physically and spiritually, the lives of suffering survivors of the blast. "He came to this country in 1951 and told me that he wanted to find some help for many of the young girls in Hiroshima who had survived the atomic bombing, but who had been so badly disfigured that they had withdrawn completely from society. He told me that they desperately needed plastic surgery, and could I help him find the wherewithal to bring them to the United States so that the work could be done here."

Edwards took over. "Ladies and gentlemen, on Monday, May 8, twenty-five girls from Hiroshima arrived in New York City via U.S. Army transport. They are being treated surgically at Mount Sinai Hospital at absolutely no cost. Tonight we would like you to meet two of these girls. Both have lived through the terror of an atomic bombing. Both are badly disfigured." He pointed to a glass door at one side of the stage and his voice lowered. "To avoid causing them any embarrassment, we will not show you their faces. May I present Miss Toyoko Minowa and Miss Tadako Emori."

The silhouettes of two women standing on either side of a floor microphone was all that could be seen. First one girl spoke in Japanese, then the other. Marvin Green translated: They were happy to be in America and thanked everyone for what the United States was doing for them. The camera lingered on their images, in some way more frightfully expressive than a detailed focus, suggesting visages so awful that the audience had to be spared.

Almost for relief, Edwards brought on the kids. Tanimoto's brood of four young children came bouncing onto the stage and started climbing their father like a backyard tree.

The orchestra floated a Well-That's-the-Story-Folks tune over a Ralph Edwards benediction. "This is your life, Kiyoshi Tanimoto, a man of God who looked into the face of eternity in that awful moment when the world stood still, and who is now courageously building a monument to peace out of the ashes that

11

were Hiroshima. Hold on, Reverend Tanimoto, and we will look into your future, which you, ladies and gentlemen, can share. But first, here is Bob Warren again."

This time, Warren supported a spiel about Hazel Bishop nail polish with testimony from a Missouri housewife who said she had been amazed that after hours at the sink washing dishes, her fingernails came out looking the same as when they went in.

It had been a memorable evening for the Japanese clergyman, and in order that he might be able to relive it again and again, Edwards announced that Hazel Bishop was giving him a 16-mm print of the show and a Bell & Howell projector to view it on back in Japan. For Mrs. Tanimoto they had a 14-carat gold charm bracelet specially designed by a New York jeweler to commemorate the happy moments in her life.

"Reverend Tanimoto, we know how you have worked hard to make it possible for these twenty-five girls to come to the United States for medical aid. We know too there are many people in Hiroshima and Nagasaki who were children in 1945 who have reached maturity now and will never know a happy life without immediate medical and surgical help. Now we're sure that there are many among our viewers tonight who want to share in your dedicated life." Edwards turned to look the camera square in the eye. "And you can do so by sending your contribution, right now, large or small, to: Maidens, Box 200, New York 1, New York. You will be making it possible for a team of American and Japanese doctors to work together and provide necessary treatment."

So there, on prime-time national television, Edwards passed the plate, asking the American people to give to the cause of the Hiroshima Maidens. And first in line, Robert Lewis walked forward, handing Edwards a $50 check that he said represented his and his fellow crew members' contribution to the fund. Edwards thanked him, added that two $500 checks would be forthcoming from the show's sponsors, Hazel Bishop and Prell Shampoo, and urged the audience to be just as generous, "for this is the American way."

HIROSHIMA

1

At the mouth of the River Ota, where the muddy currents meet the lapping tides of the Inland Sea, a delta of four grassy islands gradually formed, fanning into a shallow bay like ribs on the back of a shell. With a range of pine-green mountains sloping up sharp as fins to the north and the sea merging with the sky to the south as if there were no horizon, it was a scenic spot —but people came to live there for the richness of the soil and the catches of the sea. In the sixteenth century, a medieval feudal lord consolidated the original settlements that sprang up on the riverbanks when he constructed a baroque, five-storied castle that jutted over the thatched roofs like the ornament on an ancient helmet, and crowned Hiroshima, meaning "broad island," the capital of his domain.

Over the next three hundred years this new castle town grew into a bustling coastal community. It was controlled by different family clans according to the rise and fall of various shoguns, but overall its history was remarkably free of military disturbances, characterized more by the development of rich cultural traditions.

Its direction as a city was determined in the late nineteenth century by two major construction projects. An area of shoals that hindered navigation was filled in to create a harbor that would accommodate shipping, and at about the same time, a national railway line linking Kyoto to Kyushu and passing through Hiroshima was completed. As a land-and-water gateway, Hiroshima was poised to become an important commercial center; but with the outbreak of the Sino-Japanese War of 1894, followed by the Russo-Japanese War of 1904, Hiroshima was pressed into service as the staging area for troops embarking for the mainland front. After that it became a military city, growing more prosperous and populous as wars and "incidents" occurred.

Then came the Pacific War, a land grab by Japanese military forces to expand the boundaries of the Japanese Empire, which left sun-flags rising over the Philippine Islands, the China coast, and much of Southeast Asia. When a series of combined Allied operations pushed the South Pacific front back to the point where the home islands lay within the flying range of U.S. bombers, American military planners, who had devised a special prescription for the destruction of Japan's tinderbox cities (incendiary bombs made up of magnesium and jellied gasoline), ordered the systematic firebombing of major urban areas, one after the other.

In Hiroshima, official concern was mounting because there were numerous military installations and strategic industries within the city limits, because some 50,000 servicemen had swelled the local population to over 400,000, and because a high percentage of the houses that sprawled eave-to-eave across the delta were made of wood. Anticipating an eventual incendiary attack, civil defense planners began the evacuation of schoolchildren in the grammar grades, and decided to crisscross the city with firebreaks that would allow them to contain a conflagration. Making use of the six tributaries of the River Ota that divided the city from north to south, they planned to raze houses and widen streets into fire lanes that would bisect the city from east to west. As everyone was called upon to do his and her part, all junior and senior high school students were required to alternate their educa-

tional activities with national service, which in the summer of 1945 consisted primarily of assisting demolition crews on the house-clearing program.

Although there was a sense of foreboding in the air, domestic news broadcasts never once reported a defeat or retreat, and most Japanese people were steadfast in their belief that continued efforts and sacrifices would lead ultimately to victory. When American planes dropped leaflets urging them to give up the fight, the warnings were dismissed as agitprop by the enemy. Even when it appeared that American forces would soon invade the islands of Japan proper, civilians, responding to the exhortation that this was an all-out war of survival involving the life of the nation, allowed themselves to be mobilized into a home guard that was armed with bamboo spears because there were not enough guns to go around.

It is true that such against-all-odds patriotism drew heavily on a history of loyalty to one's lord and country that dated back centuries, but there were circumstances peculiar to Hiroshima which made the acceptance of seemingly hopeless conditions almost second nature. Some three hundred years earlier a shrewd feudal ruler had encouraged the expansion of a conservative Buddhist sect whose doctrine held that one's fate was entirely bound by karma and that security in this life and salvation in the next were attainable only by frequent and repeated prayer. To peasants who had little time or energy to practice an exacting and complicated religion, this quick and simple solution to life's problems had a tremendous appeal. Likewise, it was useful to a feudal lord concerned with keeping his vassals content with their miserable lot in life; they would tolerate hardships, accept bad rulers, and endure calamities with a bow and a smile.

Hiroshima kept its affiliation with this Buddhist sect, and in due course the creed that one should leave everything to Buddha and never force things because mortals did not have the power to change or arrange fate to suit their desires found its epitome in that community. Eventually a local religious order evolved whose influence was so pervasive it created a regional temperament. The people of Hiroshima tended to be provincial, docile, and mystically fatalistic.

The introduction of this philosophy to Hiroshima was one of those historical machinations that shape the development of a whole population. And, during the late stages of the war, the kind of brave front expected by the military authorities (referred to officially as Supreme Understanding) was, in many ways, just a euphemism for an attitude that had been handed down from Hiroshima's past. No one actually believed B-29s could be stopped with bamboo spears. But with spears raised in battle readiness, the people of Hiroshima were willing to stand up to the enemy. It was with resignation rather than a fighting spirit that they assumed their positions, however; for in the belief that everything that happens is directed from the outside, they were putting themselves in the hands of a higher power. They were waiting for something beyond their personal comprehension to happen when, in the first light of August 6, 1945, it did.

The sky was blue that Monday morning, but as Hiroko Tasaka dashed out the door of her grandparents' home in the suburban outskirts of Hiroshima, she could feel the humidity like a fever. She rode the streetcar partway into the city, getting off where the line continued into the commercial center and walking along a river road toward the bay. It was early, but already the streets were teeming with soldiers, laborers, students. Although the rainy season was over, the umbrellas which sprouted with the daily downpours were still in bloom as women took shelter from the summer heat by carrying the shade over their shoulders.

This was the first day the students from the all-girls Hiroshima Commercial High School had been summoned to assist demolition crews with the house-clearing program. Until this time their national service activities had consisted of helping farmers harvest rice and packing cigarettes into cartons, but today they were to clear the debris of dismantled houses, moving stones to one spot along the street, boards to another, where they would be picked up later and carted to a dump site somewhere outside the city. Donning a white hiking cap to shade her face and white gloves to protect her hands, Hiroko began the day's work.

Perhaps fifteen minutes passed and she was struggling with a rock from the house foundation when a classmate beside her called out, "Hiroko, look. B-chan." In those days that was how they referred to B-29s, as though they were little pets.

Hiroko stopped working and looked up. She thought it made a lovely sight, gleaming in the sunlight and chalking a white contrail across the blue sky. Just thirteen, she was too young to imagine a bomb bay opening or realize that tragedy could seek her out.

"Where?" another girl asked. "I can't see it."

Hiroko raised her arm and pointed, and at that very instant the air seemed to catch fire. There was a searing white dazzle that pricked hotly and she had time only to think she had been shot before she blacked out.

When her senses returned, she was lying on her back in the middle of an unfamiliar darkness. Not a single star shone and no light could be seen. She rose shakily to her feet. Nothing she could remember explained where she was, and it was impossible to see more than a few feet in any direction, but she sensed some danger threatened her there and with one hand held out in front, she groped forward through the nocturnal haze. A gust of smoke stung her eyes and she spun around. When she started to walk again she was unable to tell if she was heading left, right, or in a circle, and she was close to panic when the strangest thing happened. There was a sudden change of wind and before her eyes the swirling vapors spiraled into a human shape. Like the dancing devil of a sandstorm, a saintly old man appeared, his long beard and loose robes flowing, and his crooked finger urgently pointed the direction she should go. In a moment of fear her mind pressed the vision aside as a trick her eyes were playing on her, and before she knew it the figure vanished, dissolved, became the smoke itself. But alone again and absolutely lost, she had no idea which way to go so she started to run the way she had been shown.

In just a few steps she thought she could see more clearly, and a short distance further she broke out into the daylight. In front of her the Kyobashi River shimmered, and without hesitating she slid down the embankment and plunged into the cool current.

It was ebb tide, so the water in the channel was low and flowing swiftly toward the sea. Keeping to the shallow parts, Hiroko looked around and saw that scores of other people had sought shelter in the river. The tattered remains of their uniforms identified practically all of them as schoolmates, but it was impossible to distinguish individuals because every face was swollen to a piteous likeness. That led her to examine herself and she was startled to discover that her half-sleeved blouse was scorched and, even though she felt no pain, the skin on her bare arms had split open, exposing the pink tissue underneath.

No one knew what had happened. After an excited exchange, however, it was decided a bomb must have exploded directly on the work site. Just then a woman whose hair was singed, wearing rags that smoked as if they were about to burst into flames, rushed up to the riverbank crying, "The city is no longer safe. We must try to get back to school." With a choking sensation, Hiroko realized the command came from the teacher who had taken the morning roll call.

As a group they scrambled out of the water, trotted across Hijiyama Bridge, and proceeded down the road that wound around the base of Hijiyama, the only rising land formation to break Hiroshima's uniformly flat terrain. On both sides the houses that were not ablaze were leaning at an angle away from the city center, making it difficult to believe only one bomb could have caused so much damage and causing her to wonder how many had been dropped. When the path ahead was obstructed by flames and further progress was impossible, the group abandoned the pavement and charged the slopes of Hijiyama that rose into a low cloud of ash like an island surrounded by fog. There was no path to follow and the scrub oak bushes dotting the hillside were igniting with a whoosh, so everyone went in different directions. In her quest for the safety of higher ground, Hiroko took a route that went straight up, though more than once the loose rock underfoot gave way, carrying her backward on a clattering landslide.

It took her almost an hour before she reached a clearing near the summit where she paused to catch her breath and look back. Though the view was obscured by dense clouds of smoke, she was able to make out a few scattered concrete buildings standing like tombstones in a vast fireswept cemetery. It was an appalling sight, but she was too weak to feel anything but her own exhaustion. In a daze she sat down on a rock and watched others come up from below. As she saw that every single face was puffy and blood-smeared, her hand went automatically to her own face and she wondered if hers might be the same. It was getting hard for her to keep her eyes open. In front of her a woman was working her way up an outcropping, and when she made it over the top Hiroko called to her, "Excuse me, but would you tell me what my face looks like?"

With hardly a glance the woman responded, "We all look the same," and passed on.

As she picked her way carefully down the far side, tears streamed down Hiroko's fattening cheeks. Until now she had thought everyone was more badly hurt than she.

A military medic was daubing oil on wounded civilians in a first-aid tent at the corner of her schoolgrounds, so she took her place in line; but before she could be treated the roar of enemy aircraft overhead sent everyone rushing frantically for the nearest air-raid shelter. Limping on blistered bare feet, Hiroko was unable to keep up and chose to take her chances under a small umbrella-shaped tree where she hoped she would not be seen. Apparently it was a reconnaissance and not a bombing mission because, after making several passes, the planes flew off; but it was some minutes before people ventured tentatively back onto the street.

Hiroko would have been content to stay where she was in the shade if she had not heard an authoritative voice call all who could still walk to proceed to the station where a rescue train was due. She was rapidly losing her vision and knew soon she would be blinded by the swelling. As it was, she found the depot by clutching the clothes of those walking in front of her.

As the hours passed, direct exposure to the sun turned up the heat of her burns, and just when Hiroko was beginning to give up hope that the trains were still running, someone shouted, "Here it comes." As no one wanted to be left behind, people swarmed over the engine and climbed through the windows before the wheels rolled to a stop. Hiroko tried to stand up, but to her mortification her legs gave out each time and she was unable to crawl the last part of the way across the platform before the train pulled slowly away.

Through swollen slits she watched the afternoon sun sink into a plume of purple smoke rising over Hiroshima, passing through the different discolorations of a deep bruise. As the darkness fell over her, she resigned herself to the fact that her fate was out of her hands; she had done everything she could to stay alive.

How long she lay like that she does not remember. Twice she was moved. Once she felt herself swooped up off the platform and carried to another place. Later a soldier picked her up, walked with her in his arms, and delivered her to an elementary school that was being used as an emergency medical center. For the next three days she lay on a thin straw mat on the floor of a classroom in limbo between life and death. Mercifully, she was conscious only at intervals, and delirious much of the rest of the time. All around her the badly wounded moaned and ranted for water, water, water, and even though she tried to stay calm and bear her pain in stoic silence, soon her own thirst became unbearable and she joined the anthem of agony. The only relief came from the orderlies who made the rounds with a dipper of cool water, but because it was widely believed that fluids were dangerous to burn patients, they were sparing in their servings. Hiroko, in fact, drank even less because she was unable to part her lips, and most of the water ladled out dribbled over her chin. Evidently one of the water bearers felt a particular sympathy for her because he returned later with a steamed rice ball and stayed to wave the flies away while she ate. She thought maybe he had a daughter her age because the next time he came he sang to her the way her father used to when he wanted to raise her spirits.

Late on the afternoon of the third day she dreamed she heard a voice call her name. It was so distinct it woke her up, but when she listened for it again all she heard was the relentless moaning. Over the previous days many people had come to the classroom and called out the names of the people they were looking for, so on the chance she had not been dreaming she uttered a feeble, "Yes."

Footsteps came from the other side of the room, stopping beside her. "Hiroko?" a young man's voice said.

Her lids fluttered but would not open. With great effort she pried them apart with her fingers and peered up into the boyish face of her cousin, a sailor home on leave from the navy. While, under the circumstances, her reaction might have been much different, at that moment she had only one thought: She craved a taste of fruit and the first words to leave her mouth were a request for a tin of mandarin oranges. She asked so casually, as if there was nothing out of the ordinary about her circumstances, that her cousin laughed out loud. For a brief moment the moaning stopped. When it resumed, he lowered his voice and told her to hold on, he would be back soon with help.

Shigeko Niimoto was bent over trying to untie the air-raid hood she had left on after an earlier alarm when she heard her Middle School classmate say, "Look, Niimoto-san. Something's dropped from that plane." She stopped what she was doing and tilted her head back. Using her hands as a visor to shade the sun, she looked up just in time to witness an explosion of light, white and blinding. Screaming, she covered her face with both hands and dropped to her knees. The last thing she remembered was a violent blast of wind slamming her sideways.

She returned to this world slowly. Her mind was fuzzy and everything around her blurred. As she got to her feet she peered into a thick, shifting mist through which she saw flickering fires and forms beginning to detach themselves. She was unable to make out anything distinctly until the floating mists parted to reveal a frightening procession of figures that looked to her like cadavers making an exodus from their graves. They moved slowly, almost dreamily, without making a sound. They held their hands out in front of their chests like sleepwalkers. At first she thought they were wrapped in wisps of smoke, but as her vision increased she saw it was their skin peeling from their bodies. She drew a deep breath, holding it in. Something terrible had gone wrong and she wanted no part of it.

"Niimoto-san. Niimoto-san."

At the sound of her name being called, she turned. One of the nightmarish figures was moving toward her. Instinctively she recoiled. "Who are you?"

"Araki. Sachiko Araki."

To Shigeko's astonishment, it was her best friend. "Oh, Sachiko, what happened?"

Having seen the way she was looked at, her friend asked, "Do I look that bad?"

"No," Shigeko lied, "it's just slight." Then, noticing how Araki-san's eyes were fixed on her, she asked, "How about me?"

"Just slight too."

Without any discussion of what might have happened, Shigeko found herself pulled by the arm to a street not far away where her friend's mother was trapped under the wreckage of their completely collapsed home. The roof had come down on top of the woman and only her head stuck out. Shigeko stood dumbfounded for a moment, wondering what she was supposed to do, before joining Araki-san, who was frantically pushing splintered timbers and shattered tiles aside.

But there was a mound of debris to move and not much time. The house next door had erupted in fire and the heat grew more intense by the minute. Araki-san's mother was the first to admit it was useless. "There's nothing that can be done for mother, dear," she said in a surprisingly calm voice. "Go and find father."

When Araki-san sobbed she could not bear to desert her mother, they would die together, she was ordered away. "Do as I say. Hurry. Right now."

As they backed away the house became a raging funeral pyre. "Good-bye," her friend cried. "Good-bye, mother." The last they saw of Araki-san's mother her face floated in flames but she was still smiling.

Shigeko wanted only to find her way home, but huge billows of smoke were rising in that direction so she ran after the eerily silent procession that streamed the other way. She was no longer afraid of them or concerned about where they were going now that she knew what they were escaping from; all she could think of was following the person walking in front of her. As for the people rolling on the roadside and voices calling for help from under crushed buildings, it wrenched her heart to pass by without offering any assistance, and when a woman ahead of her stumbled and fell she automatically stopped to help her up. From behind someone bumped into her, knocking her to the ground also, and to the great surge of people who kept coming she shouted, "Wait. Please wait," as she realized they were both in danger of being trampled. It was all she could manage to get back on her feet, and as she plodded onward she resolved that from then on she would think only of her own safety.

Before long she came to a place in the road that was blocked with fallen telephone poles and tangled wires. Some people were attempting to pick their way around the obstacles, and some were trying to turn back. Shigeko followed the lead of those who detoured to the Motoyasu River, where she waded in until she was submerged up to her shoulders. Thinking she was safe for the time being, she luxuriated in the wet relief from the heat; but suddenly there was screaming and splashing behind her. When she looked all she saw were hands thrusting out of the water. It took only a second to figure out what was happening; there were so many people seeking refuge in the river that those who stood in the shallows were being driven deeper until they could no longer touch bottom. Clawing back toward shore, Shigeko ran for her life along the river's edge.

Of the hours that followed she remembers very little. Her movements were automatic, her eyes half-closed, and everything there was to see was beyond her brain's understanding. Her only thought now was to get back to her school, which she knew had been designated as a medical center in times of emergency. She dimly recalls staggering into a schoolyard where she fainted in the grass.

When she regained consciousness, she was lying in an auditorium. She tried to rise and fell weakly back. An insane thirst intensified the pain of her injuries, and quietly she wept, dreaming of a black mountain and a big white waterfall, falling, falling, so close and cool . . . but she could not reach it though it made a noise like thunder in her ears.

In the morning she doubted she would live until sunset, and that evening she was sure she would die before dawn. Every so often someone searching among the wounded would pass by, and although it was agonizing, she would raise her body slightly, whisper her name and address, and beg them to contact her parents. Once she heard someone say, "That poor child is going to die," and from then on she tried her best to stay awake, afraid if she let herself doze off it would be her last sleep.

On the evening of the fourth day after the bombing of Hiroshima, she heard her mother's voice in the distance calling her name, and a joyous cry rose in her throat, "Here I am, mother." But the hoarse sounds that came out were barely audible over the dirge of sighs and whimpers that had become a constant background noise, and a dreadfully suspenseful minute passed before her mother's voice came again, this time just above her.

"Shigeko?" There was a pause, and then in an altered tone

of voice, as if her mother couldn't tell for sure or was reluctant to have it confirmed, she asked, "Is your name Shigeko?"

Blubbering yes, yes, Shigeko's relief was so vast that a second after she felt herself cradled in her mother's arms, she was asleep.

When student workers around her began chattering about an airplane, Toyoko Morita looked up; the next thing she knew she was waking up on the ground and it was utterly quiet, as though she had fallen asleep in a forest. She had no idea how much time had elapsed, and at first the only indication that something eventful had happened was that a cloudless summer sky had turned into an overcast day. But when she moved to stand up, with a start she discovered her clothes were torn and she was naked from the waist up. And when modesty caused her to look quickly about, she saw that all the houses around were leveled as though the demolition crews had completed their work while she slept, and not a single member of the student work force remained—she was alone.

She did not know what to make of it, but as she stood staring at the disarray in disbelief, a faint and faraway fluting sound reached her, and she found herself drawn toward it. Block after block she walked through what seemed like a dream—no street-cars were running, stores were empty, there was no one on the streets. It was as if she had the whole city to herself. Then, turning a corner, she saw a crowd of people in the distance and it quick-ened her step; but as she drew closer she slowed to a stop. A parade of men, women, and children dressed in rags and visibly injured filled the street. They were wailing in chorus as they trudged along. It was a quivering mongrel of a cry that crossed a moan with a whine, and because it could have been the protest of people marching toward their doom rather than away from it, she wanted to ask where they all were going. But in their mass movement was the presumption everyone knew more than she did, and lacking an argument to go a different way, Toyoko fell into step.

The rest of that day is lost for her. Only now and then some incident stood out clearly: She recalls taking pity on a woman walking beside her who was struggling under the weight of a newborn baby and offering to carry it for her, only to find her own physical strength completely drained and having to hand the child back. After that, she does not remember clearly anything more.

It was late afternoon by the time she passed out of the devastated area and came to a hospital on the outskirts of the city, only to find the facility was already overflowing with the wounded. Medical orderlies were directing people to other first-aid stations. By this time, Toyoko's sight was going and she had difficulty standing, so she lay down on the lawn and stayed there until morning, when she was taken by truck to a suburban elementary school that had been designated a medical center in times of emergency. But there were few qualified medical personnel to tend to the multitude of patients, no other medicine than Mercurochrome, and all she could do was lie and wait to be found and pray that death would not claim her first.

For three horrible days, Toyoko listened to people die slowly and painfully around her, one after the other. Their misery would mount in intensity, peak in feverish supplications for help; then suddenly they would quiet down and the attendants would come. She did not need to ask what had happened or where they were being taken—she could hear the thud of bodies hitting the ground outside and the acrid stench of burning flesh was unmistakable. At night it was chilly and sometimes she found comfort in the warmth of the crematoriums.

On the evening of the fourth day she felt a hand touch her shoulder and thought surely it was her turn. Not until she heard her sister whisper, "Thank heaven, you're alive," did she realize she had been given a reprieve.

2

Although Hiroko Tasaka's grandparents lived several miles outside the ring of fire, the blast from the bomb had made a wreck of their suburban residence so they had moved to a vineyard across the street and set up a camp under a tent of mosquito netting. Without hospitals or medication to turn to, Hiroko's mother, who was a trained nurse, was forced to resort to home remedies, and in the shade of the grape vines she dressed the blistering portions of Hiroko's face and arms with a concoction of herbs and oils.

Hiroko's convalescence was gradual because her burns festered as though they never intended to form scabs. But it was the long strands of hair that stuck to the bristles of her brush that had her family worried the most. Knowing nothing about the special nature of the bomb that had obliterated Hiroshima, Hiroko was unaware that hair loss was an early symptom of the dreadful "atomic disease" that was continuing to kill people. She felt no great sense of alarm until whole tufts came dislodged from her scalp while brushing. During the war she had received instruc-

tions to follow in case of injury, but nothing had been mentioned
about loss of hair.

"Don't worry. It's happening to everyone," her mother tried
to reassure her. And yanking hard, she managed to uproot a few
hairs from her own temples to prove it.

Hiroko found the bizarre twists of her brutal fate mystifying.
Her very presence in Hiroshima seemed part of her destiny, or
doom. Just two years earlier, after receiving notice that her father
had been killed in action in New Guinea, she, her mother, and
her younger brother and sister had moved from Osaka to her
grandparents' home so she could attend the highly regarded Hiroshima Commercial High School. And there had been more than
a hint of the miraculous in the lifesaving apparition of the old
man. If she had stumbled off in the opposite direction, it would
have taken her into the city center and certain death. She was
convinced that there was too much luck and coincidence involved
for it all to be a matter of accident; and though she had no idea
of the purpose, she had no doubt that her descent into hell, as
well as her escape, had gone according to the will of the gods.
With this encompassing view, the poignancy of her misfortune
receded.

As the months went on, it was left to Hiroko's mother to
worry—first, that pillaging and rape by American soldiers would
bloody the wake of defeat; and second, when that didn't happen
but a series of drastic reformations were enacted that pushed
Japan through centuries of social change almost overnight, that
the Tasaka family would be hurled into instant poverty. She had
been living off the income generated by tenant farmers who were
cultivating her late husband's estate on a small island in the
Inland Sea, and a land reform law was about to be passed by the
Occupation authorities giving ownership rights to those were
working the estates of absentee landlords.

Faced with the prospect of losing their large holdings, Mrs.
Tasaka made plans to return to the island. She intended to take
all her children with her and was startled when her oldest daughter expressed a different desire. Hiroko was beginning to feel that

her strength was almost back to normal again, and she seemed to be cured of that other strange affliction—her hair was growing back. But more than that, word had reached her that her school was going to reopen in the spring, and she had resolved within herself to proceed with her education. After all, that was the reason she had come to Hiroshima.

When she announced her intention at a family conference, her grandparents were outspoken in their concern that school-work would be too much of a strain for her, suggesting she should wait another year. They said they were worried about her health, but Hiroko heard something else. She felt that their real objection was a protective anxiety about what was going to happen to her when she ventured outside the family circle and would be forced to endure indignities for the grisly way her burns had healed.

Hiroko was fourteen years old—an age when the slightest irregularity in an otherwise clear complexion could be disconcert-ing—so the first time she assessed the damage to her face in a mirror she wanted to die. The brim on the hiking cap she had worn that morning had spared the high cheekbones and wide eyes that opened her face with a placid prettiness, but the features on the lower half of her face looked as if they had been wholly reshaped. Her neat snub nose could have been smudged by a heavy thumb: Two tiny holes peeked out of mashed cartilage. Her rosebud mouth was a memory; the lipless opening that passed for a mouth now was more like a thin tear in an overlay of angry red scar tissue that stretched over her chin and clutched her throat, cocking her head awkwardly to one side, and made such ordinary functions as eating, sipping, kissing, or smiling utterly graceless if not impossible.

Of course, she too knew the severity of her deformity meant there would be trouble ahead. But it was a corollary to the creed that one's life was decided elsewhere that certain problems could be overcome if met with serious determination, and Hiroko was a girl of stronger than average will. She realized that sentimental grieving would be futile; she would just have to work harder than others to make herself happy.

When her mother saw how much it meant to her to take up her life again where she had left off, she let Hiroko have her way, and in April she resumed classes in an abandoned military barracks. All but ten of the fifty-three girls in her original class were dead, so most of the students with whom she attended school were newcomers, daughters of demobilized soldiers who had been raised in other parts of Japan and had no notion of the terrible things that had happened in Hiroshima. Some snickered when they saw her, others blanched, and a few looked away grimacing. Only one ever said anything, and that was, "If I looked like you, I could not bear to go on living."

Her retort, "Yes, it's hard to live like this, but dying isn't any easier," had been less than satisfying, for she was a girl as sensitive to the feelings of others as to her own. And even though her attitude was that, come what may, it was her life to live not take, she decided to do something about the face she showed the world. In the privacy of her home she tried powdering her cheeks and painting on lips, but rather than smoothing the defects the make-up exaggerated them like warpaint, and she felt like she had put on some tribal mask. She thought she would be better off wearing a real mask, which gave her the idea of shrouding her disfigurement with a large gauze mask of the kind worn throughout Japan by people suffering from colds who did not want to pass their germs on; such a mask would cover her face from below her eyes to her neckline, and people would no longer have to look away from her in disgust.

From that day on, Hiroko never left home without tying on her mask first, which settled one problem created by her injuries but left another. Her thin arms, bared to the elbow that day, had been severely burned, and the contracting scar formation, like a cable strung between the biceps and forearms, had locked them at right angles. The result was that she walked around with her hands held rigidly out in front of her as if she were carrying something, making such simple tasks as dressing very laborious. It was her most inconvenient injury, and when the newspapers carried a story about surgeons at one of the hospitals who were conducting "reconstructive surgery" on physically handicapped victims of the A-bomb, Hiroko made an appointment to see if it could be fixed.

She would never forget the initial reaction of the doctor who examined her. Upon seeing her disrobed and without her mask on, he had gasped and rather than saying, "You're lucky to be alive," his comment was, "It's unfortunate you didn't die."

She had stepped lightly as she entered the examination room and shown a brave face when she exposed herself; but his remark was piercingly hurtful. Trying not to show what was churning inside and afraid if she tried to speak at that moment she would begin to cry, Hiroko said nothing. And after observing her injured expression, he must have realized the callousness of his comment because the doctor went on to look at her wounds closely and tenderly; when he was finished he said that although she was a serious case, he thought plastic surgery would do her good.

When school broke for summer vacation, Hiroko entered the hospital, but from start to finish it was all wrong. The hospital was poorly stocked with medical supplies and there was no anesthesia, so several orderlies held her down while the doctor began to cut. Her eyes brightened in pain as he excised a massive scar on the inside of her right arm, then sliced a series of thin strips of skin from the inside of her right thigh which he sewed over the open wound in patchwork fashion. Then he moved to her left arm, cutting sharply down through the band of scar tissue that bound her forearm to her upper arm, and she screamed and screamed and screamed. There was blood spurting everywhere, and Hiroko was thrashing on the operating table and kicking and begging them to stop. Her mother, who had accompanied her into the operating room so she would not have to go through it alone, fled into the corridor so she would not have to listen to her daughter plead for help.

The violence of the procedures left Hiroko terrified, and the surgeons came back the next day to finish the job. Inch by inch, snapping tendons and ripping muscle tissue, they wrenched her arm straight and tied it down to a wooden splint. When she was discharged several weeks later, they called the surgery a success; but by the end of summer her arms were back at angles, and the best reason they could give was that it must be another pernicious phenomenon peculiar to the A-bomb.

Hiroko devoted a kind of ascetic energy to her schoolwork, and when she was rewarded with the high school diploma it had been so important for her to get, she joined her family on the island. Her mother's efforts to hold onto the rights of the family estate had failed, but a sizable parcel of land with enough orange groves on it to provide her with a modest income had been deeded over to her by an uncle. The same uncle gave Hiroko a job in the office of his shipping company.

Considering her handicap, she knew she should have felt fortunate. She was putting her education to use and contributing to the family expenses. But it did not take long before Hiroko overheard nasty comments whispered by her co-workers: "Is labor so short they have to hire a girl like her?" And although filing and typing was fine for now, she knew it was not the kind of work she would be content to do for the rest of her life.

For as long as she could remember she had wanted to be a schoolteacher. She could no longer picture herself standing in front of a classroom full of students, but she was still interested in providing some sort of service to others. She came up with the idea of designing clothes, which seemed to perfectly order her feelings; rendering beauty to others would compensate in some personal way for the outrage inflicted on her. Hiroko had a long talk with her mother, who understood her desire to make something more of herself and tried to help by contacting an old friend in Hiroshima who had recently opened a sewing school. When the woman wrote back to say not only that there was an opening but that Hiroko could work off part of her tuition by handling the bookkeeping chores in the administrative office, she departed for Hiroshima to further her education once again.

As it happened, she returned at a time when the people of Hiroshima were preoccupied with the atomic bomb and its delayed effects. Within a year after the bombing, the "atomic disease" appeared to have run its course. Indeed, after her hair had grown back, Hiroko had exhibited no other symptoms of exposure to radiation. But the horrible enigma of an atomic bomb was that its secrets revealed themselves over time, and disclosures in 1950 that leukemia was epidemic in both Hiroshima and Nagasaki had been supplemented by the admission by scientists researching the aftereffects that the risks of contracting a variety of cancers was high among irradiated survivors. They could not say what diseases would turn up next.

The news sent a wave of hysteria over the community. An enormous range of complaints was suddenly attributed to the bomb, some real and some fanciful. There were wild rumors of babies born to survivors without brains, with eyes on the top of their heads. And it was in this highly charged atmosphere of paranoia and possibility that Hiroko noticed an unusual swelling in her feet. She ignored it at first, hoping it would go away. When it did not, she made an appointment with a doctor who diagnosed it as a simple infection caused by an ingrown toenail, which he removed. But the condition persisted, and when a rash of tiny red spots bloomed between her toes, he asked her to come to the hospital for a second opinion from a celebrated specialist in radiation effects, who had come to Hiroshima for the sole purpose of examining A-bomb survivors.

By the time Hiroko arrived, the waiting room was packed to capacity with more journalists than survivors. In compensation for the censorship policy enforced during the Occupation, which had restricted all references to the A-bomb, the media was taking an intense interest in what happened in Hiroshima and Nagasaki now that control of the country had been returned to the Japanese. Conspicuous with her white mask and her contorted arms, Hiroko was instantly noticed by reporters, who sidled up to her for an interview. She answered their questions cordially but was relieved that her name was called soon after her arrival.

In the examination room a group of grim-faced physicians huddled around her.

"Very strange," commented the specialist.

She could not have been more alarmed. "What is it? What's the matter with me?"

When the examination was completed the medical men conferred privately. She heard someone say, "I've been waiting for this kind of trouble to show up, and now it has come." The rest of the conversation was conducted in hushed tones.

The whole thing could not have taken more than several minutes, but it seemed like hours. After a prolonged pause, the doctors returned with their judgment.

"I'd rather not go into it now because if this gets out, then others will worry," the specialist began. And he went on to say some things too medically cryptic for Hiroko to quite get straight, but yes, her affliction was related to the atomic bombing, it was something that had not been seen before, and at the moment there was no known treatment. The doctor's advice was to go home, get plenty of rest, and wait and see what happened next.

Despite the much-publicized studies that indicated there remained much to be understood about the consequences of the bombing, Hiroko had had great faith in the future because she could not believe that she had survived the acute effects only to succumb to the late effects. This news made her realize how vulnerable she was, and her composure was totally undermined. She did not even think to ask how much time she had left before a nurse ushered her out of the examination room.

The journalists circled her immediately, asking questions, their voices raising when she refused to speak. Above her mask her black eyes seemed to bulge and roll in terror as she pushed her way past. Too upset to go back to school, she hurried to the place where she was boarding; sitting by herself in silence, she tried to collect her thoughts. Although the symptoms amounted only to a scaly itchiness between her toes, the message the doctors had imparted was chillingly clear, with overtones of imminent death. It was true they had not been able to diagnose the problem with medical certainty, but that was the insidious character of atomic diseases—they showed up in unexpected forms. No one could be sure that the slightest ache or pain or itch did not signal the early stage of a malignant growth.

Hiroko decided to keep the results of the consultation to herself and act as if nothing out of the ordinary had happened. Then, early the next morning as she was preparing to leave for school, there was a knock at the door. It was her neighbor, calling to extend her sympathies. At first Hiroko didn't know what she was talking about, and then the woman handed her the morning edition of the daily newspaper that featured an article about the latest manifestation of the "atomic disease," and its first victim, Hiroko Tasaka.

The newspapers had as much as printed her obituary, but Hiroko did not die. With the cooler weather of autumn, the rash cleared up as mysteriously as it had appeared. Nor was her confidence in doctors shaken. She wanted to believe they knew what they were doing more than she was willing to accept that nothing could be done. For that reason, when she read about a local surgeon who was getting rave reviews for the work he was doing in his own small private hospital, she went for a consultation. After looking at her arms and face, he told her about a new and intricate technique of transplanting skin that had been newly mastered and proven successful in 99 out of 100 cases, and a date for surgery was set.

His facility was not equipped for general anesthesia, so Hiroko was awake throughout the procedure, sitting slumped forward on the edge of an operating table. The surgeon had decided to take a large flap of skin off her back, and after the shots of novocaine took effect, he reached for his scalpel and she closed her eyes. For the better part of an hour he worked, talking to his nurse all the while and explaining what he was doing. And it was while listening to his running commentary that Hiroko realized her enormous misunderstanding: When he had said this new technique was 99 percent successful, he had been quoting a statistic in an article on plastic surgery he had seen in an American magazine. This was an experimental attempt to duplicate a procedure he knew only from a written source.

As though suddenly awakened from a troubled sleep, her eyes snapped open. Looking left, she saw a tube of bloody flesh draped over her shoulder, with a pair of forceps clamped to one end to weight it down. Realizing it was too late to stop now, she suppressed her nausea and did her best to pretend this was not really happening to her.

The graft did not take hold. The day after it was attached to her face it started to discolor. She was given an injection to stimulate the flow of blood to the area, but it did no good and a second operation was required to remove the dead transplant.

So long as there was any hope at all that the resources of medicine could help, she was willing to take a chance. But after eleven unsuccessful attempts at a graft over the next six months, Hiroko realized she now had as many wounds on her body from surgeons' knives as from the atomic bomb, and decided there would be no more cutting.

Shigeko Niimoto was eased onto a stretcher improvised out of boards and carried to her parents' summer house along a river on the western edge of the city. Her charred clothing, singed hair, and scorched skin made it difficult to distinguish the front of her head from the back, so with ruthless efficiency her father pruned everything loose away. Three days of heat and filth had infected her wounds, but with no other means of treatment available, all her mother could do was anoint the burned parts with cooking oil.

For a girl who had so recently measured her life by the hours between dusk and dawn, Shigeko's recovery was remarkable. By the middle of October she was sitting up in bed. She required assistance at mealtimes—the hands she had held up so she could see what was falling from the airplane had caught the lightning flash, leaving her with two clusters of stiff nubbins bunched at the knuckles—but she was no longer in danger of dying.

Like a child who has been on her best behavior indoors too long, she soon grew restless with nothing to do. One morning when she was alone, she disobeyed her mother's instructions to stay in bed and crawled over to the dressing table. Picking up a mirror, she glanced at her reflection, and for a moment thought a trick was being played on her. She could not bring herself to believe her eyes. Understanding came at her with a sickening rush, giving her a delayed, frightened start. Instead of the little imp she expected to see grinning back at her, a beast held her gaze. A hideous red-faced beast without hair, brows, or lashes whose eyes stared dully from sunken, drooping circles, and whose chin . . . a moan escaped as she realized her chin had all but melted into her neck.

With a deep, choking breath and a wanting beyond hope, she looked away, prayed "Please, God, let it be a bad dream," and glanced back. Once again the mirror refused to reflect the face she was used to seeing.

At just that moment her mother entered the room. Trying to smile in an unbearably pathetic way, Shigeko ventured, "Oh mother, it must be they aren't finished healing yet."

Convinced that her condition was temporary, Shigeko stayed indoors while waiting for her wounds to heal. She occupied herself by reading books, making up stories, and doing things with her older sisters, both of whom had been out of the city on the morning of August sixth. When she finally did gather the courage to take a walk down a neighborhood street, a funny thing happened. This was about the time that the American soldiers moved into the region and were frequently seen strolling through the ruins of Hiroshima. Few Japanese had ever seen live Americans before and found them odd-looking with their bulging eyes, prominent noses, and pink complexions. All the weight Shigeko had lost showed most in her face, so she, too, appeared all eyes and nose and there was a fiery glow to the raw tissues of her face. When the neighborhood children saw her coming, they ran up to her shouting things she did not understand but was sure were insulting, and turning, she sprinted home. For some time afterward she considered going for a walk a perilous journey, and it wasn't until one of her sisters saw her lingering at the front window gazing apprehensively out at the road and heard her version of what had happened, that it was explained to her that she had probably been mistaken for the daughter of an American soldier. The neighborhood children had not been hurling insults, but had been using English words to beg for chewing gum and candy.

Shigeko was able to pass the episode off as an example of how ludicrous it was for her to let her fears get the upper hand. Perhaps the implications of her disfigurement would have been more disturbing if she had been older; but she was just thirteen, and she had always been a free spirit for whom impulse and play were primary. When something upset her or made her unhappy, she had only to go to sleep and when she woke up it was all better; and even though that would not be the case this time, and she had no real idea how drastically her life was about to change, she was unable to think of personal setbacks in less than hopeful terms. Likening herself in her mind to the dharma doll, that small figure on a rounded base that bounced up again when it was knocked over, Shigeko made a promise to herself that from that day forward she would be the same pixyish girl, full of pep and piquancy, she had always been. Though deformed in body, she was determined not to let her spirits suffer.

There were times when it seemed her life was going to be one long trial putting that pledge to the test. When she walked down the street, children call her "Pika-don," slang for atomic bomb, and when she entered a store adults would make excessive room for her, as though she had something that was somehow contagious. She so often returned home with tears in her eyes that her mother finally pleaded with her to wear a veil that would hide her scars from public view. Adamantly she refused, saying, "I didn't do anything bad, Mother, so why should I hide? If there hadn't been a war I would look like everyone else. Let them look, I don't care."

Most of all she missed her girl friends. Few had survived and she had not returned to school—what was the point when her hands could not even hold a pencil?—so she had made no new friends. More and more, with nothing else to do, she would take long, solitary walks, wandering down dusty, shadeless streets and across old bridges in partial disrepair, hoping that along the way she would encounter someone she knew. But nothing was familiar. Approximately 140,000 people were estimated to have died by the end of 1945 from the bombing, and many of the surviving residents, having lost their homes, assets, and places of work, and suffering from acute and lingering chronic effects, had relocated in their ancestral homes in inland villages and never returned. Meanwhile, a new Hiroshima was growing on the grave of the old dead city; a shantytown of sheetmetal sheds and scrapwood shacks knocked together by demobilized soldiers and repatriotees who were staking their claims on the wasteland like pioneer settlers. And here, where one would think that deformed was the natural state of the people and the scarred would far outnumber all others, she did not once meet someone else like herself, while often *she* was made to feel like the trespasser.

On one of her sojourns she came upon several young men who started conversing in abnormally loud voices when they saw her approaching. "Looks just like a damn monkey, doesn't she?" "I wouldn't have her for my wife if they gave me a million yen." An abrupt hush fell over them as they pretended they had just noticed who was coming, but it ended in mocking laughter when she had passed.

Another time she saw a group of girls her own age who were smartly decked out in the latest Western fashions, and she was so taken by their stylish garb that she went straight toward them for a closer look. With disarming innocence she extended a friendly smile, forgetting completely about what she must look like to them until they recoiled—eyes wide with terror, mouths open to shriek.

Sometimes in her reveries a magical transformation gave her back her original looks; it would happen just like before, in a bright flash from the sky.

Shigeko was seventeen when her older sisters married. It being the custom, both marriages were arranged by a go-between who introduced the prospective partners and planned the wedding ceremonies. Although she too was approaching marriageable age, Shigeko's prospects were never the topic of family discussions, and inquiries from the outside never got very far. Matchmakers continued to come to the house because it was listed on the family register that the Niimotos had three daughters, but the conversation never included Shigeko. Crouching on the other side of a closed sliding door, she would listen to the exchange. "Good afternoon. I'm inquiring as to the status of your daughter." "Thank you," her mother would reply, "but my daughters are married." "Oh really? Even the youngest?" The voices would lower to a murmur, and though she strained to hear her mother's response, she could make out nothing, and soon the matchmaker would depart.

Those years after the war were bearable somehow as long as she had her sisters around for company, but once they were gone she felt a strange and desolate kind of loneliness. For the first time she began to think about herself and her life, and to realize just how restricted a sphere her existence had become. Not only had she depended on her sisters for a social life, she had entrusted them with her education, for most of what she knew they had told her.

Disenchanted and bored, Shigeko was smart enough to know that if she didn't do something about it, nothing would bring about a change in her circumstances, and she began to seek out opportunities to make new acquaintances. And that was her frame of mind the summer afternoon in 1951 when she was returning home from the city by bus and mistakenly got off at the wrong stop. While waiting for the next bus to come along, she found herself staring at a church diagonally across the street that, from its dilapidated appearance, seemed to be a structure that had somehow survived the bomb. She crossed the street, pausing at the door of the chapel because she had never entered a strange door in her life, then pressing it open to peer inside. A small congregation was in assembly, their attention focused on a preacher who stood before an altar delivering a sermon. Out of curiosity, she slipped in and took a seat in a back pew.

The preacher was talking about the Christian message of hope, love, and belonging offered by a man called Jesus whose story was written in a book named the Bible; and sitting in the cool, dark chapel and hearing about someone who had devoted his life to comforting the wretched of the earth so they would not feel forsaken gave Shigeko a sense of serenity she had never felt before. When the service ended she was in such a state of euphoria that she did not have time to sneak back out before the preacher approached her. He introduced himself as Reverend Kiyoshi Tanimoto, and his friendly manner had the effect of putting her instantly at ease. They talked briefly, and when she said this was the first time she had ever been inside a Christian church, he gave her a Japanese language Bible to take home with her and asked her to come again.

But it was he who called on her. She was in the middle of reading the Old Testament as if it were a school assignment (and was surprised to find how similar the stories were to the neatly crafted moral tales she had heard the Buddhist monks recite in temple) when the Reverend Tanimoto stopped in on his way to a meeting in a neighborhood of Hiroshima people injured by the atomic bomb. He invited Shigeko to come along and without even bothering to consult her parents, she did.

It was an evening of far-reaching import, though it did not start out that way. The meeting was held in the sitting room of a private residence that was crammed to capacity by the time they arrived. From the back, Shigeko searched the crowded room for others as young as she. Finding none, she settled down to listen to the discussion that was already underway and quickly realized this was going to be no fun at all. The people present told how miserable their lives had been since the bombing and talked of schemes to get money out of the government. It was all too political for Shigeko, and when she determined there was no one in attendance she was interested in getting to know, she whispered to the Reverend, "Let's go."

It was on the way back that the point of the evening was made. Shigeko was explaining why that was not a group she wanted to be part of, and that she had come seeking friendships, when it suddenly occurred to her, "Wouldn't it be neat to form a group of just girls hurt by the A-bomb?"

It was an idea that appeared to impress the Reverend greatly, for after thinking about it for a minute, he said he knew of at least a dozen others who might be interested. Before saying good night, he promised to let her know as soon as he had arranged such a meeting.

That night, Shigeko fell asleep dreaming of a roomful of girls, all of whom bore the characteristic scars. When they first came together they eyed each other's deformities with solemnity, but by the end of the evening they clung to each other, laughing.

Waiting for her sister to get help, Toyoko Morita alternately wept and wondered, Why me? As excruciating as the pain of the burns was, a greater torment came from knowing that if it had not been for a last-minute change in plans she would have been far enough away from the center of Hiroshima to have escaped the blast.

A week earlier there had been a knock at the door of the Moritas' luxurious landscaped mansion and a uniformed officer had told her that the house-clearing program was being accelerated and each household was required to send a representative to a neighborhood work site the following Monday morning. Although there were nine children in the family, with her father —a wealthy banker and moneylender—bedridden with a stomach ailment, her mother evacuated to her rural hometown with the four youngest, her older brothers already enlisted, and her older sister married, that left Toyoko and her younger sister. As Toyoko had been employed since graduating from high school at an office job at the port of Ujina, a forty-minute ride by streetcar from her home where she reported for work each weekday by eight in the morning, and since her sister was a student who happened to have that day off, she thought it was obvious who would represent the family. But come Monday morning, she awoke to discover her sister had slipped away early and gone off with a friend, so it was she lying there in critical condition waiting for help.

Soon her brother-in-law came for her with a truck, only to be told that if she were moved now she would not reach her destination alive. She was willing to take the chance, but he thought it unwise and left saying he would let her mother know where she was.

Feeling abandoned and utterly helpless, Toyoko kept asking herself why she had been singled out for such suffering. The irony of her fate demanded an explanation, but she did not know whom to blame. Her sister for acting so selfishly? The Americans for bombing innocent, unarmed civilians? The Japanese military for waging war in the first place? She even added the Emperor to her list of guilty parties when she heard he had announced the surrender of Japan. Why had he waited so long?

When her mother came from the country to nurse her as was the custom in Japanese hospitals at that time, she learned for the first time that the damage to their family extended beyond herself. Of their beautiful house with its central garden nothing had been left standing except her father's safe; and in the lawless aftermath of the bombing, looters had pried open the doors and made off with his personal savings and the family jewels. Somehow her father had managed to extricate himself from the wreckage of their home and had been evacuated to their country house, but even though his physical injuries seemed slight, his health was steadily deteriorating because of a persistent fever that the doctors found impossible to identify.

It was October before she was out of danger and well enough to travel, and although she had counted the days until the end of her confinement, when it finally came time for her to leave she panicked, for the wounds on her face had barely begun to heal. The side that had been turned away from the blast was spared to a large extent, but the other half looked as though some foul disease that rotted flesh was trying to bore its way out from the inside. While brushing her hair in preparation for the journey, she stared at her disfigurement in the mirror for the longest time.

During the war years she had thought little about the implied risks to herself. In fact, although in those days the authority of the state was not to be questioned, she had flagrantly disregarded the dress code for civilian women and worn skirts instead of pantaloons, causing more than one military policeman to reprimand her. To a slender twenty-year-old who had always basked in the assurance that young men found her attractive—at eighteen she had already refused one suitor because she thought she could do better—it was an exciting time, a chance to meet soldiers and sailors before they went off to battle. This was the reason she had not followed her older sibling's scholarly footsteps and attended a university; she was more interested in going to teahouses with girl friends and mixing with junior officers on leave from the nearby naval base. But looking at herself now, it was difficult to keep her hysteria in check.

They took the train to her mother's native village where the rest of the family was staying, and Toyoko took a seat nearest the window, angled so the bad part of her face pointed away from the aisle. As she stared fixedly out the window it seemed to her mother she was lost in thought, but in truth she was watching the reflection of her fellow travelers on the pane of glass and did not relax until she was convinced that no one was giving her undue notice. Surprised as much as she was relieved, she wondered if people were just too preoccupied with their own problems to mind anyone else's business; secretly she hoped it meant she was not as startlingly ugly as she appeared to herself.

When the train reached their stop and they deboarded through a swirl of steam and started to cross the platform, she realized she had only been fooling herself, for the villagers who had come to greet the arriving train gaped, nudging others to look. All the nervousness and anxiety that had been simmering inside boiled up, and as much to conceal her face as to hide her emotions she tucked her chin into her coat collar and trained her eyes on the ground. It was possible these people were inordinately curious because the war had not come to the countryside, and they had heard rumors about what the atomic bomb did to the survivors; but whether or not that explained why they stood and gawked long after she had scurried past, their rudeness made her want to turn and shout, "Go ahead and stare, damn you. But just wait. Before long I'll put your oafish country girls to shame."

Though it had been only months, her father had aged years. He was an old and ill and broken man, and it withered her spirits to see him struggle for a smile when he first set eyes on her. Three days later he was dead, and he did not go in peace but grieving the loss of his home, a lifetime of work, and the future of his daughter.

It was hard for all of them in the years that followed. Her mother borrowed a small section of land and started a vegetable garden so there was food on the table, and they rented a house from a relative so they had a roof overhead, which made them more fortunate than many of their countrymen; but compared to the life of luxury and leisure they had enjoyed in Hiroshima, it was a difficult existence, and for Toyoko it could not have been worse.

Throughout her childhood they had come to this village every summer vacation and she had always looked forward to it. She liked the quaint, thatch-roofed homes that had been passed down to generation after generation of farmers, and she thought there was no sound as lovely as women singing melodiously as they weeded rice paddies on a crisp golden morning. Now, everything was different, and she hated the countryfolk for making her feel like the village freak. Children would gather when they saw her coming, and adults stopped working in their fields to watch her pass. The only time she felt wholly at ease was when she went off by herself on treks through the thick timber on the hills above the valley to gather firewood. Traipsing around the green woods brought back the summer memories, and in her complete absorption she sometimes forgot the time of day and her reason for coming, returning home in the evening darkness apologetic and empty-handed.

Only the faith that this condition was a crisis that would pass in time kept despair at bay, and even that was beginning to seem like a miscalculation. After the scabs had come a thick rubbery overlay of a pearly luster that looked like nothing less than a crab clutching one side of her face, its claws extending up to her cheek and down to her chest. Time had done nothing to heal her scars; on the contrary, the creature they resembled seemed to gradually tighten its grip so she could no longer raise her head naturally or open her mouth wide.

In the midst of her depression, her only defense was to conjure an image of Hiroshima as the one place on earth where people would be able to empathize with her feelings, because they had history and circumstances in common. There, she believed, she would not be fair game for the curious but could walk among fellow sufferers with a feeling of community. She had not reached the point of planning to return, however, until she read in the newspaper that Hiroshima doctors had begun to perform reconstructive surgery on badly burned victims of the A-bomb. From that moment on, all her dreams led back to Hiroshima.

When she made up her mind to return, she trembled with anticipation, remembering the city as she had seen it last—like the ruins of an ancient civilization, the mounds of collapsed buildings the only vertical shape in an endless plain of rubble and cinders. When she stood once again in front of the railway station, two years had passed, and looking about, it struck her that in that time Hiroshima had been to hell and had not come all the way back.

Across the wide plaza where buses and streetcars made their drop-offs and turnarounds, a congested, noisy, and obscenely fecund black market had sprung up, replacing the commercial district in the former downtown area that had been leveled in the bombing. Trying to absorb the changes all at a glance, she thought there was almost a fairground quality to the crudely carpentered stalls and booths that lined the dusty streets spoking out from the plaza, the crowds drifting past secondhand shops and fresh fruit markets, the smoke pluming out of cheap cookshops, sending out whiffs of fish and crabs frying in oil. Nervously poised at the alleyways were "pan-pan girls," identically painted in rouge and lipstick, keeping one eye out for customers and the other for the police, and gangster types, sporting GI haircuts and jackets tailored to resemble the tight-fitting Eisenhower jackets worn by their conquerors, who surveyed the scene behind aviator sunglasses like sentinels.

Toyoko was beginning to feel a queer sense of dislocation when she realized that several young men loitering at the entrance to the waiting room of the station had found her worth watching. Out of the corner of her eye she thought she saw them giving her their intense scrutiny, but when she turned and looked directly at them they appeared to be busily engaged in a private conversation. Or were they just pretending to talk to each other? One of them laughed and she looked away, certain she was the butt of a joke and suddenly feeling extremely exposed. Or was she being paranoid in her suspiciousness? After a pause she glanced over again and this time caught the eye of one of the men. As it turned out they had not noticed her before, but heads turned now. Picking up her bags, she started to walk and her quick steps became a little hurry of escape, as much from the unwanted attention as from the dreadful thought that maybe she had been wrong about Hiroshima.

Previous arrangements had been made for her to rent a room from family friends who lived on the outskirts of the city, and as soon as she was settled in, Toyoko took a bus to the hospital. It was a depressing place with dark corridors, grimy walls, and a sharp odor of disinfectant that gave a stronger impression of filth than cleanliness. Only a flower and vegetable garden in the inner compound rescued the atmosphere from total dreariness; it had been planted to test the effect of radiation on plant life. Radishes, carrots, and potatoes bulged from the ground, while Chinese bellflowers, dahlias, and early chrysanthemums were in magnificent bloom. Radioactivity apparently had a perversely stimulating effect on vegetation.

The cheap wooden benches spaced at intervals along the hallway were filled with expressionless patients. Room was made for her, and taking a seat, Toyoko composed her hands in her lap and stared straight ahead until it was her turn to be examined.

The staff surgeon, who took his time assessing the extent of her injuries, was quite different than she expected. His young face gave him the look of a serious high school student, but his clear eyes and steady hands seemed to vouch for the maturity that had come from two years of diagnosing medical problems brought on by the A-bomb. A high shelf behind him that sagged under the weight of several thousand case cards spoke too for his experience.

All Toyoko wanted to know was, "Can you give me back my face?"

He looked her in the eyes and replied, "Let me be straightforward with you. You may not look exactly as before, but it will be very close."

But it was not close. Like the orderly in the hospital who had told her earlier that her wounds were nothing more than a bad sunburn and would mend in time, he was either being kind or did not know what he was talking about. Either way, she felt cruelly deceived. Two major operations and nearly a year later, Toyoko looked no different than when she had been admitted.

She was crestfallen, and for some time afterward did not feel like doing anything. The excitement that had expressed itself in her optimistic return to Hiroshima congealed into a big lump inside. Until now, she had not let herself think of her condition as a permanent and unalterable fact of her existence. She had refused to believe that this was the face she would look at each morning in the mirror and show the world every time she went out. As it came home to her that this might be the way it would be for the rest of her life, a kind of dullness settled slowly upon her. And even this was not the limit which she would be forced to withstand.

When an old friend of her father who was employed in the city government offered her a position as a clerk in the social welfare office, she accepted it to shake herself out of her apathy. It was decent work at a fair salary that enabled her to support herself while she struggled with the question of what to do next. She was twenty-three, and there was so much that was still young, soft, and female alive within her; but when she honestly asked herself if any man would have a woman like her she was unable to deceive herself. Feeling the need to do something interesting and worthwhile with her life if she was never going to marry, she spent several months contemplating her future before she came up with what seemed like a reasonable and satisfying alternative. She decided to pursue the solitary life of an artist by going back to school, following up on the violin lessons she had taken as a young girl and eventually playing in an orchestra. The more she thought about it the more she liked the sound of it; filling her life with music was just what she felt she needed.

Toyoko's heart was set on attending the St. Elizabeth School of Music, a prestigious conservatory established in Hiroshima by Catholic missionaries, and to cover the cost of tuition she sold the silk kimonos her mother had taken to the country for safekeeping on the black market. Acting on a definite plan in which some degree of personal happiness seemed possible took her thoughts away from her condition for a while, but this did not last. She was never comfortable around her classmates; they represented life and laughter, and she could not help feeling jealous at how carefree they acted. Nor did the violin give her the pleasure it once had; in fact, in addition to music lessons she was required to take liberal arts classes and she found her philosophy class much more interesting. Her faith in God had never been the same since the bombing, and at that time an atheistic form of existentialism was popular among Japanese university students. Then, before she knew it the semester was ending and the fees for the upcoming term were due. Until the last minute she pretended that her family's prosperity still stood behind her; but the school carried things forward on a businesslike basis and when she was unable to post tuition, her name was dropped from the school rolls.

All that Toyoko had worked to achieve had come to naught, and she felt she had exhausted the possibilities of her situation. Perhaps some could bear up with stoicism and dignity, but having been raised in affluence she had taken it for granted that comforts and conveniences were a birthright to a girl of her social standing, and nothing prepared or equipped her to cope with endless drudgery and one degradation after another as her daily bread.

In certain morbid moods it seemed like nothing more than her death could happen, and when she asked herself, "Why do I go on living in this world?" she found herself envying her father and wondering if it would have been better if she had died with him. She had no will to live without hope, and neither did she have the nerve to take her own life, but thoughts of suicide plagued her like a sickness. Alcohol was the only thing that put a temporary stop to her suffering, less the ritual glass of sake than a bottle of whiskey which she drank in blighted, numb solemnity.

Moved to pity and then dread by the vacant, far-away look in her daughter's eyes, Mrs. Morita tried to stimulate her interest in the future again by arranging to pay for a follow-up operation to the earlier surgery. Toyoko had reached the point where she no longer cared, but she did not have the strength to resist. At least in the hospital she was around others affected by the A-bomb.

While waiting for surgery, Toyoko received a visit from another young girl marked by burn scars as a victim of the bombing. One morning Shigeko Niimoto simply walked into the ward and introduced herself. Toyoko could barely disguise her surprise. She had continued to ask herself why she had been singled out for this tragedy, and Shigeko was the first girl she had encountered who was branded the same way. Just as significant, Toyoko thought the poor girl's disfigurement was worse than her own.

They talked, and Toyoko found her new friend's buoyant cheerfulness startling. The girl seemed oblivious to her injuries. In their conversation, Toyoko inquired delicately how she managed to keep her spirits up, and Shigeko told her that she too had been somber at one time, but she had been pulled out of her hole of unhappiness through her association with the Reverend Tanimoto. She explained that once each week girls like themselves met in the basement of his church, and she invited Toyoko to attend a future meeting.

Toyoko's operation did little to help her, but this time she did not despair. Her release from the hospital meant she could accept Shigeko's invitation, and the two girls met at an agreed-upon street corner and walked together to the Nagarekawa Methodist Church. Toyoko was a little nervous and uncertain as they entered a brightly lit basement room in which a group of girls were seated on folding chairs arranged to face a man she soon came to know as the spiritual leader of the gathering. After bowing through the introductions, she was glad to take her seat.

Over the next two hours, Toyoko came to relax in a way she had not in the seven years since the bombing. The Reverend Tanimoto read to them from the Bible and they sang hymns together, but most of all she liked the discussion period that followed when the girls talked among themselves. All had lived in a kind of dark exile since that day, and like herself, each was able to cite an odd set of coincidences that seemed to ordain their fate. A week before the bombing a girl named Atsuko Yamamoto said she had gone with several of her girl friends to have her fortune told. While some took it seriously, she had gone just for fun and the whole walk there had ridiculed the idea that anyone could peer into her future by looking at her palm. However, when the gypsy fortuneteller told her, "You will be a girl whom people will turn and look at," Atsuko had suddenly been willing to give the superstition the benefit of the doubt, for the prophecy pinpointed her ambition in life. Her father managed movie theaters, and a significant portion of her childhood had been spent sitting in her father's theaters watching films and dreaming of becoming an actress when the war was over. She had thought the reader meant people would turn and look at her because they recognized her as a matinee idol; it was the cruelest of ironies that people did now turn and look at her, but it was to stare at the angry purple welts that tore along both sides of her face in clawing sweeps from nose to ear.

Likewise, it seemed each girl had seriously considered killing herself. Michiko Yamaoka told how her mother had saved her life twice. Once, after the blast from the bomb had buried her alive under a collapsed stone wall, her mother had stayed behind while everyone fled to lift, one by one, the rocks that would have been her daughter's grave. The second time came several months later. They had evacuated to a coastal resort that was now occupied by Hiroshima refugees and were staying in a reed shack that had once served as the dressing room for bathers, when Michiko saw her ruined reflection in the mirror for the first time. Her pale scalp had been visible through thin, shedding hair; an eruption of scar tissue seemed to spurt out of her left cheek, flowing lavalike down the side of her face, over her jaw, and into her shoulder, where it had hardened; and when her hands came up in a gesture of horror, the webbed fingers completed the portrait of something better off dead. She had been crawling across the white sand of the beach toward the sea to drown herself when her mother found her and dragged her back.

So many times Toyoko had felt the need to unburden herself, but there was no one she felt she could talk to. She had not been able to relate to any of her schoolmates, and her sisters accused her of feeling sorry for herself when she complained to them. Besides, she had never felt she could reveal the complex feelings churning inside her to anyone, for apart from the pain it caused her to talk about the past, she was unable to believe that anyone could comprehend her feelings without having lived through the same. Now, among these other scarred girls, she felt an instant kinship. As she heard them talk about the bombing and what they had experienced, their ordeals and frustrations in the years since, the humiliations and heartbreaks, Toyoko found herself thinking that the very experiences that set the members of this group apart from the rest of society bound them to each other, and they were, in a vital way, closer than family.

3

Among the thousands who survived that fateful August morning, the thinly clad, young schoolgirls were the unluckiest. In a fraction of a second their lives took a tragic turn. Many had witnessed the atomic flash with their faces lifted, and the intense heat charred exposed flesh and left scars that wrenched their facial features into grotesquely symbolic expressions. One could not smile because the contractions tugged her lips over her teeth into a permanent snarl. Another had her right eyelid seared away; unprotected, the eye watered steadily as though possessed with a grief of its very own.

A society that placed such great emphasis upon aesthetic presentation and losing face in every sense offered no place for their kind. Some were kept in back rooms for years by parents ashamed of them, while others were so afraid of public ridicule that whenever they ventured out in daylight they scurried down side streets with shawls wrapped tightly around their bent heads. Employers refused to hire them because, they said, it would be too demoralizing to have them around, and marriage was out of the question because it was roundly believed they would give birth to a generation of genetic monstrosities.

The first time the Reverend Kiyoshi Tanimoto set eyes on them was when he was distributing clothes and medicine at a relief center in the years shortly after the war. Only a few showed up, just long enough to fetch their goods and go. They woke such a deep sorrow in him that he visited them at home. All had lived for a period of time after the bombing under a mosquito netting to keep the flies away from festering wounds, and in some of the homes he entered he found the gauze still draped over the beds in which they slept. In the dark of their rooms it had come to serve as another kind of shelter behind which they lived like shadows.

Somehow it seemed unjust that they had suffered so terribly, while he had come through without so much as a scratch. As a minister he was ashamed that he had no such cross to bear, and he wanted to do all in his power to help. But at the time he was not in a position to do anything more for them, and it would be five years later before his circumstances changed.

It began with an interview he gave to a young American journalist that was published as part of a long article in the *New Yorker* magazine. John Hersey's account of the atomic bombing as told through the prism of six Hiroshima citizens became a literary sensation when it was put between covers and released as *Hiroshima*. For the Reverend Tanimoto, whose daredevil dash into the fiery city to rescue the wounded was cast in a heroic light, the publicity stimulated a variety of Hiroshima Projects in church organizations, schools, and community groups across America. But nowhere was his popularity greater than among his fellow ministers from the Class of '39 at the Candler School of Theology. They were well placed in respectable churches throughout the country, and when they read about the Reverend Tanimoto and how he was struggling to resurrect his ministry from the atomic ashes, they petitioned the Overseas Methodist Mission Board to invite him to the United States for a speaking tour.

He hit the sawdust trail, speaking at crossroads churches in every state in the nation, chilling congregations with a firsthand account of the day Hiroshima erupted into a flaming hell, but leaving them with an inspirational conclusion: Seeing an atomic bomb explode over a city had been an experience almost religious in nature; it had convinced him that the promise of peace offered by Christianity was the only hope for the world, and his thinking was reflected in the attitude of the people of Hiroshima itself. When asked what they thought of the atomic bomb, they replied, "I hope it will bring peace to the world." To be sure, many found it impossible to believe that animosity toward America was not the primary reaction (particularly in southern states where stories of Sherman's March were still told to children), but it made a great testimonial on behalf of Christian brotherhood, and the people in the pews gave generously when a free-will offering was requested.

A year and a half of evangelical barnstorming netted the Reverend more than ten thousand dollars, enough to rebuild his church from the ruins. But the most promising aspect of his tour was the success he had in interesting a group of world-minded literary figures in joining with him in an ambitious enterprise intended to reconstruct Hiroshima in a larger sense. In response to a proposal he drafted for the establishment of a Hiroshima Peace Center Foundation that would attempt to dress the wounds of atomic warfare and "explore the ways of peace," he had enlisted the support of John Hersey, Pearl Buck, and Norman Cousins. Cousins had been impressed enough by the idea to give it space on the editorial page of his magazine, the *Saturday Review*.

Six months after returning to Hiroshima with the good news, Tanimoto flew back to the States at the invitation of Norman Cousins to raise funds for the newly incorporated organization. In terms of the money, the friends, and the impression he made, his second speaking tour was even more profitable than his first. The highlight would have to be his visit to Washington, where he was received like a distinguished statesman. A luncheon was given in his honor by the members of the House Foreign Affairs Committee, and later that afternoon he delivered the opening prayer as guest chaplain at the United States Senate, the first foreign clergyman upon whom that honor had been bestowed since the war, and the first Japanese ever. But the most important issue was the formation of a Hiroshima Peace Center Associates, with a Board of Directors chaired by Norman Cousins, whose purpose was to coordinate charity benefits in America with humanitarian projects undertaken by the Reverend's Hiroshima Peace Center Foundation. When he returned to Hiroshima he was now in a position to initiate programs to help the walking wounded.

He began with the innocent victims of the bombing—the orphaned children, the widowed women—placing them in homes and organizing classes that would give them practical knowledge to earn their own livelihood. He helped found an Atomic Bomb Victims Association that launched a campaign for a national medical treatment bill, for as he saw it the survivors of the atomic bombing were being systematically neglected by the government that had placed them in jeopardy in the first place by continuing the war to a disastrous conclusion. And when the idea of forming a separate group of scarred single women was suggested, he arranged, out of deference to their sensitivities, for them to meet in the basement of his church.

Though he quoted passages from the scriptures and led them through chorus after chorus of Christian hymns, all the women came from Buddhist backgrounds and most were there for the fellowship rather than the faith. Only a few knelt before the altar to be baptized. Coming together gave them a chance to experience a unity of spirit, and him the chance to lighten their burden by offering fresh ways of thinking about the violence done them. Consistent with his personal philosophy that private tragedies should be used for great spiritual ends, he saw something larger in their bereavement than any of them did. He talked of an ongoing connection between the survivors of the bombing and those who were killed that brought an exciting new nuance to that experience. It was his contention that those who died were sacrificed, and the only way their souls would rest in peace was if what happened to them never happened to another ever again.

He was trying to give them a new basis for dignity and self-worth; as message-bearers telling the nightmare truth of an atomic bomb they could find meaning for their lives and redemption for their losses. And a measure of success could be found in the ending of an essay written by little Shigeko Niimoto, who had become Exhibit A: "The scars will remain always on my hands and face, but I think that's all right. I am sure that at the sight of me those who feel sorry for me and those who do not wish another girl to endure the same will want to cry out, 'No more Hiroshimas!' I am crying to each and every one of you for Peace in order to prevent the making of people like me again."

As important as it was to maintain a positive attitude, it was only a first step toward rehabilitation. Before long it became apparent that what these women needed was practical feelings of self-worth that would only come if they were able to feel useful, maybe even manage their own livelihoods, for they were all still dependent on their parents. Jobs were scarce, however, and few had completed their education or possessed marketable skills.

In an effort to create employment opportunities the Reverend hired several girls to work in a dormitory for blind children, another of his Peace Center projects. Endeavoring to teach them a trade he purchased three sewing machines and organized sewing classes four nights a week; as seamstresses, they could work at home and not have to face the public. Very quickly, however, he realized that many of them were so functionally disabled they had trouble threading a needle and that before anything further could be done for them they needed special surgery.

The saga of the Reverend Tanimoto's struggle to obtain medical help for his group of girls from within the community of Hiroshima is a shameful episode of neglect. When he went to the Hiroshima Medical Association he encountered immense resistance; first they pleaded poverty, then they told him to mind his own business. When he approached public officials, he found that they were so intent on establishing a new identity for Hiroshima as a "Peace City" and placing it on the world map, that they were interested more in constructing monuments and memorials to the dead than in helping the suffering thousands who still lived.

The way he saw it, if he was going to get help it was going to have to come from sources outside the city; with that in mind, he attended the Japan PEN Club conference in Hiroshima the following year. There he met Shizue Masugi, a prominent Japanese novelist and newspaper columnist for the *Yomiuri Press*, a widely circulated Tokyo-based paper. Miss Masugi was a warmhearted woman who had taken a special interest in Hiroshima's problems. When she asked him what he thought the city needed most, he replied without hesitation: Help for the young women burned by the breath of the atomic blast who would be condemned to a life of endless degradation and despair unless they received reconstructive surgery. When Miss Masugi left Hiroshima at the end of the conference, the Reverend saw her off at the station and brought along several of "his" girls so she could see for herself the extent of the problem. Miss Masugi was aghast. As the train pulled out of the station, she promised to do something on her end.

Two weeks later a wire came from Tokyo, inviting the Reverend Tanimoto and his group of girls to come as soon as possible; everything had been arranged and all expenses would be paid. For the nine girls who went, it was as if all the field trips they had missed as schoolgirls were rolled into one grand excursion. They were entertained royally and whirled around town on Miss Masugi's connections. Their plight appealed to the newsmaking dictates of the time, and the press dubbed them "Genbaku Otome—Atomic Bomb Maidens," an image of horror defiling innocence. At the Tokyo University Hospital a team of specialists examined each girl to determine what the chances were of restoring her original appearance and functional abilities. When the overall prognosis was optimistic, Shizue Masugi announced the formation of a Hiroshima Peace Center Cooperating Society, whose board was composed of high society matrons and whose purpose was to raise the funds necessary to bring the A-bomb Maidens back to Tokyo for surgery.

Hiroshima

Within a month after the Reverend and the girls had re-turned to their native province, they reboarded the train to Tokyo for an elaborate series of operations. While the Maidens were hospitalized, the Reverend campaigned extensively for their cause. Promotion had become his specialty and he delivered countless speeches to women's groups and church meetings. When a national magazine arranged for some of the country's most popular screen actresses to put in benefit appearances on behalf of those less fortunate, the Reverend Tanimoto was amply supplied with a stack of autographed photographs which he sold to the crowd of fans who turned out. A poem written by Michiko Sako, an artistically inclined Maiden, entitled "Smile, Please Come Back," was put to music and became a hit song. A short movie about them was produced and distributed to Japanese theaters. The resulting publicity carried to Osaka, where another Hiroshima Peace Center affiliate was formed, and in December 1952 twelve other Maidens were invited for treatment at Osaka University Hospital and Osaka City Medical College. As interest in treatment for these girls reached a peak, a group of Hiroshima surgeons, smarting at the implication that they were unable or unwilling to foster care for their own citizens, announced plans for a program of their own.

Almost singlehandedly the Reverend had propelled the fate of the A-bomb Maidens into national prominence at a time when no one else spoke out in their behalf. But all the media attention *he* was receiving created a backlash in his own hometown. His gutsy, independent style of promotion contrasted with the tradi-tional Japanese approach that persuaded in quiet ways. There were those who thought a minister should stick to the pulpit and address questions of God, instead of straying down into the pit of controversial social issues. And by playing every conceivable angle, he opened himself to the charge that he was manipulating the Maidens.

During their first trip to Tokyo they had visited Sugamo Prison, where the Japanese "war criminals" were incarcerated. According to the press, a remarkable reconciliation occurred when the Japanese three-star general who had commanded the army divisions in Hiroshima bowed deeply before the girls and volunteered responsibility for "forcing this tragedy on you." At that, one of the girls had burst into tears and cried, "We never thought it was your fault. Let's all make an effort to put an end to war once and forever." Flowers had been exchanged, everyone prayed for "No more Hiroshimas," and altogether it made for a stirring story—except in Hiroshima, where many found it strange that the victims of war should want to console those who had been convicted of initiating and profiting from war. Even if the girls genuinely felt no personal antagonism, as it was reported, the intention behind arranging such a meeting was unclear. Whatever was going on, it was unlikely that the meeting had been a spontaneous act by the Maidens, and more likely it had been staged by the Reverend for private reasons.

In early 1953, when the Reverend was asked by leaders of the Japanese Teachers Union to cooperate in the making of a semidocumentary film about Hiroshima, he agreed to permit the cameramen to take footage of the Maidens praying for world peace in his church. It was not until he saw the movie premiere that he realized he had made a mistake. The storyline was melodramatic; in an attempt to illustrate what happened to children in the aftermath of an atomic attack, the camera recorded the grisly fate of an orphan who ended up an embittered delinquent raiding graves for the skulls of bomb victims to sell to tourists. And the message of the film, rather than pointing a finger at the crime of war itself, appeared political in purpose and seemed edited to agitate anti-American feelings in the viewers. To protest the context of their appearance in the film, the Reverend and several Maidens demonstrated outside the theater, demanding their scene be edited out; but the damage had been done, and to many the incident served as a confirmation that the Reverend was willing to go to any extreme for the sake of publicity.

In defense of his actions, the Reverend Tanimoto maintained that there had been no other way to get things done than to opt for maximum exposure. He pointed out that only after working very hard through "official channels" and receiving disappointingly slight attention had he turned to his own devices. But for the most part he disregarded the criticism because there were other more pressing problems occupying his attention. The money to finance the surgery for the Maidens was almost spent, and even though some of the girls had been operated on as many as a half-dozen times, their conditions were not markedly improved.

At first he had put the failure down to the complexity of the injuries caused by the atomic bomb; but while it was true that the particular scar formation that disfigured and crippled the Maidens was unique, it was not a phenomenon associated with the atomic bomb alone. The growths of scar tissue that exceeded the normal boundaries of the skin, swelling like hard tumors and contracting on all adjacent movable tissues were called keloids. It was not known why or how keloids developed, though apparently they had something to do with the pigmentation of the skin, because they were uncommon in whites but more common in Orientals; the higher incidence of keloids among A-bomb survivors also suggested an enhancing effect of radiation. Perhaps their most distinguishing property was their tough resistance to scalpels; when cut away, they promptly grew back.

But the nature of the injuries was not the only stumbling block to progress. The level of reconstructive plastic surgery as it was currently being practiced in Japan was an equally impressive obstacle. It was not a medical specialty, and its techniques were primitive at best. When he looked into it further the Reverend found the reason had something to do with the fact that Japanese medicine was largely modeled after German medicine, and traditions of plastic surgery were worked out in France and England. Apparently there were no courses on plastic surgery offered in Japanese medical schools, very little was written on the subject in Japanese textbooks, and there was not one surgeon in the country who could transplant skin with a reliable degree of success.

From a purely medical standpoint it was logical then for the Reverend to think of taking the Maidens to America for treatment. The best, most challenging plastic surgery was being done in American hospitals, he was told. But apart from that, the idea seemed perfectly ordered to him on two other grounds as well. First, he felt that such an undertaking would foster a more favorable image of the United States, which was urgently needed to slow the surging left wing movement in Japan that was attempting to make the Hiroshima bombing the symbolic rallying point against the "American militarization" of Japan. Second, it had been a source of considerable discomfort for him that a Christian nation had used the atomic bomb first—and twice; and it seemed to him that if the country that had the scientific genius to create such a weapon could show it also possessed the moral courage to repair the human damage it had wrought, it would make a story that could unite the people of Japan and the United States, so recently at war, in their common humanity.

He knew that getting the girls to the States was going to require the intervention of an influential person, so he took every opportunity to make an appeal to visiting Americans. In June of 1953, he spoke with the wife of none other than the man who had initially approved the development of the atomic bomb, Mrs. Eleanor Roosevelt, when she came to Hiroshima. After meeting with several Maidens, Mrs. Roosevelt was willing to express her sympathies in a public statement but reluctant to get more deeply involved. Then in the fall of that year, Norman Cousins came to Hiroshima, accompanied by his wife, Ellen.

Sensing that if anyone he knew had a conscience about Hiroshima and the power to make things happen, it was Norman Cousins, the Reverend made arrangements to pick them up at the airport. And on the drive into the city he gave a brief report on the Hiroshima Peace Center activities and his frustrations surrounding the A-bomb Maidens. This was the first Ellen Cousins had heard of the Maidens and she expressed the hope that they might be able to meet the young women. The Reverend replied they would be coming to his church the following evening for one of their get-togethers, and he urged the Cousinses to join them.

They met the next night on the steps of the renascent Nagarekawa Church, and after leading his guests on a tour of the chapel, which had been restored with American donations, the Reverend led the Cousinses downstairs to the community room where the A-bomb Maidens were waiting. There were fifteen girls present, whose ages ranged from sixteen to twenty-one, and they sat in a circle on wooden chairs, their legs tucked under them, hands folded primly in their laps. Cousins had been expecting something of the sort, but was still not prepared for what he saw. He tried not to scrutinize the details—a shorn-off ear, the caved-in side of a face, a nose shoved into a snout—but it was impossible not to stare. Once seen, they were faces never forgotten.

Cousins and his wife attempted to carry on a normal conversation through the Reverend's translation. He asked them what they liked to do most, and one girl answered, "Just be together, like this." Another said they liked to sing songs and a third added, "Go to the movies." When he asked them what kind of movies they enjoyed most the answer was unanimous, American movies, and their favorite actor was Gregory Peck, with Gary Cooper a close second.

When the Reverend asked several of them to roll up their sleeves and hold out their hands, Cousins swallowed hard. Elbows and wrists were yanked out of position as if from some muscular frenzy and locked into place by gristly straps of scar tissue. One girl held up both hands, revealing fingers that were curled and webbed like talons clutching at prey.

The Reverend spoke softly. "I can give them things to do, and I can help restore some of their self-respect, but the important thing now is medical treatment." He had come to realize, he said to both Cousinses, that there was neither the means nor the expertise to go much further in Japan. He went on to say that if miracles did happen, he would like to take the girls to America for the help they so badly needed.

Before he could utter a word, Norman Cousins's wife turned to him and said, "It may not be as difficult as you think."

What happened in Hiroshima and whether the atomic bomb should have been used in the manner it was had preoccupied Norman Cousins's postwar writings and dominated the editorial pages of the *Saturday Review*. As one of the earliest critics of the bombing, he felt that most people had been convinced by President Truman that it had shortened the war, that nothing short of an all-out invasion would have made Japan surrender, and that before the last surviving Japanese soldier was dug out of a cave on top of Mount Fuji, a half million GIs would have lost their lives. Cousins did not believe that an invasion of mainland Japan was necessary because he felt the outcome of the war was already evident; it was simply a matter of the terms of surrender. He was convinced that the atomic bomb had been dropped so Japan could be defeated before the Soviet Union could enter the war and stake a claim in the Occupation, an intention revealed by the use of a second atomic bomb on Nagasaki just three days after Hiroshima. "It was a matter of racing against a deadline to prevent Russia from getting in on the kill, and not to spare American lives, that explained why all those people in Hiroshima and Nagasaki died."

In the forties and fifties the *Saturday Review* burned with a purer flame than most other magazines of the day, due mainly to the visionary humanism of its editor—a man with mild, pleasant features, fit-looking in build, thick brown hair with a well-defined part, but nothing in his appearance that stood out as remarkable except his luminous brown eyes. Since taking over the helm at the *Saturday Review*, Cousins had expanded a literary weekly into a widely circulated journal dealing with world affairs and committed to a policy of cultural enlightenment, as well as the arts. In the process he had demonstrated a unique ability to inspire a sense of family among his readers, and no greater proof of his devout following existed than the response that followed his moving report on the plight of the "atomic orphans" he wrote after his first visit to Hiroshima in 1949. Observing that thousands of children who had been evacuated to country villages during the war had lost their mothers and fathers in the blast, and were roaming the ruins or were penned up in draconian orphanages, he had invited *Saturday Review* readers to contribute the funds for a "Moral Adoption Program" that would shelter, feed, and educate the "atomic orphans." More than six hundred Americans had answered his call, anteing up more than $70,000.

Cousins had a special feeling for orphans. When he was eleven years old he had spent a harrowing year in a sanitarium because the doctors thought he had tuberculosis, and that experience had left its mark: He knew what it was like to face a future dark with doubts. That feeling, coupled with the fact that he had four daughters of his own, accounted in large part for his strong reaction to the A-bomb Maidens; but it was his disagreement with the American government's policy toward the survivors of Hiroshima on a general humanitarian level that ultimately provoked him into action. Within a year after the war had ended, the United States had set up a research facility in Hiroshima called the Atomic Bomb Casualty Commission to study the long-term effects of radiation on the survivors. Sponsored by the Atomic Energy Commission, the facility was a scientific institute run by American authorities with the exclusive purpose of carrying out research on what parts of the human body were affected most by radiation. It was not a therapeutic establishment designed to treat patients. There were those in Hiroshima who felt that their city had been used as a laboratory for a spectacular American scientific experiment and that they were now being studied like guinea pigs, and Cousins was of the same opinion. He thought it was indecent if not immoral for the government to study A-bomb survivors for the scientific purposes of calibrating how close they were to death while denying them medical treatment. Feeling as he did that any doctor who examined a patient had an obligation under the Hippocratic Oath to treat the patient, he was determined "to shame the bastards," if that was what it took to rectify the injustice, beginning with the A-bomb Maidens.

On his own, he attempted to calculate the costs of the enterprise he had talked about with the Reverend Tanimoto. He started with transportation and figured it would take approximately $25,000 to bring about twenty girls over and fly them back. He estimated that the cost of room space and operating time in a hospital might round off to $40,000. When he added up the cost of surgery—an extremely difficult branch of surgery, involving a series of operations—and realized this might exceed $100,000, he stopped counting.

As he thought about the options and courses open to him, he slowly realized that a project of this magnitude would obviously need the support of a foundation. For the next six months he visited officials of various foundations that seemed to be concerned with America's relationship to other nations, particularly in Asia, but foundation after foundation turned him down. One was fearful of what repercussions might follow should any of the girls die accidentally while in treatment. Another was concerned about the political views of the girls. Anxieties generated by the Cold War, the controversy over atmospheric nuclear weapons testing, and the current anticommunist crusade made them wary of any associations that might furnish ammunition to some future Congressional investigating committee.

When it became evident that the best chance, perhaps the only chance, was for the venture to take shape as a volunteer project, and that it depended entirely on what support he himself could rally, Cousins turned to his large circle of New York contacts. First he took up the medical and surgical aspects with his friend and personal physician, Dr. William Hitzig, who divided his time between a lucrative Park Avenue private practice and Mount Sinai Hospital, where he was an internist on staff. A short, stout man with receding white hair brushed straight back from a florid face that was frequently flushed by an excitable temperament, Dr. Hitzig responded with alacrity when asked for the name of a plastic surgeon who would be equal to the towering surgical challenge. "Why not start at the top," he said. "Arthur Barsky sounds like your man. I'll call him right away."

In a profession not generally known for humility, Dr. Arthur Barsky was the exception. Gentle-mannered, soft-spoken, and almost shy, he had an air of ancient learning about him that was consistent with his position as founder and chairman of the Plastic Surgery Departments at both Mount Sinai Hospital and Beth Israel Hospital in New York City. Nor was he a stranger to war injuries; during the Second World War, Lieutenant Colonel Barsky had set up an independent center for plastic surgery in the army camp at Tuscaloosa, Alabama, where as well as handling three or four wards of regular patients, he was given a separate ward and the right to select interesting cases that presented him with challenging problems. There were no restrictions on his activities in this regard, which were left up to the surgeon and his conscience: The range of injuries he saw, and the innovative techniques he used to treat them led to a joke around the camp that Dr. Barsky could mend anything but a broken heart.

Barsky listened carefully as Norman Cousins outlined the project, and afterward he said it was hard to know how much good plastic surgery would do these people without actually seeing them. At that, Cousins pulled out a folder containing photographs sent to him by the Reverend Tanimoto. After studying them for a long time Dr. Barsky said he thought surgery would most definitely be of help. Next, he expressed a concern about the way a project like this would be handled in the media. He said he did not want to get involved in anything that would become a sensation in the press. Cousins assured him that he would see to it the project was handled with restraint and dignity.

Shuffling through the photographs again, Barsky said, "A detailed examination of each patient will be essential before any basic decisions can be made."

"Then I'll explore the possibility of an on-the-site inspection in Japan," Cousins replied.

For a moment or two Dr. Barsky leaned back in his chair and

said nothing. Of that moment Cousins would later write: "It was the kind of calm and deliberateness that spoke unusual strength. A small smile played around the corner of his lips, as though to indicate he was going to say something that he knew would change the course of his life."

Barsky suddenly nodded. "All right. Count me in."

Wrote Cousins: "There was something in the way he said it that made me think he knew far better than the rest of us what we were letting ourselves in for."

After that, one good thing happened after another.

Since Drs. Barsky and Hitzig were both attached to Mount Sinai Hospital, it was the logical place to approach in the search for hospital facilities. The director of the hospital, Dr. Martin Steinberg, readily grasped the significance of the project, but he said the hospital charter did not allow them to underwrite charity, no matter how worthy the cause. The solution was provided by the chairman of the board of trustees, Alfred Rose, a wealthy New York lawyer, who agreed to pay personally for all hospitalization costs, though for reasons of his own he insisted that his role remain anonymous and the hospital be credited for supplying the operating facilities and bed care.

As important as the surgery was, Cousins knew that the Maidens would be spending a substantial amount of time outside the hospital and that the kind of experience they had, the people they met, what they did and learned would probably be crucial to the overall success of the project. So he selected the Religious Society of Friends to handle the hospitality in between operations because he believed they were "honed by history" to carry out a project of this sort. One of the distinguishing principles of the Quakers is their opposition to war, reflected not only in their refusal to fight but in their tradition of carrying out relief work. Collectively he felt they "understood the possibilities of compassion as well as any people." Working through the American Friends Service Committee, Cousins was put in touch with the New York Friends Center, where he was told that an immediate affirmative could not be made until the matter was discussed with all the Meetings involved, but they had every reason to believe that the Friends would rise to this "opportunity for service."

Next, he turned to the issue of transportation, and for a while it seemed the project would quite literally not get off the ground. Every trans-Pacific airline he approached to discuss the possibility of supplying "courtesy flights" for approximately twenty persons politely informed him it was out of the question. For several months the progress of the project was stalled at this point, and it might never have gone further had not a friend, recently returned from Japan, suggested he let the Japanese see what they could do on their end. He was given the name of the American-born and -educated president of the *Nippon Times,* an English language daily newspaper based in Tokyo, and told that if anyone would be sympathetic and resourceful enough to make it happen, it would be Mr. Kiyoshi Togasaki. Only later did Cousins learn of the chain reaction his letter to Togasaki set off. Sufficiently intrigued by the largesse expressed in Cousins's appeal for help, Togasaki had given the matter his full attention. Working quickly and quietly on his own, he made unofficial calls on the Foreign Office and the U.S. Ambassador; and once he determined that passports and visas would be granted when they were needed, he flew to Hiroshima to make certain the project had the blessings of the mayor of the city and the governor of the prefecture. With all these assurances in hand, he went to Japan and Pan American air lines, the two commercial carriers with routes between the Orient and the States, but got no further than Cousins had. Temporarily stymied, he arranged another meeting with the American Ambassador and sought his advice. Casually, in the manner of a government official leaking a delicate piece of news to a reporter, the Ambassador reminded Togasaki of how progressive General John E. Hull—commander-in-chief of the Far East Command—had shown himself to be in his attitude toward improving U.S.-Japanese relations.

It so happened that a few weeks earlier Togasaki had met the general at a kabuki performance, so he felt comfortable calling Army Headquarters and asking for an appointment. But an aide answered whose job it was to screen all calls to the general, and he wanted to know the exact purpose of the request for a meeting. Afraid that if he were truthful he was taking a risk on being turned down out of hand by an underling, Togasaki said he wanted to invite the general to an upcoming banquet; knowing that was often the way social business was conducted in Japan, the aide scheduled him for ten o'clock the following morning.

It was impossible to know what General Hull was thinking when he heard the background to the project. He gave no indication of whether he was for or against it, and even when he asked to be sent a copy of Norman Cousins's letter, it seemed to Togasaki like a perfunctory way of ending the meeting. He was speechless then when, four days later, he received a communiqué from the general giving written confirmation that a U.S. military plane would be placed at the disposal of the responsible parties in charge of escorting the Maidens to America. Togasaki forwarded the letter immediately to Norman Cousins in New York.

The project was materializing quickly, but Cousins knew that everything could be voided by the shake of a bureaucrat's head, and the time had come to approach the American government. As everything being done was organized under the auspices of the American-based Hiroshima Peace Center Associates, he sent its treasurer, the Reverend Marvin Green, former classmate of the Reverend Tanimoto, to Washington, D.C., to meet with a group of high-echelon State Department officials, who made it known immediately that they were less than sanguine about the idea. Their objection was that treating these girls in America could give the appearance of admitting America's culpability in dropping the atomic bomb. They argued that the girls' presence would embarrass the United States and might well be turned into anti-American propaganda by communists.

A hard line from the State Department had been anticipated, and a full complement of rebuttals polished. While admitting that the project involved certain risks, the Reverend Green said it was his group's intention to show that Americans today were understanding of the problems facing other people in the world and that a person-to-person campaign to rehabilitate the innocent victims of war could only have a salutary effect. He pointed out that the disfigured Hiroshima girls held a special symbolic importance for the Japanese people, and to the extent that they could be given decent care and consideration, much of the sting of the anti-American propaganda generated by the Atomic Bomb Casualty Commission's hands-off policy could be removed. Indeed, he said, the girls they wished to bring to America would become symbols to the entire nation of Japan of American generosity and enduring friendship. And finally, he said that the State Department might as well know that the girls had already been approached by communist leaders, who wished to exploit their plight through international publicity. So far they had refused to cooperate, but it was his opinion that if his group was not allowed to do something soon for these poor girls, the Russians might get to them first.

After two hours of tense, heated discussion, the Reverend Green succeeded in convincing the State Department that the Hiroshima Peace Center Associates would be sensitive to the potential for misinterpretation and distortion and would keep publicity limited and tasteful. In return, while not officially endorsing the project, the State Department agreed to give it implicit approval by not standing in the way, as long as it was not billed as an act of expiation or atonement for dropping the atomic bomb, or confused with a form of government restitution.

Norman Cousins had succeeded in obtaining guarantees for transportation, hospitalization, surgery, and home care free of charge, but he knew that once the Maidens were in America the project would accrue substantial expenses. The Hiroshima Peace Center Associates, unfortunately, were not in a financial position to cover them. But confident that whatever act of fiscal serendipity was necessary to prop the project up would be there when it was needed, Cousins proceeded to plan as though the coffers were full, for in anything he had ever done, one way or another the money had always come. As it turned out, this project was no exception. About this time he chanced upon a newspaper account of a recent *This Is Your Life* television program that had featured a seventy-year-old Negro educator who had started a school for black children in a ramshackle sheep pen in the Mississippi backwoods, and how an appeal over the air for contributions to endow a larger facility had brought in close to $1,000,000. So he wrote the show's host, Ralph Edwards, and suggested a tribute to the the Reverend Kiyoshi Tanimoto, a man admired throughout the country by those who had read John Hersey's bestseller, that would frame a similar fund-raising campaign on behalf of the A-bomb Maidens. Edwards, who liked to feature people who had distinguished themselves in admirable ways, found what Cousins had to say of great interest, and agreed to book the Reverend for his May eleventh show.

Conceding that there were probably dozens of things he had not yet thought of, Norman Cousins put in a call to Drs. Barsky and Hitzig and told them the time had come to go to Hiroshima and select the girls who would be brought to America.

The news that an American medical team was coming to Japan to select a group of female atomic bomb survivors to be taken to the States for treatment was prematurely leaked to the Japanese press, so by the time the Americans assembled in Tokyo, they found themselves facing an army of reporters. No one could have anticipated the tremendous amount of interest and emotionalism their arrival generated, nor the difficult questions that were asked. This was a time when American hydrogen bomb testing in the South Pacific was dominating the news in Japan, and the press wanted to know if this was a secret ploy by the U.S. government to offset the negative publicity created by the irradiation of Japanese fishermen following a test explosion on the Bikini Atoll the previous year. If not, who was putting up the money? What were their reasons? Where was the catch? And what about the rumor that the project was only a facade for a circus group which planned to take the girls on a coast-to-coast exhibition tour of America at a fancy admission charge?

So that the unfriendly speculation did not get out of hand, Norman Cousins decided it was best to open up and hold a press conference. Most of the questions were easily disposed of. As for the volatile question about motives, Cousins portrayed the project as an expression of traditional benevolence for disaster victims. The Japanese press was divided in its response. The answer apparently registered with the establishment papers, but the leftist press saw only ulterior motives and claimed to have confidential information that proved the Maidens would be studied, with the results benefitting the United States government so it could build more deadly "imperialist atomic weapons."

The question of motives was more involved for Norman Cousins, who felt a strong personal responsibility as a citizen of the nation that had been the first to use atomic weapons against other human beings, than for Dr. Barsky, who felt the use of the bomb was defensible as a military decision that had saved lives by shortening the war. Beyond that, Barsky had not given the subject much thought, and it played no significant part in his desire to participate in the project. It had been the convergence of the professional and the human aspects of the case that had prompted his involvement: He was fully aware of the fact that the advancement in modern surgical techniques was tied to the kinds of injuries sustained in successive wars, and initially he had been intrigued by the challenge presented by atomic burns. But he was also concerned for the innocent children caught in the crossfire of war who would carry their injuries for the rest of their lives.

The situation that awaited the medical team in Hiroshima was extremely complex. Everyone was suspicious about what was going on. The public was puzzled; people found it incomprehensible that American doctors would come all the way to Hiroshima to help a small group of survivors for nothing. The local medical profession was ready to take offense because having citizens from its community treated by outsiders made it appear that they were either incompetent or uncaring. Indeed, the very presence of foreign surgeons seemed like a slap at the Japanese medical profession in general. Perhaps the greatest hostility, however, came from the men at the Atomic Bomb Casualty Commission, because the emphasis of this new project highlighted the callousness of their program design.

Although the project as originally conceived had been structured to accommodate girls who were members of the Reverend Tanimoto's group, it was decided that the selection process should be opened to any young female disfigured or crippled in the bombing, and newspaper and radio announcements went out giving the time and place of the examinations. According to city officials there were hundreds of eligible women, but the rumor that they would be experimented upon apparently had a discouraging effect, for in all, forty-three women, ranging in age from their late teens to their late twenties, presented themselves for consideration.

As the senior medical man on the project, Dr. Barsky did his best to avoid any discussion with his Japanese counterparts about the comparative levels of Japanese and U.S. medicine, and he solicited their opinions at every turn. His professional manner, which bespoke dignity and high competence, won him a certain degree of respect, but it was his shrewd handling of the eternally vigilant and infinitely demanding press that ultimately won over his Japanese colleagues. Just before the examinations were to begin at a local hospital, reporters insisted that they be allowed to watch in order to make sure that nothing "untoward" was going on. Out of courtesy, Barsky had invited several Japanese physicians to sit in, but he drew the line at allowing the press to observe his inspection of disrobed young females. In the interest of community relations, however, he welcomed them to listen to what was going on from the far side of a partition he erected out of sliding panel screens.

To handle the large number of patients efficiently, Barsky divided them into two groups. While Dr. Hitzig administered a thorough physical exam to half the girls (checking for heart disease, tuberculosis, and disorders from any of the so-called atomic bomb disease syndromes), he inspected the injuries of the other half, and then they switched. What he saw were the late effects of severe thermal "flash burns." Even though the heat had come from a radiation source, the injuries were identical to those that might have been inflicted on someone sitting in a gun turret when there was an explosion of a powder magazine. He found that most were burned in two places: the face and neck region, and the hands and arms. Reconstructing the moment of the blast in his mind, he saw them turned in the direction of the fireball by the sound of the plane overhead, and instinctively raising their hands to protect their eyes from the blinding light. Although most of the girls reported they had exhibited the symptoms of radiation sickness shortly afterward, Dr. Barsky could find no physical evidence of actual radiation injuries per se, which would have affected the function of tissue cells.

When the examinations were completed and Drs. Barsky and Hitzig compared notes, they found that twenty-five of the forty-three candidates met the required guidelines. Reconstructive plastic surgery could significantly improve their appearances and disabilities, and they were deemed healthy enough to withstand the rigors of surgery. Since the project had been planned to accommodate twenty-two at the most, a decision had to be made whether to cut the list to the original figure or go ahead with twenty-five; at the last minute it was resolved that they would take everyone who was eligible.

Notifications to this effect went out to General Hull, Mount Sinai Hospital, and the Quakers, and individual letters were sent to the entire group of forty-three girls. Those who were selected to make the trip were given instructions regarding passports and visas and final preparations; those left behind were given no promises, but it was made clear to them that the possibility of bringing treatment to them and to the thousands of others, men included, in Hiroshima who were reported to be deformed by keloids would be explored in the future.

Dr. Barsky was grateful for the decision that had been made to enlarge the project to include two practicing Hiroshima surgeons who would accompany the girls to America in order to observe and learn American techniques of plastic surgery. When the idea was first proposed it had reminded him of the Chinese proverb, "Give a man a single fish and he will eat for a day. Teach him to fish and he will have food for a lifetime." Even though the services of the Japanese physicians were not essential, he thought it would be good for the patients to have them around, and adding an educational dimension to the project would broaden the way people evaluated the results. After all the Japanese media attention, Barsky also found himself thinking it was a smart move from a diplomatic standpoint as well. The Japanese doctors could serve as witnesses for more than techniques; they would function as reliable reporters that nothing "untoward" was going on.

There remained one other slot to be filled. The Maidens were going to be airlifted to a foreign country and admitted to a strange hospital for major surgery by men who could not speak their language. It was felt that a person was needed who could be with them when they were going into surgery, who would be there when they were about to be anesthetized and when they recovered, who would explain when things did not go according to plan or to expectations. Finding such a person had been on the agenda since the group arrived in Japan, but the search had been unproductive. They wanted a mature female, preferably someone who had raised children, who was familiar with medical procedures and terms, and, of course, who spoke both languages fluently. While in Tokyo they had interviewed a number of candidates, but few middle-aged Japanese women spoke English at that time, and the younger ones who presented themselves seemed too eager for the job, leaving the impression they were more interested in a free trip to the United States than anything else.

Time was running out when another one of the coincidences that seemed to charm this project brought the perfect person onto the scene. One afternoon Norman Cousins went to the Atomic Bomb Casualty Commission for the shots he had been in too much of a hurry to get before coming to Japan, and while there he talked to the head nurse about the difficulty they were having locating someone to assume the combined responsibilities of interpreter and chaperone. When he described the person he had in mind, she said that sounded like the woman whose desk he was leaning against.

Turning around, Norman Cousins was introduced to Mrs. Helen Yokoyama, an aristocratic-looking woman born in America of Japanese ancestry, who was a graduate of UCLA in psychology and who had married a Japanese and moved to Japan before the war and lived there ever since. She was the mother of three children and the wife of a man who had lost most of his estate holdings in the postwar land reformation, which was why she had taken a job at the Atomic Bomb Casualty Commission in Hiroshima, where her bilingual skills as well as her understanding of the different cultures had made her a valued employee. Whenever there were labor tensions between the American staff and Japanese hirelings, Helen Yokoyama's office became the mediation room. Whenever the American doctors had to break bad news to a patient's family, they would call in Helen Yokoyama, whom they trusted to translate a death sentence in a way that did not arouse resentment. She was still an American citizen and she considered America her home country, but she had come to love Japan too, and felt at one with its people. The satisfaction of acting as a bridge between the two countries was the main reason she stayed on at the Atomic Bomb Casualty Commission and why, when Norman Cousins offered her a position in the Maidens Project, she did not say no.

But she had not made up her mind to say yes either, nor fully discussed the matter with her husband, on whom the burden of taking care of the children would fall if she went, before a party was given at the Reverend Tanimoto's church for the twenty-five chosen girls and she was asked to attend as interpreter. By the time she arrived there were twenty-four seated at a long table, and their suspicion of her was profound. The twenty-fifth girl was standing on the dark side of a pillar, half in shadow, her face partly hidden behind a gauze mask and her whole countenance projecting a wounded-animal vulnerability. Their eyes met, and thinking suddenly about her own two, very lucky daughters, Helen Yokoyama knew now that she had no choice but to go.

It had been ten years since the world had seemed to come to an end for the A-bomb Maidens. They all thought the bomb that had destroyed their city and killed friends and family had robbed them of their futures. In her hit song, Michiko Sako wrote that people were different from flowers because blossoms might wither and die but would bloom again in the spring. Not so, the Maidens. Perhaps if the situation had not been so desperate at home they would not have had the courage to seek help from their former enemies. At the time, they had only one thought: They wanted to undo what had been done to them. Not to have gone to America would have meant they had abandoned all hope. They felt they had nothing to lose. Dr. Barsky had gone out of his way to impress upon them that plastic surgery would not be able to make their scars vanish without a trace, and they should not expect miracles. But for them the chance to go away and come back looking a little bit more normal was worth any risk.

Besides, there was little time to sit down and reflect on their fate. From the time of their selection to their departure only two weeks elapsed. They were kept busy with dozens of practical preparations, and then the necessary travel procedures had to be handled.

The day before they were to leave, the American Consul from Kobe, Ralph Blake, arrived in Hiroshima and opened a temporary branch office. Blake had been the first Foreign Service man to raise an eyebrow when he learned of the official clearance granted this project, for it sounded to him like a rash action with explosive foreign policy implications. He had cabled his concerns to his superiors at the State Department, questioning whether this was in keeping with "our worldwide efforts to deemphasize the destructive effects of nuclear weapons." While his views were under consideration, however, he was following standing orders and cooperating fully. Indeed, with an eye toward the favorable comment the gesture was bound to bring forth for the Foreign Service, he had come to Hiroshima himself instead of requiring the group to come to his office in Kobe, and he had thoughtfully waived the requirement for photos on the Maidens' passports.

In addition to the visa applicants, several dozen newsmen, photographers, and news cameramen were on hand, and they asked Blake to make a statement concerning the trip. Aside from wishing the participants an enjoyable and successful journey, he declined further comment, but in the spirit of goodwill he did grant a request to take pictures of the issuance of visas. Immediately he regretted it. As he reported in the dispatch he filed to Washington: "When several photographers and moviemen attempted to take close-ups of the girls, one in particular attempting to take movies of a girl with hideously deformed hands laboriously signing her visa, the reporting officer covered the camera lens and refused permission for continued photography."

Early on the morning of May 5, 1955, the departing party assembled in front of the Hiroshima City Hall. The twenty-five Maidens all wore dark blue suits purchased with the 20,000 yen that a local civic organization had donated to each of them to help them get ready for the trip, and they each carried one suitcase. Accompanying them were the Reverend Tanimoto, Helen Yokoyama, Drs. Tomin Harada and Goro Ouchi, and an entourage of escorts and interpreters headed by Dr. Hitzig. They boarded a charter bus and left for the American Air Force Base at Iwakuni, a half-hour's drive away, making one stop along the way at the Peace Park, a swatch of land in the center of Hiroshima that marked the hypocenter of the atomic blast. After laying flowers before the memorial to the 140,000 who would never make this trip and pausing for a moment of silent meditation, they went on.

Some 150 jubilant well-wishers had come to Iwakuni to wave the Maidens off, and standing among them was General John E. Hull, whose cooperation from the start had played a chief part in the good fortune that had brought the project this far. The girls had already walked up the boarding ramp and the propellers on the Skymaster C-54 were whirling when an aide dashed up to the general with an urgent cable from Washington. It was one he read with dismay: Senior officials at the State Department had apparently decided at the last minute that the risks of the program outweighed the potential benefits, and they were ordering the flight canceled.

For a long minute the general said nothing. Then, with a heavy sigh, he handed the cable back to his aide. "Unfortunately, I don't have my reading glasses with me," he said. "Be sure to remind me to read this later."

The aircraft made a sweeping circle over Hiroshima before disappearing in a southeasterly direction. When it was out of sight, General Hull reread the cable and then wired the State Department saying that the plane had departed by the time he received their message, and to abort the mission at this stage would, in his opinion, so sour relations that unless he immediately received a countermanding order from his direct military superior, the flight would have to continue on its prearranged course.

AMERICA

4

Even though foam rubber seats had been installed for their comfort, and a galley added so they might have complete meal service as on a commercial flight, the trip to New York was a noisy and grueling one for the Maidens, most of whom were too airsick to think about eating. This was their first airplane flight, and the slightest turbulence was enough to send up screams all around. The make-up of the crew was an added concern; for brawny Air Force men and not stewardesses were the flight attendants, a reminder that only ten years separated this flight from the one that had brought disaster to Hiroshima. The similarity ended there, for in fact this mission was almost the reverse of the other, and the men smiled reassuringly as they moved up and down the aisle serving cold beverages and handing out moistened towels. Nevertheless, the awareness of each other as another day's enemy charged the air with something extra—until one of the uniformed attendants who knew rudimentary Japanese attempted to make friendly conversation with several girls in the front seats. The ensuing reach for a medium of communication led one girl to bring out a songbook of traditional American tunes that they had each been given before leaving, and it proved to be the icebreaker, for soon the pure sopranos of the Maidens were harmonizing with the basses of the servicemen over old-fashioned campfire ditties. The women in back crowded forward to join in on the sing-along, which had evolved to an exchange of national anthems when suddenly the plane began to buck wildly, tossing the passengers into the air, spilling water out of the temporary latrine that had been set up in the tail section. It was a terrifying moment that seemed like nothing less than the prelude to a plunge into the sea, but as the men sprinted toward the rear the plane quickly stabilized, and when word came back from the pilot that the disturbance was the result of the unbalanced distribution of weight and they should stay close to their assigned seats, everyone had a good laugh.

After twelve hours in the air the plane reached Wake Island, where it stopped for refueling. From there it was scheduled to head straight for Hawaii, but a typhoon forced it to depart from the normal flight plan and veer south. Circling around the bad weather meant a detour stop at Johnston Island and another fourteen hours before arriving at last at Hickam Air Force Base where, despite the delays, more than a hundred Japanese residents of Hawaii were on hand to garland the Maidens with colorful leis in a traditional island greeting.

They were billeted in the bachelor officer's quarters, ate at the plush Officer's Club, and the next day taken on a sightseeing tour of the island that included an hour of relaxation in the sunshine at famous Waikiki Beach and a visit to the Punchbowl National Cemetery where Americans who had died in the Japanese attack on Pearl Harbor were memorialized. The following morning they departed for Travis Air Force Base in California, and a murmur spread among them as the plane passed over the city of San Francisco and the view from the air revealed block after unbroken block of bungalows and buildings in clear relief. It was their first glimpse of America, and what struck them most forcefully was the absence of a single sign of war. They saw none of the reminders of bombings and fires that still scarred most urban areas in Japan; and for the first time it dawned on them that Japanese warplanes had never gotten any closer to America than Pearl Harbor.

After resting for several hours they flew on to New York, landing at Mitchell Air Force Base on Long Island early on the morning of May 9, 1955, to a raucous reception. At a briefing beforehand, Norman Cousins had told the press that the girls did not mind group shots but they were understandably sensitive to close-ups, and a rope had been put up behind which everyone was asked to stand. But along with the gentlemanly New York papers like the *Times* and the *Herald Tribune* were the *Mirror* and the *Daily News,* and thrown together they made a tough bunch of reporters who would go to any lengths to beat each other out for a story. As soon as the small, dark-haired women stepped one by one from the Air Force transport, huddling at the foot of the exit ramp, uncertain and visibly scared, the pressmen forgot the agreement and charged across the runway like they were on their way to a prizefight. All the representatives of the project could do was try to get in their way. Big flash cameras exploded over their shoulders and between their legs, and a fistfight nearly broke out between Norman Cousins and a photographer from the *World Telegram & Sun* before the girls could be hustled into the terminal and the door locked on the angry, cursing mob of reporters who had not gotten all the pictures they wanted and were demanding interviews.

With their faces pressed to the windows, the Maidens rode into Manhattan on an Air Force bus with a New York Police Department motorcycle escort. After a formal registration session at Mount Sinai Hospital, they checked into an uptown hotel and rested for a few hours before assembling at Dr. Hitzig's five-story Park Avenue townhouse for a catered welcome party. In some ways it was their debut into New York society, for the reception and dinner was attended by a strong representation of the city's medical elite and embassy officials, who came fashionably dressed as though they were attending a ball. But the various supporters of the project were also present, and afterward people commented that no one who saw the overwhelmed and miscast Maidens clustered in one corner of a room where the plainly clothed Quakers joined them, linking arms in a united kind of front, could question Norman Cousins's wisdom in asking the Society of Friends to handle the hospitality.

As a point of fact, the Quakers had agreed to take on the responsibility of boarding the Maidens with serious and protracted reservations. Many had felt that as well-meaning as Norman Cousins was, he did not realize what lay ahead of him. At meetings held in advance of the Maidens' arrival, concern had been expressed that they would become homesick and be unable to make the adjustment to a different culture with a different diet. No one knew what these girls were like, or what their attitude toward America was. Mothers with young children wondered if they were safe to be around after having been exposed to high levels of radioactivity. After all the misgivings had been voiced, a core group in twelve Friends' Meetings in New York, New Jersey, and Connecticut, two in conjunction with other churches in their towns, took the initiative to respond positively; but by that time the flight of the Maidens was already in progress. Although Norman Cousins's penchant for going forward and letting the details work themselves out was once again vindicated, actual homes had in fact not yet been located for all twenty-five women.

Up until now, Helen Yokoyama had been reacting to what was in front of her without a clear understanding of what her duties were or what precisely was expected of her. She had assumed that the project had been carefully planned and that her responsibilities would be spelled out in due time. That many details had been unforeseen, overlooked, or simply not given a great deal of thought became distressingly clear the morning after their arrival. First, when the Maidens came down for breakfast they found that the hotel did not have a restaurant on the premises and that no arrangements had been made for their morning meal. At the Reverend Tanimoto's suggestion they went in search of a coffee shop, trooping down the street and into a corner drugstore where they filled the seats at the counter. The astonished waitress dropped a plate as they entered and threw a glance of supplication to the short-order cook, who came out wiping his hands on his apron. "What's this?" he asked. "It's all right," Helen Yokoyama assured him, and when she ordered breakfast specials of ham and eggs down the line, it was fine with him. The girls loved it, too, every second of it, but Helen could not eat for worrying, for if it hadn't been for the American currency she had brought along to take care of her own personal expenses, she would not have been able to pay the check.

Then, when they got back to the hotel, a charter bus was waiting to whisk them out of town; as the move was explained to her, the Maidens were going to be taken to a Quaker retreat in eastern Pennsylvania until their housing arrangements were worked out. All she could think when she heard the news was, *They don't know where the girls are going to be kept. We're going to this place because there's nowhere else to go. . . .*

As they rolled out of the Holland Tunnel and across the New Jersey flats, an American woman accompanying them noticed several girls gazing intently out the window at the landscape of marshlands and oil refineries and she hastened to assure them that where they were going and where they would be living would be much nicer than this. Compared to A-bombed Hiroshima, the girls thought the view was already picturesque, but when they stepped off the bus at Pendle Hill, a Quaker retreat a dozen miles southwest of Philadelphia, and found themselves surrounded by glorious green lawns and grand old trees, with the fragrance from flower beds scenting the soft spring air, it was less an arrival than a deliverance.

Designed to provide spiritually centered people with a place to gather and study and reflect in an atmosphere of serenity, Pendle Hill had the look of a small private college. The center of "campus" activity was a fieldstone mansion, actually a spacious farmhouse that had been converted into a combination dining hall, library, and meeting room. A large barn had been remodeled into a dormitory, and several other buildings used for a variety of purposes were scattered over some seventeen acres that had been partially landscaped, with enough lush woodland left to give the grounds the atmosphere of a park. Each morning after breakfast the residents would gather in a meeting for worship, which was followed by an hour or two of cooperative work, then classes in religious thought, social change, and literature, with time available to pursue individual study projects. As there had been no official orientation program devised for the Maidens, the daily routines of the sixty current residents at Pendle Hill became their starting point. After a day or two to recover from the fatigue of five days of travel, they attended the morning meetings, which consisted of an hour of meditative silence; they pitched in on the common tasks, cleaning their rooms and cutting vegetables in preparation for the evening meal; and during the time of day set aside for educational activities, they sat in the grass and listened to Helen Yokoyama as she tried to prepare them for the year ahead.

That there was indisputably an improvised element to this whole enterprise had been disconcerting in the extreme to the woman who felt herself caught in the middle, for it led her to question the thoroughness of the rest of the preparations. She did not know what to do at this point, but when she let herself feel the full gravity of the situation she knew that if the project flopped there could be disastrous international repercussions. Realizing it was too late to turn back now, however, she made up her mind that if it did fail it was not going to be because of any neglect on the Japanese side.

The job she assigned herself was neither enviable nor easy. First of all, the twenty-five girls in her charge had only the dimmest idea what the country they were visiting was like. Aside from what some of the older girls had studied in geography class at school, they knew next to nothing about Western customs, they spoke and understood no English, they could not even write their names in Roman letters. Most of what they did know about America came from American movies they had seen, usually westerns. As the plane had taxied to a stop at Mitchell Air Field, one girl, eyes glued to the window, asked, "Where are all the cowboys?"

For that matter, their familiarity with Japanese customs varied greatly. Though she had been "den mother" for less than a week, it had been long enough for her to observe that not all the Maidens were model Japanese girls. Watching them eat, she had been appalled at their table manners. Some of them ate like common laborers, devouring their meals in as little time as possible. Apparently some of them had come with an unreasonable load of expectations, too; a group of girls went on a food strike as soon as they arrived at Pendle Hill, refusing to accept a Western menu and demanding Chinese noodles at the very least. Eventually the girls had come around out of sheer hunger, but that had not been the only instance of rudeness.

To a certain extent that was to be expected. After all, these girls were inexperienced and uneducated; they had been selected on the basis of their disfigurement, not their backgrounds, and most had lost homes and family members so their home training lacked the discipline and instruction in etiquette that were mandatory in a traditional Japanese household. That being the case, and knowing that soon they would be entering American homes as guests, Helen Yokoyama felt it was most important for them to have a standard of conduct to guide them in their daily interactions. So in addition to leading them through a crash course in the ABCs of conversational English and American customs, she conducted an elementary class in etiquette.

Her method of tutoring was to let the instruction flow from the girls, for instinctively she knew better than to criticize them, which would only make them more self-conscious. "Imagine yourselves as perfect Japanese daughters," she would say. "What would you do for your own parents to make them happy?" When one girl replied she would help her mother prepare meals and clean dishes, and another said if her father came home tired she would give him a massage, Helen would say, "That's fine. Do just the same for your American parents."

She stressed the fact that politeness and courtesy were virtues recognized and appreciated around the world and that if they always presented a pleasant, gracious self it would add to their attractiveness, for people would notice their presentation more than their appearance. She said that whenever they were in doubt as to how they should think or speak or act in a given situation, they should remember that they were Japanese ladies and that, in their own way, they were going to be perceived as emissaries from Japan. And it seemed she had found just the right tone to use, because looking at their eyes she saw they almost seemed relieved to have a code of conduct to hold onto in the days ahead.

They stayed at Pendle Hill for two weeks, and in that short time Helen Yokoyama came to feel that even though they had ended up there through a hurried, last-minute arrangement, it could not have worked out better. Those two weeks not only gave the Maidens an opportunity to prepare for their future in a casual, easygoing atmosphere but also gave them a chance to develop relationships with foreigners in an ideal situation. Although none of their feelings about the war and the bomb had been particularized against the American people, nonetheless, they felt a certain apprehension being around the citizens of a country they had been raised to despise. Pendle Hill had been set up expressly to create a shared sense of community among those who stayed there, however; and as the Maidens meditated and worked side by side with the residents, they found themselves growing fond of them. The Quakers were friendly and helpful. They were unable to speak Japanese, of course, so through pantomime they tried to communicate the customs of daily living, which added a kind of sporting element to their exchanges. Amused, drawn out of themselves, the Maidens would reciprocate by singing folk songs of Old Japan in the evenings after dinner when the dining hall was cleared. The most memorable was a plaintive one about a lone maiden who sits apart waiting patiently in the gathering dusk for her lover to come.

Although predictable excesses showed up in the headlines announcing their arrival (25 JAP GIRLS SEEK NEW FACES) and in the descriptions of their appearance ("The face of every girl was scarred. One had an eye burned out. The flesh of another's throat had the corded appearance of manila hemp. The nose of another girl was all but burned off and the mouths of many were like twisted and distorted livid gashes. Through the girls' stockings could be seen red and white fire scars."), the nation's newspapers generally gave the story wide and fair play. The Hiroshima Maidens, as the American press called them, were characterized as a peace-loving and appreciative group, and the project was portrayed as a "mercy mission."

The majority of Americans were introduced to the Maidens on a live television broadcast, however, for the day after their landing in New York, the Reverend Tanimoto and two girls who had been with him from the beginning were flown back across the country to Los Angeles to appear on Ralph Edwards's *This Is Your Life*. "This Is Your Life—Kiyoshi Tanimoto" was strong material for the mid-fifties, and the messy spectacle of a captain of one of America's proud airships crying over what he had done to the enemy in wartime—on national network television, no less —provoked an immediate and angry response. Minutes after the show had ended the switchboard at the NBC studio was blitzed with phone calls.

The Reverend Marvin Green had been put in charge of the post-show public relations, and he could not handle the calls fast enough. Every caller was a member of the American Armed Forces, and to the man they were outraged. To watch a decorated Army Air Force man all but apologize for his part in a mission that to their minds had put an end to the war in the Pacific made them mad. On the phone Green did not argue; none of the callers wanted to talk anyway; they just wanted him to hear them out and then they banged the phone down. But Green alone knew there was more to the matter than what had been seen on the air, and that Captain Robert Lewis had been under the influence of more than strong emotions when he had broken down. As he would recall the incident years later, "Lewis claimed that Edwards's office had worked out a deal with him ahead of time and he thought they were going to pay him a big fee for appearing on the show. When he got there he found they weren't going to pay anything but expenses, and he hit the ceiling. Around noon the day of the show he started visiting the grog shops. He didn't show up for the afternoon rehearsal and the producers were going crazy. They sent me out to find him and by the time I tracked him down he had already hit four taverns. And he was drunk. I got him back to the studio in time for the show and we tried to sober him up, but, you know, coffee only makes a drunk wide awake instead of sleepy."

Green had no doubt that what Lewis had said on the air was deeply felt, for he knew too that while stumbling around backstage waiting to go on, Lewis had peered into the room where the two Hiroshima Maidens were also waiting. His face was white when he turned to Green and whispered, "And there are a hundred thousand more who look like that?" But Green did not believe Lewis would have cried if he had been straight.

The media reviews ran the gamut. *Time* magazine called it "First-rate entertainment. . . . Easily the most dramatic and affecting moment of the TV week." John Crosby in the *New York Herald Tribune* awarded it a "new low in taste" rating and wondered if "an adorable little gold bomb [was] attached" to the charm bracelet given to Mrs. Tanimoto as a souvenir for appearing on the show.

As for Norman Cousins, he felt that the purpose of having the Reverend on television had been decent and that there had been nothing staged or wrong about what Lewis had done. The man had expressed genuine emotions, which were natural under the circumstances. Rather than defend the program, however,

Cousins preferred to let the viewing public cast its vote by mail. Fourteen letters of criticism were received, seconding the opinion that the show was in poor taste (while Ralph Edwards saw historic irony in arranging for the Reverend Tanimoto and Captain Lewis to cross destinies on his Hollywood stage, others could only remember the shadows cast by the two deformed Japanese girls) or stating that Japan had a long way to go to atone for Pearl Harbor before she was entitled to American sympathy. Against those fourteen letters stood more than twenty thousand pieces of mail warmly supporting the project with contributions. The proceeds did not amount to a million dollars, as hoped, but the $55,000 eventually collected would help to to solve the petty cash crisis of the Hiroshima Maidens Project.

Meanwhile, at the State Department the program had been watched with mounting dismay, for during May 1955 a series of overlapping articles and events were putting America's nuclear policy on parade. On May 5, the very day the Maidens departed from Hiroshima, Operation Cue had been carried out at Yucca Flats, Nevada. This thirteenth U.S. atomic blast of the year was given the full glamour treatment through promotional and public relations techniques. Busloads of middle-aged Americans wearing civil defense caps and badges, coming from as far away as Kansas City, Akron, and Terre Haute, had been transported to the detonation site where they tramped through dust and sagebrush to inspect the test homes of frame and brick and concrete block: a mock town such as you would find on a Hollywood set that was carefully designed to simulate a typical American community, right down to department store dummies seated at kitchen tables. Comedian Dave Garroway was reported to have conducted his morning show from the GI-filled trenches two miles from the blast, which had twice the destructive force of the bomb dropped on Hiroshima; the show was carried live over national television into millions of homes at breakfast time.

A week later the magazine *US News & World Report* carried a cover story on the findings of the Atomic Bomb Casualty Commission in Hiroshima and Nagasaki. Dr. Robert Holmes, the current director, tried to dispel some of the rumors and fears about radiation effects by equating the nervous public reaction to the hazards of the Atomic Age to "the panic that the first steam engine produced among the Indians as it crossed the Western prairie, and the consternation of the people at the first automobile as it roared along at the tremendous speed of about 25 miles an hour." But under questioning, Dr. Holmes was forced to admit there had been a dramatic rise in the incidence of a whole range of cancers in the A-bomb survivors, with more due to come because of cancer's incubation period. Ten years after the bombing he confessed, "The end is not yet in sight."

That same week the semidocumentary Japanese film *Hiroshima* that had so disturbed the Reverend Tanimoto that he had picketed it, opened commercially in New York City to favorable reviews.

Then along came *This Is Your Life*, wherein a commercial organization had presented a sensational story to the public without investigating its possible ramifications in a very sensitive area of Japanese-American relations. Even if the show had been designed for the purposes of entertainment, some felt the picture of the teary-eyed American co-pilot of the *Enola Gay* shaking hands with an atomic bomb survivor and presenting him with a check from his squadron, could be dynamite in the wrong hands. There was concern it could serve to dramatize the demands of aggressively active groups in Hiroshima who were seeking funds from the United States government for the rehabilitation and care of all persons affected by the atomic bomb. There was little doubt that the film would do much to reinforce leftist propaganda of American guilt and could even provoke further anti-American demonstrations in the Far East.

It was time for a talk. Officials at the State Department were well aware that Norman Cousins was a vocal critic of its nuclear policies and active in disarmament and antinuclear testing campaigns. They needed to be assured that the Hiroshima Maidens were not going to be used to attract publicity and followers for his political objectives, and become the darlings of the Ban-the-

Bomb Movement. Norman Cousins was eager for a meeting, too; he wanted to find out why the State Department had tried to halt the flight of the Maidens.

The face-off took place during the summer of 1955 at the State Department in Washington, D.C. Behind the desk sat Assistant Secretary for Far Eastern Affairs, Walter S. Robertson, and in front of it sat Norman Cousins, who would remember the exchange this way: "I asked him why he had sent a wire to General Hull canceling the flight, and he said the reason was he was afraid if the girls came to this country they would produce sentiment for outlawing the atomic bomb. I said, 'But Mr. Secretary, President Eisenhower has declared it to be a prime purpose of American foreign policy to find a way to outlaw the atomic bomb.' He fudged at that point and said that we had to create a formulation to indicate that we would be second to none in our interest to produce peace, but that the atomic bomb would not be outlawed, not in the interests of American security—which ran directly counter to the President's stated policy."

A recently declassified State Department memorandum supports this account of the conversation, which rapidly degenerated into a debate. Robertson took the position that "the single major factor now keeping the world from a third world war is the deterrent power of nuclear weapons," and Cousins argued that "disarmament carried out by foolproof methods of enforcement is the only feasible course to try to follow." The meeting concluded with the assistant secretary of state stressing that "helping victims of misfortune is a very worthwhile endeavor, but every effort should be made to keep the project involving the Hiroshima girls from stirring up propaganda against nuclear weapons," and Norman Cousins summing up his case with the opinion that the treatment of the Hiroshima Maidens could only further the cause of peace and goodwill on an international level.

Of course, Cousins was aware that the Hiroshima Maidens Project probed a sensitive nerve at the State Department. At that time the government was defensive about anything that the "Red press" could possibly exploit for propaganda purposes. But while he did not hesitate to speak out publicly, calling the double-barreled atomic bombings of Hiroshima and Nagasaki "the greatest stain on our national history," or opposing the brinksmanship of building and stockpiling more and bigger nuclear weapons, or advocating certain unilateral measures "to demonstrate our own good faith, since we took unilateral measures in dropping the bomb," he did not want the Maidens to feel part of a larger symbolism. They were not pawns in a political game, be it relations between the United States and Japan or the issue of nuclear weapons. Some of his friends were concerned about America's nuclear policy and thought the Maidens ought to go around lecturing about the A-bomb "to bring about a larger awareness of the menace and immorality of these bombs." But again, Cousins did not want them to feel they were being used for something greater than themselves. "If their presence aroused public opinion, it was all to the good. But to have them travel around as part of a demonstration, or attend meetings or rallies for that purpose would have exploited the girls, as well as the emotions of the people."

For that reason, when the producers of the Japanese film *Hiroshima* attempted to obtain his endorsement of the film in exchange for one-half the box office proceeds of the first week's run in New York as a benefit for the Hiroshima Maidens, he refused. Although he was determined to challenge the American government for ignoring the special sufferings of the Japanese people hurt by the atomic bombs, he was not indifferent to current political realities.

Cousins wanted to keep the project a personal event. "That, for me, is what history consists of. One makes an impact on history in terms of example, not pronunciamentos. I was trying to create relationships and I thought the relationships would spread and endure. If there was anything to this, the power of the example would find its meaning."

The day before the Maidens were to leave Pendle Hill for their American homes, the Reverend Tanimoto escorted the first two girls scheduled for surgery to Mount Sinai Hospital. There they found themselves barraged by a sequence of wholly unexpected physical checks before they could be admitted. First, a nurse came to take their temperatures. In Japan, the thermometer was placed under the arm, so there was an awkward moment of embarrassing confusion when the American nurse attempted to take their temperatures rectally. It required an explanation from the Reverend before they understood and, with grimaces, skeptically submitted to the procedure. Barely had they gotten over the humiliation of this when a young doctor showed up to conduct a gynecological examination. While this may have been a common procedure in many American medical institutions, it was not done in Japan. The Reverend had left, so there was no one around to explain. It was not until the nurse herself assumed the proper position on the examination table that one of the girls, evidently more experienced in these matters than the other, guessed what they were talking about and hopped onto the table. Even then, it sounded like a wicked inspiration to the other girl, who cooperated when it was her turn, but was burning with shame and afraid to imagine what they would want to do next.

After breakfast the following morning, seeing there was no one in authority around, one of the girls suggested they have a look around. Her shyer companion did not think it was a good idea to leave the ward without permission. "What are they going to do, send us back?" the bold one demanded. And when she indicated her willingness to venture on her own, her wardmate was not about to be left behind. Together they wandered down a maze of corridors, peering around corners and scurrying down empty hallways, riding an elevator all the way to the roof where they gasped at the vertical grandeur of midtown Manhattan, and then taking the elevator down to the very last stop. They were exploring the catacombs of the basement when a security guard spotted them. "Hey," he called, "where do you think you're going?" From the way they looked at him he must have realized they didn't understand English. Holding his hands out in a wait-right-here gesture, he ran to make a call upstairs. One girl had the terrible feeling they were about to be arrested and was on the verge of tears, but the second the man's back was turned the other girl bolted for the elevator, grabbing her companion by the hand and pulling her along like a doll. They were breathless by the time they found their way back to their ward; and though they hung their heads in shame before a lecture from a stern nurse who made it clear they were not to leave the ward unaccompanied again, when they were alone they laughed and laughed, and even the shy one had to admit it had been an exciting first twenty-four hours.

Mount Sinai Hospital consisted of two buildings, each over ten stories high, standing side by side on Fifth Avenue at 100th Street across from Central Park. On the fourth floor of the surgical pavilion a four-bed suite at the back of the general ward for females had been converted into a private ward for the Hiroshima Maidens. To assist him in performing the operations, Dr. Barsky had recruited his second-in-command at Beth Israel Hospital, Dr. Sidney Kahn, and at Mount Sinai, Dr. Bernard Simon. When they were first approached, each man had had personal reservations about donating time to this project. Aside from the fact that they were both already maintaining steady hospital and private practices, Dr. Simon, who had served in the Army during the Second World War as an evacuation hospital surgeon in Germany, suspected this might be a political ploy put together by Norman Cousins to dramatize the effects of nuclear weapons. Dr. Kahn had not quite overcome his resentment toward the Japanese as a ruthless enemy and was loathe to be part of an action that implied regret over the use of a weapon he credited for putting an abrupt end to the war. Moreover, he knew there were a good number of Americans who could benefit from free treatment, and he felt that if they were going to start opening their services to charity, they should begin with the people in New York. But both men had been trained by Dr. Barsky and held him in tremendous respect, and when he told them matter-of-factly that this was what they were going to do, they forgot their reservations.

Dr. Barsky had decided it would be best to begin with several uncomplicated procedures so that the progress could be immediately seen, thus raising the morale of the rest of the Maidens. Before operating, he let each girl know what he had in mind, giving her a sense of what was going to happen and what she would have to put up with. He did not feel that their emotional backgrounds posed an obstacle; he believed they would respond to complete gentleness, compassion, and honesty, and he treated them the same way he did every other young patient.

In his own mind, Barsky was thinking function first, appearance second, knowing that in most cases there was an interrelation between the two—that restoring an eyelid, for example, not only saved vision, it looked better. But these were young women who obviously wanted to be made more presentable, so sometimes he would discuss the options with them, and there were those who were willing to accept a slight functional restriction in trade for a better look.

Four girls were operated on in rapid succession. A keloidal adhesion was removed from the back of a girl's neck, allowing her head, which had been frozen in a bowed position, to move freely. A scar that had locked another girl's right hand to her forearm was excised and replaced by a small skin graft, restoring an elementary function that had been missing for a decade. An ulcerated lower left eyelid was replaced by a graft taken from the inside of a right upper arm so a third girl could close her eyes at night. And a graft of full-thickness, hair-bearing skin was taken from behind a fourth girl's right ear and implanted over her eyes, giving her a new and complete set of eyebrows.

Where just the surface of the skin had been affected, "free grafts" could be drawn directly from another part of the body. But where the deeper structures were damaged, the transfer of fat and subcutaneous tissue was also called for. The first step in this process was the selection of a "donor area" that resembled the recipient area as closely as possible, in color, texture, elasticity, and thickness of skin. The abdomen was generally recognized as the most suitable area to draw from, but as Barsky and his associates quickly discovered, with the Maidens the best tissues were not always available because they had already been used up on procedures attempted by Japanese surgeons—procedures that had been improperly chosen and inadequately carried out. He never said it would have been better if the girls had been left alone, and he would not use the fact that he had to go to secondary selection sites as an excuse if the operations did not turn out satisfactorily, but Barsky was glad for the presence of the two Japanese surgeons who had come along, and who could not help but see the handicap he was working under.

Once the donor site was determined, a "pedicle graft" was the procedure of choice. It was an extraordinarily complicated process of moving skin that, in short, called for the transportation of middle-body tissues to the face in stages, using the arm as a carrier. Typically, the patient was put under general anesthesia and two parallel cuts were made in the abdomen, approximately 9 inches long, 4 inches apart, and 1/2 inch deep. The flesh was then pulled up, folded in on itself, and sutured between the incisions to form a cylindrical roll. Several weeks later, one end was severed and sewn to the wrist, connecting the blood vessels. A month was generally considered time enough for new blood circulation to be established in the tube, and then the other end was detached from the abdomen and planted in the face. In the final stage, the roll of flesh was disconnected from the arm and slit open, the facial keloid was excised, and the graft spread over the gaping wound. Since straight scars often healed in a pucker, the edges of the graft were Z-stitched, and an effort was made to put the seams along a natural crease in the face.

These were demanding and exhausting operations that required a great deal of patience and attention to the most minute detail, and which lasted anywhere from two to four hours at a time. It was a slow process, day by day, operation by operation, without any dramatic climaxes that represented turning points. After three months, Dr. Barsky was cautiously pleased with the progress but less than delighted with the publicity. Not that the newspaper notices he was receiving were negative or unfriendly. The headline that bannered the front page of the *World Telegram & Sun*, SURGEON'S KNIFE BATTLING A-BOMB, while a little too dramatic for his liking, caught the spirit of the majority of press reports. But he was disturbed by rumors that had come back to him that some of his distinguished colleagues were suspicious of his motives and, behind his back, accused him of participating in a publicity stunt. An ill-timed article in *Time* that left the impression Barsky and his associates were America's three foremost plastic surgeons did not help matters; but it was the antics of his medical counterpart on the project that he held accountable for the impression they were playing this up for their own gain.

Dr. William Hitzig's bombastic personal style was at complete odds with Dr. Barsky's reserved, professional manner. An alternately exuberant and moody man who dressed dapperly, Hitzig could be both a charming character and an unsufferable egotist. His penchant for baring his soul whenever he spoke his mind and his transparent attempts to ingratiate himself with the press made him seem at times like the public relations manager of the project. (Somehow he always managed to wind up in the center of the newspaper photographs with his arms draped around two Hiroshima Maidens like a proud papa; for some reason the accompanying articles were consistently unable to get his title and position straight, and compositely referred to him as a Quaker plastic surgeon who was director of Mount Sinai Hospital, when he was neither.) For Dr. Barsky, Hitzig was one more thing to worry about, and it came as no surprise that Dr. Hitzig turned up at the center of their first crisis.

One day, unannounced, Dr. Hitzig, accompanied by another gentleman wearing a white coat, appeared on the ward and asked Helen Yokoyama to bring one of the Maidens who was in line for surgery to the nurse's station. Thinking this was just another pre-operative interview, she followed his instructions, and after all four of them had taken a seat in the private cubicle, Dr. Hitzig said, "This is Dr. Kauffman and he is a member of the Mount Sinai staff. If you don't mind, he would like to ask you a few questions."

Through Mrs. Yokoyama's translation, the girl said she would be glad to cooperate, and everything was fine until Dr.

Kauffman went from general questions about how she was enjoying her stay to a more probing inquiry into her personal history. She glanced at Helen Yokoyama and said she did not understand the meaning of this line of questioning. Neither did Helen Yokoyama, and she asked Dr. Hitzig what was going on. Hitzig then explained that Dr. Kauffman was the chairman of the hospital's psychiatry department and was interested in doing a psychological study of the Hiroshima Maidens. Helen Yokoyama tried to translate, but the direct translation of *psychiatry* into Japanese connoted "mental illness," and when the girl heard that, she yelled, "I'm not crazy," and ran down the hall to alert the other girls on the ward that the critics in Japan were right, they were going to be put through all kinds of tests just like guinea pigs.

Helen Yokoyama turned on Dr. Hitzig. "Why didn't you give me time to explain if that was what you intended to do? You should have told me beforehand."

Flustered, he protested. "But it's a common practice . . ."

"In the States, maybe, but in Hiroshima it's virtually unheard of."

At a subsequent meeting, in Norman Cousins's *Saturday Review* office, of a steering committee formed to deal exclusively with the Maidens Project, Dr. Hitzig defended his decision to bring a psychiatrist onto the scene by making the case that the Maidens had lived through the single greatest disaster known to man, and surely it had left them with lifelong psychological problems that would benefit from analysis and counseling. At the same time, he said, they constituted a test group like no other in history and were in a position to make a contribution to medical history and posterity.

Dr. Kauffman proceeded to elaborate. From the scientific point of view, the opportunity to interview Hiroshima survivors and document the impact of this sequence of events in which they were involved could supply the kind of information which was not available in any other circumstances and which until now his profession could only imagine. An investigation into the Maidens' reactions to the atomic bomb, the inner emotional turmoil they endured, the adjustment required to seek salvation from the very perpetrators of their misery, were fascinating components of an extraordinary psychological constellation.

In a soft but firm voice, Helen Yokoyama countered that such a study was impossible. Psychiatry may be fashionable in the United States, she explained, but in Japan few people were familiar with the practice. Putting aside for the moment the question of whether the theories and therapies of Western-oriented psychological studies would be of help in maintaining the mental health of the individual Maidens, it was her opinion that such a study could not be conducted without implying that the girls were either losing their minds or being brainwashed; and if word of that got back to Japan, she warned, even though it might be a misinterpretation of what was really happening, it would be disastrous.

"Besides, the girls won't understand the need of it. It's a departure from the original purpose. They are here for surgery, and are not interested in posterity."

Listening to all this, Dr. Barsky had to will himself to stay calm. When patients in a hospital were assigned to a particular service, it was considered proper procedure to discuss with the chief of that service any projects involving those patients before proceeding, and he was irate that Dr. Hitzig had taken it upon himself to initiate this study without even discussing it with him first. He knew that successful plastic surgery considered every aspect of the patient's well-being and not merely the local symptoms in a problem area, but he was unpersuaded that psychiatric care was required. If no one in Japan saw a psychiatrist unless they were psychotic, which these girls were not, then that was all he needed to hear.

What Dr. Barsky said was, "We can't judge this by our standards; we must judge it by theirs. The information to be gained is not worth the risk of misunderstanding and the bad effects of probing." What he did not say but thought was that disturbed females made bad patients, and he would not permit any activity that upset them as long as he was in charge.

After considering the various viewpoints, Norman Cousins

wondered if a compromise might not be worked out so that such a study could be useful both to medicine and to the girls.

During the ensuing discussion the question of whether or not the data would be true to the facts if the girls did not cooperate willingly was raised. It was suggested that perhaps they could each be approached personally, alerted to the possible value of this phase of treatment and asked to participate on the basis of making a contribution to science, as a way of repaying the people who were doing so much for them.

At this point the Quaker representative, Mrs. Ida Day, a slender, bespectacled former school counselor who was the project's designated Hospitality Coordinator, spoke; her voice was choked with indignation. "I speak for the Friends and we think it would be a shabby exploitation of the girls. We feel the only person who would profit from such a study would be the person publishing the article or writing a book about it. We feel strongly that rehabilitation is the most important thing, and psychiatrists are not the only ones who can do this. What is already being done for the girls, from the human angle, is enough. They are adjusting just fine."

There was silence in the room. His arms folded, chin upraised, Dr. Barsky rocked back in his chair. He thought she had answered wonderfully. Indeed, the voice in favor of a psychological study of the Hiroshima Maidens was never heard from again.

When the Maidens' idyllic interlude at Pendle Hill drew to its conclusion, Michiko Sako, in a gesture of gratitude that humbled the residents, who had come to feel they had received as much as they had given, gave the director of the retreat a handful of morning glory seeds that she had brought from her garden in Japan. Exactly what the Pendle Hill experience had done for them would be difficult to describe, but each girl felt it and showed it the day the American families came to take them away. Where once the move would have filled them with apprehension, now they were bursting with anticipation.

The decision had been made to send them into American homes in pairs, as a way of minimizing loneliness, and the task of deciding upon roommates was left up to Helen Yokoyama. It was her idea to put girls together who were not only compatible but who would be good for each other, and for that reason she tried to mix rather than match personalities, placing the more outgoing girls with shy, introverted partners. But since she did not know any of the girls well and there was not enough time to learn about them in any depth, she had to go with her first impressions.

Nor had there been enough time for Ida Day to carefully investigate the suitability of individual homes. She had thought it a good idea to place the women in homes outside the New York metropolitan area because living in the city was apt to produce confusion and not the sense of community that she felt would be valuable in terms of a representative American experience. Other than insisting that the homes be located within a reasonable driving distance from Mount Sinai Hospital, the only guidelines she was able to pass down were that the chosen homes should be able to offer a comfortable, private living space for the guests, and the mother of the family should be a housewife who stayed home during the day. She left the screening of the homes up to the special committees each Friends Meeting had formed to handle this concern. In recognition of the haphazard character of the pairing process, however, Helen Yokoyama and Ida Day agreed that it would be best if the first home-stays were considered a trial period to see how well the girls got along—with each other as well as their new families.

The Quakers went all-out to make the Maidens' move to their new and strange homes a smooth one. The Ridgewood, New Jersey, hostess, for example, brought along the Japanese wife of a neighbor, a war bride who had married an American GI, as interpreter; and in an effort to make her house seem familiar to the girls, she had arranged for a "Japanese evening," complete with koto music on the phonograph and an American version of sukiyaki for dinner. A similar evening was planned in Rockland County, New York, but there the hostess did not have the advantage of an interpreter and learned quickly that the language barrier, coupled with the inherent timidity of the girls, doubled the chances for misunderstanding. It was late in the afternoon when she took her guests to their room and told them dinner would be ready when they were. Hours passed and it was getting late but the girls had not appeared. When she finally went to call them, she found they had changed from Western dress into silk kimonos to make a ceremonial occasion of their first meal, but after dressing had been sitting, waiting, afraid to go downstairs.

In every household a special effort was made to make the Hiroshima Maidens feel welcome, but the most effective gestures were the unplanned and spontaneous acts of thoughtfulness. Her first evening in an American home, Hiroko Tasaka retired early to her second-floor bedroom, only to be wakened at dawn by sunlight streaming in the east-facing windows. She could find no curtains to draw, nor could she hear any stirrings in the rest of the house, so she just lay in bed thinking when she heard the creak of a door opening and footsteps quietly enter the room. She lay perfectly still, pretending to be asleep, and through half-closed lids watched her hostess tiptoe over to each window and lower the venetian blinds. The room was dark when the hushed footsteps left, but Hiroko was unable to go back to sleep. The good lady would never know how much that simple act meant, or in what giant way it relieved; but Hiroko could palpably feel the foreignness of her surroundings and the nervous uncertainties that had collected since arriving in America melt away.

As it happened, such moments were taking place in many of the homes opened to the Maidens, which was reassuring to the host families for whom all this was new, too. One of the most touching occurred in Flushing, New York, where Yoshie Harada had gone. Yoshie was one of the shyer girls because she had not been a member of the Reverend Tanimoto's original group. Because of her injuries, she was unable to get around and she had not even known of the existence of the other girls until she read about the project in the newspaper. For a year and a half after the bombing she had lain on the floor on her right side, unable to move, unable to roll over, and as a result her entire right side was nerve-dead. When she walked, she dragged one leg behind like something stepped on, she had trouble holding things in her right hand, and one side of her face was pinched as if she were screwing her eye up. After a quiet meal, Yoshic Harada was left sitting in front of the television set while her host and hostess disappeared into the kitchen to clean up. Shortly, the picture on the television turned to vertical lines. She did not know what had happened or how to fix it so she soon limped toward the kitchen to see if she could be of help. At the entranceway she stopped, suddenly unable to remember the names of the people she was staying with. She wanted to address her hostess but was at a loss when all of a sudden she recalled a doll that her father had given her as a child that had been made in the United States. When it was stood up its mouth opened and a two-syllable sound came out, "Mom-mee." Softly, Yoshie said, "Mommy?" Her hostess turned, astonished. She was so moved, tears sprang to her eyes as she embraced Yoshie in her arms. Yoshie was not sure what she had done, but she would always remember that incident.

On the whole, the Maidens were eager to conform to the customs of their host country, and over the ensuing weeks their thoughts and interests were turned fully to learning the ordinary ways of doing things in America. They learned, for example, that they did not have to take their shoes off before entering the house. They learned how to sit in chairs rather than Japanese fashion on a floor mat, and how to eat with a knife and fork instead of chopsticks. They learned that Americans would just as soon stand under a shower as soak themselves in a tub when it came to bathing, and that they slept on boxed mattresses instead of bedding spread on the floor.

The customs of every country are strange to first-time visitors, but an extra measure of difference was added in this case because of the enormous gap in living standards between the two nations at the time. The austerity and privation of postwar Japan was not only a world away, but decades behind the America of the mid-fifties. Coming from war-ravaged and impoverished Hiroshima subtracted another ten years in time, making the airlift to the progressive, modern suburbs of New York tantamount to traveling through time to the future.

Landing in upper middle class homes, the Maidens were dazzled by the latest in automatic amenities. And while they marveled over the way music and movies could be brought into the living room at the touch of a button, they were naturally just as curious about the work and time-saving devices that allowed the American housewife to do her chores in a fraction of the time it took a Japanese wife to complete the routines of housekeeping. To date there had been little progress in modernizing the Japanese kitchen. Except in certain urban areas, gas was not generally used for cooking, so women had to rise early to make a charcoal fire in the brazier. Lack of refrigeration meant food spoiled rapidly, which meant going to market on a daily basis, sometimes prior to each meal. Because so many more bowls and plates were used than in Western cooking, washing dishes was a tedious process. So it was with amazement and delight that the Maidens discovered that the modern American kitchen was a virtual appliance center. Everywhere they turned, a shining gadget beckoned —an electric stove, a toaster, a Mixmaster, "the fridge," a freezer, a dishwasher, a garbage disposal—and they exulted in the testing of one after another.

It was the effort to adjust to the American cuisine that presented them with the greatest challenge. Their hosts were well aware that the Japanese were inveterate rice eaters, that it was their staple and no meal was substantial without a large helping of rice. For that reason, they were fully prepared to serve rice three meals a day if that was what their guests wanted. But in their desire not to inconvenience, the Maidens did not insist on rice, and in fact even developed a liking for most Western dishes, especially those that came with a generous portion of red meat. Beef in Japan was in such short supply it was used mainly to flavor foods, so they were thrilled to find themselves eating a T-bone steak or a couple of hamburgers, and sometimes consumed more meat at a single sitting than their annual intake at home.

Marveling at their appetites, their hosts reported that the anticipated dissatisfaction with Western food was failing to materialize, and the Maidens had adapted wonderfully to their new culinary situation. What they did not know, because the Maidens went to great lengths to keep their feelings hidden, was that one reason the Japanese consumed such large amounts of rice every day was because they had so little else in the way of foods, and rice gave them a sense of fullness that no other food would. So while their nutritional needs were being served by their American diet, they were rising from the table neither satisfied nor full, and craving more to eat.

It was happening in home after home, and although the Maidens tried to ignore the pangs of hunger, it got to the point where many girls were unable to think of anything but food. Since it was impossible for them to imagine a scene where they approached their hostesses and requested larger portions, and equally as painful to think of going shopping with the $15-a-month allowance they were given and returning with a bag full of groceries, when it reached the point they had to do something, several of them, on the pretense of going window shopping, strolled to the nearest grocery store, made a purchase of sliced lunch meat and cookies, and returned to their rooms where they feasted in private.

That was not to say that an extensive effort was not made to determine their desires. Virtually every morning in every home the phone would ring and it would be another hostess calling to exchange information about what "her" girls had eaten the day before. It was just that no one wanted to insult her hostess, so no one said anything. In one household a Maiden did express a preference but was apparently ignored; the incident so upset her that she was convinced her hostess must still think of her as the enemy. "Why do you feel that way?" Helen Yokoyama asked when the girl called her on the phone to complain. "Because every morning she serves me eggs, and I can't stand the sight of eggs on an empty stomach. They look like two big yellow eyes staring up at me out of a slimy white face. And I keep telling her

I don't like them, but she serves them anyway." Later that day Helen telephoned the hostess to hear her side of the story and learned that the root of the misunderstanding was the Oriental custom of using the affirmative case as a polite way of saying no. The woman said of course she noticed that the girl was not finishing her breakfast, but every time she asked her, "Don't you like eggs?" the answer was always "Yes."

But those kinds of problems were, individually, more than offset by private acts of extreme generosity; collectively they were lost in the background of what was rapidly becoming the Time of Their Lives.

In an effort to make things interesting for them, their hosts kept them busy with a whole range of varied and rich experiences. Sightseeing tours were arranged—to the top of the Empire State Building, through the United Nations, up to Niagara Falls. Curiously, West Point was a hit with some of them; they liked to see young men in uniform marching. When they indicated a willingness to go almost anyplace and do almost anything, their hosts took them along on family outings and shared the activities that gave them pleasure. A Connecticut couple who loved the sea took their girls along on weekend boating excursions, dropping anchor at a small island in Long Island Sound where the girls swam and collected seaweed which they brought home, hung on a clothesline to dry, and later cooked into a Japanese meal.

Silencing those who had worried that they might have to make a special effort to keep things from becoming too grim or restrained in the presence of disfigured persons, the Maidens enthusiastically took advantage of every opportunity and invitation to enjoy a thoroughly active social life. They went to outdoor movies, Broadway plays, Radio City Music Hall. Partying was not a word in their vocabulary at the time, but it soon became a fact of their lives. One day Yoshie Harada was pushed out of the house with no explanation and taken for a long drive by a neighbor. She did not understand what was happening, wondered if she was being moved to another family, and was hurt that her hostess had not even said good-bye until they arrived back home. Now she was even more confused because the street out front was lined on both sides with cars. It was not until she opened the front-door on a scene bursting with balloons and bunting and beaming faces shouting, "Surprise! Happy Birthday!" that she understood. In a daze, she just stood there shaking. Not only was it a surprise party, it was the first time her birthday had ever been celebrated.

As though exuberating in their newfound freedom, as though making up for the lost years, the girls traveled to places they had never thought to see in their lifetimes, found themselves in a hundred new and exciting situations, and at the end of each day looked forward to what tomorrow would bring. There was so much happening they did not have time to be homesick, and they barely made time to write letters home rhapsodizing about life in America.

The initial plan for out-of-hospital care mapped out by a special committee of Quakers called for the Maidens to be rotated to different families for stays of at least one month, but no more than two. The idea was not to burden any one family and to expose the Maidens to different ways of living. Everyone recognized the reasonableness of the rotation plan, but when the first period of hospitality ended it was not as simple as that. Some of the girls were so comfortable that they did not want to move and their hostesses did not want them to go. In several homes there was friction between girls: An assertive girl was ignoring her subdued partner and competing for the attention of their hostess; a girl was glad to do housework and assisted her hostess at every turn and was accused by her lazy roommate of trying to make her look bad. The decision as to how best to handle each situation was made within the respective Meetings, and as a result some pairs moved on, some girls went individually to different homes, and some stayed put.

In all the Friends Meetings, when there was to be a change of homes the new hosts became acquainted with the girls by visiting them, entertaining them, and driving them to the hospital so the change would be easier. Of the American families who played host to the Maidens, most were elderly couples who resided in large houses with rooms their children had left empty, but there were also a fair share of young couples starting families and a few who did not fit into either category. In two consecutive moves, one Maiden went from a luxurious mansion to a log cabin. First she found herself occupying a room in a house that had service like a hotel. Maids did all the housework, and a black cook prepared meals that were served by a butler when a tiny bell was rung by the host. A month later she was living in the country home of a couple who operated a lumbermill, so everything in the house involved wood. The house was constructed out of logs, the furniture was fashioned out of rough planks, and the place was heated by a wood stove.

But both families had provided her with a home, not merely housing; and it was that way down the line. The American hosts were showing the Hiroshima Maidens the same interest and concern as they would their own daughters. The result was a reasonably complete family experience, and family life in America was more than just miles and an ocean away from what it was in Japan. There, expressions of affection and emotion were controlled even among family members, whereas here there was a natural openness to family relations that the girls were totally unfamiliar with. It was evident in the casual exchanges of tenderness between husband and wife: Once two Maidens entered a room and surprised their host and hostess in a kissing embrace. Blushing and giggling with embarrassment, the girls tried to sneak out but were called back. "Is it true that in Japan there is no kissing, even between husband and wife?" they were asked. They had to admit, they had never seen their parents kiss. "Oh," the couple said, "well, we do it like this," and they proceeded to put on an exuberant display of smooching American-style. And it was there to be seen in the way parents related to their children: It would be rare in Japan for a father to come home from a day at the office and play ball with his son until dark, then spend the evening reading to his daughter. It was new, it was different, and ultimately the girls discovered its particular charm. The turning point in the evolution of a relationship is sometimes the result of a dramatic event; other times it can stem from something that at the time seems inconsequential. The experience of finding themselves kissed good night at bedtime was one of those small events that took on an extraordinary significance for the Maidens.

5

A fter the initial burst of publicity, Norman Cousins thought
surely the media interest in the Maidens would settle down,
but it was soon apparent that the American imagination had been
captured by the girls. Cousins was besieged by requests for additional information from the major wire services in both America
and Japan. The television networks wanted to interview one or
two girls in their homes. National magazines wanted material for
feature stories. Inquiries were received about adaptations for stage
and screen. The producers for the *Ted and Jinx Show* called. So
did Ed Sullivan.

In the beginning Cousins tried to enforce a news blackout,
explaining to reporters that, understandably, the girls were sensitive about pictures of themselves, that there came a time when
it was too much of a burden to go through the same story over
and over again, and that they believed that publicity had the
effect of dramatizing their own good fortune in contrast to that
of the girls who were left behind. But once he realized it was
impossible to shield them from any contact with the press whatso-

ever, he permitted controlled encounters on the condition that all interviews were cleared in advance (with the girls, the families, and himself) to assure that they remained tasteful, supportive, and cognizant of Japanese sensitivities. Other than that, the primary public source of information and the most extensive coverage of the project was a series of "Reports on the Maidens" that appeared on the editorial page of the *Saturday Review*.

In these reports, Cousins never mentioned the controversy over the atomic bombing implicit in the very presence of the Hiroshima Maidens in this country; he kept the focus of the project on the present rather than the past. And far from giving the impression that everything concerned with this endeavor was being carried out solemnly and with a self-conscious realization of the symbolic value it might have, his accounts stressed that "there has been both the time and occasion for sheer joy and fun." Indeed, at times his articles sounded like dispatches from a summer camp as he recounted how the girls went as a group on a picnic at a farm in Woodstock, New York; took a boat trip around Manhattan Island as guests of the New York City Police Department; proved themselves to be ardent Brooklyn Dodger fans at a night baseball game against the New York Giants at Ebbets Field ("When Sandy Amoros broke a tie in the fourth inning by blasting a triple against the right field screen, the girls leaped to their feet in unrestrained joy. And as the Dodgers continued to pile up runs it almost seemed as though the universe were fulfilling itself").

As Cousins reported it, a heartwarming story was being written that went in many directions, crossed many barriers, and touched many lives. The extent to which his glowing descriptions of the way the appreciation, courage, and cheerfulness of the Hiroshima Maidens was winning the hearts of all who met them succeeded in creating a favorable public impression among those who only read and heard about them, was manifested in the donations that poured in from all over the country: money from schoolkids and pensioners and people on social security; presents of cosmetics, clothes, shoes; tickets for plays, movies, fashion shows; flowers, cards, dinner invitations. Gifts from individuals were usually accepted gratefully (except in a few crackpot cases, as with the alleged inventor of a facial cream that magically made scars disappear who was willing to let the Maidens use it in exchange for bus fare to New York City), whereas gifts from companies were selectively screened. When a leading American surgical supply house presented them with sutures and antibiotics the goods were welcomed; but when General Electric offered to give each girl a new steam iron on the condition that the manager of the regional office be photographed with them, the gesture was respectfully declined.

The popularity of the Maidens accounted most notably for a change in attitude within the Japanese-American community. At first they had been reluctant to get involved. There were hundreds of ways they could have helped, but most had put up with hardships and prejudices during the war and were afraid that if something went wrong with the project it would mean trouble for them. Gradually, however, as it became evident that a success story was in the making, their outlook changed. In response to the desire expressed by several Maidens to observe a program of modern Western dancing, the 442nd Veterans Association, composed of Japanese-American ex-soldiers who had fought in the European theater during the Second World War, sponsored a benefit dance in their honor, and there were no wallflowers that night.

So inspirational was the project that a group of ministers and community leaders from Mobile, Alabama, were moved to take up a similar effort, except that they wanted to bring "maidens" from the city of Nagasaki. In a letter to the State Department, Dr. Carl Adkins, a Mobile minister, explained why Mobile would be a suitable host city: "We believe this program would be particularly significant [because] Mobile is in the center of a section of our nation which no doubt in the minds of the Japanese is synonymous with race prejudice, and for us to bring these girls into the homes of the citizens of this community would be a tremendous gesture of goodwill."

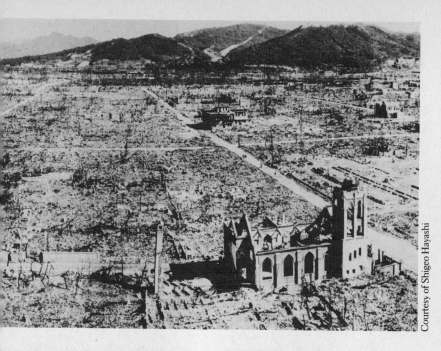

The remains of the Nagarekawa
Church standing in the ruins.

Reverend Kiyoshi Tanimoto in 1979.

A Japanese soldier offers water to an
injured young girl in the aftermath of
the atomic bombing.

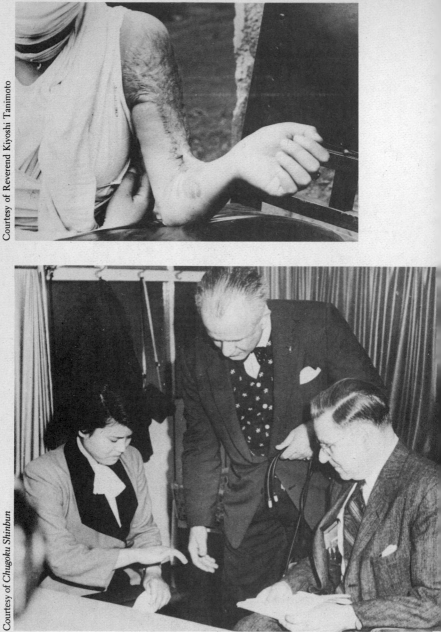

Hiroko Tasaka's left arm; the scar tissue locked it at a permanent right angle.

Drs. Barsky and Hitzig examine Michiko Yamaoka.

Jun Miki, *Life* magazine, Time Inc.

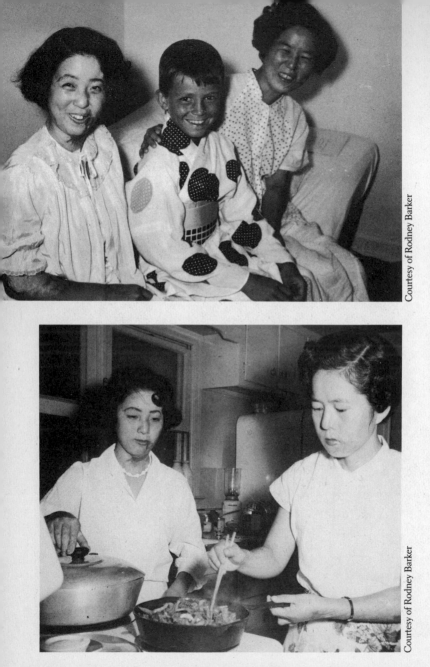

Author Rodney Barker (age eight) at home in Darien, Connecticut, with Suzue Hiyama and Misako Kannabe.

Suzue Hiyama and Misako Kannabe fixing dinner.

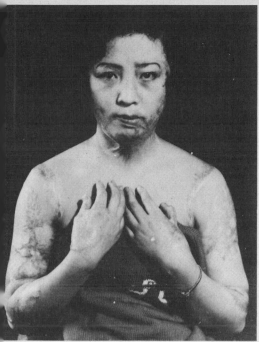

Suzue before surgery and after.

Atsuko Yamamoto opened her own Japanese pizza shop in 1973.

Yoshie Yanagibashi (Harada) on her wedding day, 1956.

Suzue Oshima (Hiyama) with her husband and two daughters, 1965.

Shigeko Niimoto and Margaret Bourke-White.

Harry Earl Harris.

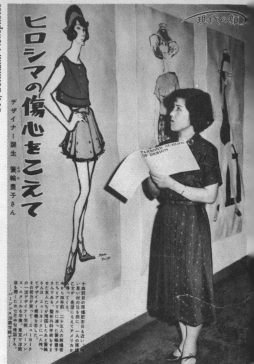

Toyoko Morita at Parsons School of Design.

The first group of Hiroshima Maidens and Dr. Sadam Takahashi—who carries the urn with Tomoko Nakabayashi's ashes inside—prepare to return to Japan.

Alarms went off when the proposal reached the State Department. Agency memorandums reveal a strong concern that "there might be a rush of 'Hiroshima Girls' projects in major American cities." Taking immediate steps to ensure "that another incident may not be allowed just to grow like 'Topsy,' " Assistant Secretary Walter S. Robertson responded with a letter stressing "the undesirable character of the 'Mobile Plan' " and asking Dr. Adkins that his group "defer action . . . until the results of Mr. Cousins's project at Mount Sinai and its attendant political implications can be more accurately evaluated." As a result, the Mobile Plan never materialized.

Insofar as public impressions of the Hiroshima Maidens Project were shaped by selective media coverage, most Americans remained ignorant of the perpetual problems and backstage intrigues that plagued the project organizers. Some were trivial in the overall scheme of things, such as the inexplicable refusal of the producers of *This Is Your Life* to reimburse the Hiroshima Peace Center Associates for expenses the Reverend Tanimoto and his family had incurred in connection with his appearance on the program, seven months earlier, which they had promised to do. Nor had their contribution of $500 been received so far. Other problems—such as what to do when it became evident that the continued activities of the Reverend Tanimoto in connection with the project were turning into a liability—were not so easily dealt with.

Officially the Reverend Tanimoto was referred to as the "spiritual counselor" of the Hiroshima Maidens, but in fact the Reverend spent most of his time fund-raising, for which he displayed a natural talent. Even though measures had been taken to make sure he did not personally handle any of the money (the Reuben Donnely Corporation, the firm that kept the accounting books for the March of Dimes campaign, had been hired to handle all finances relating to the Hiroshima Maidens Project), rumors continued to circulate that the Reverend was skimming profits and amassing thousands in unrecorded contributions. And as if that were not enough, the matter of religious freedom became a most sensitive issue for the project organizers; reports abounded that the Buddhist Maidens were being subjected to Christian proselytism by the Reverend.

When the controversy surrounding the Reverend was brought to Norman Cousins's attention, he felt bad because he knew better than anybody how important the man's role in this project had been. Tanimoto had been the first person to befriend the Maidens and champion their cause, and he had done it at considerable personal sacrifice. But Cousins also knew that for the project to have come this far it had been necessary to branch out and enlist the blessings and cooperation of many people in both Japan and the United States, and in the best interests of the project, the time had come for the Reverend to take a seat in the gallery. The only question was how to effectively separate him from the matter at hand without causing a rupture.

Naturally the Reverend Tanimoto's perspective on the progress of events had a slightly different slant. To begin with, when he had introduced Norman Cousins to the Maidens in his church and asked for help, he had assumed that if help was forthcoming, Cousins would treat him as the representative in Hiroshima. But it had been the mayor's office that had received the official invitation, the Hiroshima Medical Association had been brought into the picture (and he thought it was bitterly ironic that the same medical association that had snubbed him when he approached them was so quick to take an interest once a trip to America was in the offing), and the internal organization of the project had been taken over by Americans. Even the composition of the group was not what he had intended for it to be; rather than draw from the pool of girls he had assembled in his church, Cousins had opened the project to any Hiroshima girls scarred by the bomb, so of the twenty-five selected to go, the "Tanimoto girls" made up less than half.

The Reverend had, however, gone along with Norman Cousins's wishes, and even felt that his willingness to compromise had been rewarded when he found himself playing a starring role on national television. The surge of interest that followed his personal introduction of the Hiroshima Maidens to the American public seemed to further vindicate his cooperative spirit. Hundreds of requests for speaking engagements came his way, and each day's mail brought in five or ten more. This was before there was any indication of how successful the appeal for funds on the *This Is Your Life* program would be, and since at that time the project had no visible means of support, he departed on a national speaking tour to raise money.

This was the third time around for the Reverend, and while the lecture circuit had been good to him before, it had never been this good. The congregations that gathered to hear him speak averaged more than twice the size he had commanded on his previous visits. He was applauded in churches throughout New England; in Los Angeles and Chicago, leaders in the Japanese-American communities announced benefits held in his behalf. The only discordant note was struck on August 6, 1955, the tenth anniversary of the atomic bombing, when he placed a wreath on the Tomb of the Unknown Soldier in a ceremony conducted before the eyes and ears of television and radio coverage. Even though the prayer he offered was for all victims of war, it was unprecedented for a citizen from a former enemy nation to make such a tribute, and the veterans' organizations screamed.

The first indication that an unpleasant parting of the ways was in the offing occurred after Tanimoto had organized a prayer session with several girls who had been members of his church, only to receive a letter of caution from Norman Cousins reminding him it would be inappropriate "to exert undue influence in trying to make Christians out of Buddhist girls." His disappointment was profound. He had initiated the effort to help the Maidens as a minister, working out of his church, and he had high spiritual ambitions for its outcome. He hoped that a strong dose of Christian friendship in America would provide the Maidens with a thoughtful religious experience, above and beyond everything else. It was his secret desire that upon their return more would want to be baptized. But as things were currently being carried out, the church orientation had been nullified, and he blamed Norman Cousins for secularizing the project and giving it a distinctly medical tilt.

The matter came to a head at the end of the year, when the Reverend wound up his tour and prepared to return to Hiroshima. It had been his understanding that if the funds collected through the television program were sufficient to see the Hiroshima Maidens Project through to a successful conclusion, then the money he personally raised on his speaking tour would go toward his work in Hiroshima. Like any business, the Hiroshima Peace Center operated on a budget and needed a steady infusion of funds if it was to stay on top of the movement to bring comfort and aid to the victims of the atomic bombing. Since the fifty thousand produced by the solicitation on *This Is Your Life* was more than enough to cover the Maidens Project expenses, Tanimoto requested that the tour money be sent to his bank in Hiroshima.

But Norman Cousins did not see things that way. He was of the opinion that all the money the Reverend raised should go into one fund out of which the Maidens Project was operated and that no money should be released for anything else until the project was over, at which time it should be spent according to the wishes of the Maidens themselves.

Tanimoto felt double-crossed. Not only had his position of leadership been usurped and the entire focus of the project altered, but he was being cheated out of money that he felt rightfully belonged to his organization. In a passionate appeal before the project steering committee he said that the Hiroshima Maidens Project was just one part of the total program of rehabilitation he had had in mind from the beginning; he reminded the group that for them this was just a project, while it was his lifework.

It was left to the Reverend's former schoolmate, the Reverend Marvin Green, to communicate the decision of the committee. "As I see it," he wrote Tanimoto, "Mr. Cousins feels the moment you agreed to come to America you agreed to play on a bigger team than the team you played on in your work with the Hiroshima Peace Center. . . ." Though the Reverend's definition of which team he was playing on was quite different, he was not in a position to argue. The money in question amounted to more than ten thousand dollars, of which one thousand was forwarded to his church in Hiroshima as remittance for "borrowing your services." He felt it was a paltry sum to show for having been away from his duties as full-time minister for so long, and did nothing to quell the rumor that he had a private fortune stashed in a secret bank account somewhere in the States. Maybe everyone else was calling the Hiroshima Maidens Project a triumph, but according to the indices by which the Reverend Tanimoto measured its success, it was a profound disappointment. To close friends he confided, "Norman sold me out."

The real drama, meanwhile, was being acted out under the operating lights at Mount Sinai Hospital where, far from finding themselves the subjects of medical experiments, the Maidens were being treated to the best modern medicine had to offer. To those girls who in Japan had been forced to walk to the operating rooms and return to their hospital beds under their own power and lie for weeks in a frail postoperative state, weak from the combined loss of blood and appetite, the experience of being wheeled to and from surgery on a gurney and having their recovery period expedited by such things as plasma, blood transfusions, and intravenous feedings, all of which were new to them, was comforting as well as confidence-inspiring. They were also finding American doctors less authoritarian than their Japanese counterparts, and, most reassuringly, more objective when it came to evaluating injuries relating to the atomic bomb. When the mysterious skin infection returned to Hiroko Tasaka's feet, Dr. Barsky simply treated it with a topical lotion, unlike the specialist who had declared it to be a disturbing new symptom of the A-bomb. When it cleared up immediately, Hiroko asked him what the problem had been and was told that in America the condition was called athlete's foot.

As for the surgery, it was not something one got better at or learned to like with experience, but in time it became less dreaded, and on occasion something the girls could even joke about. They would talk about the roll of skin taken off their abdomen as a being in its own right, and like a baby gave it a name. Though it was sometimes difficult for them to imagine pretty results by looking at the gruesome stages, they never once questioned or doubted that the doctors knew best.

So trusting had they become that even when there was an occasional mishap, it never occurred to them to fault those in charge. Once, on the operating table, the anesthesia mask was not properly fitted over a girl's face, allowing air to slip in, and rather than counting her way into unconsciousness she felt as if she were drowning. Panic seized her. In her mind she was clawing reflexively for the surface while in reality she was thrashing in the grip of a nurse who was trying to hold her down. After a terrifying struggle she was allowed to sit up. Over her gasping sobs she heard Dr. Barsky's voice, "She'll be all right now. Let her rest. We'll try again tomorrow." Afterward, back on the ward, she was ashamed of herself. All she could think was she had let everybody down. She was determined to be brave the next day and was even looking forward to the chance to submit to the ether calmly just to show the doctors she had not lost faith in their procedures; the second time, however, they stuck a needle in her ankle and seconds later she was asleep.

It was still too early to tell the extent to which the surgery would succeed, but the good news was that the special difficulty in treating keloids was being effectively dealt with through the use of radiotherapy. Although administering radiation for a benign condition was rare in view of the cumulative and unpredictable delayed reaction, the dose was small, consisting of "soft" beta rays which were absorbed in the first few millimeters of the skin, and the treatment succeeded in suppressing the formation of keloids in the donor area and along the borders of the grafts. The bad news was they were finding the pigmentation factor difficult to control. Something in the general architecture of Oriental skin caused grafts to become darker upon healing than the surrounding area. As a result, they would take skin from another area that was perfectly adequate for the functional purpose, even the contour, but it would end up standing out on the face as a bright yellow patch.

Dr. Barsky also felt severely constrained by the fact that he had only one year to work on these patients. Plastic surgery involved a series of operations and you could not simply operate week after week. It took time for tissues to heal, relax, soften; if a patient was going to need three operations, then a year or so should pass between them. But he did not have that kind of time with the Maidens, and working under a deadline he sometimes had to bunch operations more closely than he would have otherwise.

By the same token, it had become increasingly apparent that the medical success, was all but secondary to what was happening outside the hospital. When the girls came in, there was already a lift to their expressions that had nothing to do with plastic surgery. There was none of the defensiveness or circumspection commonly exhibited by patients about to undergo major surgery; they arrived in high spirits and were capable of kidding the doctors and being teased in return. Shortly before one of the girls was wheeled into the operating room she asked Helen Yokoyama to give this message to Dr. Barsky: "Tell him not to be worried because he cannot give me a new face," she said. "I know my scars are very, very bad and I know he is worried because he thinks I may expect that I will be as I once was. I know this is impossible; but it does not matter because something has already healed here inside."

The way the Maidens spent their free time between operations was largely left up to the energy and interests of the individual; but where at first they had shown a desire to go everywhere and do everything, once the operations got underway many of them found their schedules tiring and welcomed the days when no activity was planned for them. In general, they required very little home care during their convalescent periods other than occasional assistance when bathing and dressing; even when a girl was in the more awkward stages of surgery—such as when her arm was attached to her abdomen or face—she usually found a way to perform most normal tasks with her free hand so the only care required from her hostess was a massage to relieve an aching shoulder.

Around the house they could do as they pleased, but often they tried to make themselves useful. There were certain similarities in the maintenance of American and Japanese homes, and the girls enjoyed the opportunity to help with the housekeeping and marketing. In homes with children they gladly played the role of babysitter. Some hosts had feared that the girls' disfigurement might shock the children or arouse excessive curiosity, but such fears proved groundless. The girls adored children, taught them finger-games and new things to do with blocks and toys, and were adored in return.

All was very different from home life in Japan, and not just for cultural reasons. Many of these girls were estranged from their own parents, for whom they had become financial burdens. Some had been kept out of sight by parents who subscribed to the belief that malformation or any gross irregularity was due to some unknown wrong committed by an ancestor and that this child had been chosen to bear the punishment for the family sins. Consequently, the world had been a vast unfriendly place for them, and they had lived with a sense of loneliness and insecurity that seemed to grow cumulatively with the years. Now, however, they were accepted with affection as an integral part of the homestead. Family relations were normal and wholesome once again. And not only were their foster parents making them feel as wanted as natural daughters of the house, but they were determined to give them all the tangible benefits of American living. When they realized the girls had come to this country with only the clothes they could cram into a single small suitcase and had no winter-wear, they took them shopping and bought them new outfits. Appointments with optometrists were made for those who needed glasses, and those whose teeth were bad were taken to the dentist. One hostess who was particularly fashion-conscious taught her girls to walk like models and wear flattering clothing —and she took them to a salon where they were coiffed in the latest hairstyle.

Of course there were different opinions among the host families about the manner in which parents can assist their children to achieve a sound foundation for an enjoyable life. While some were content to make the Maidens' stay a thrilling social occasion, others felt a more constructive program of activity than sightseeing and entertainment was in order, and undertook to make it an educational event. Within the group there were a variety of talents, abilities, temperaments, and aspirations to be found, and after consulting with individual girls to determine their level of formal schooling and their area of interest, special educational agendas were designed. Some had little training or talent on which to build and were satisfied pursuing personal hobbies such as handcrafts, music, and art; but others were eager to take advantage of the opportunity to further a skill or trade in the hope that the education they received in America would help them earn a living when they went home. With that in mind, several girls who had studied English conscientiously on their own, keeping notebooks in which they recorded all new words and phrases, were enrolled in language classes at a local high school; one girl who had been told before she left for the United States that if she learned to type in English she would be given a responsible job in an import firm, was placed in a secretarial class; two girls who had expressed an interest in social work were introduced to various welfare organizations and instructed in the use of a braille typewriter so they would be qualified to work with the blind in Hiroshima; a few studied design, one took a training class to become a beautician, and all were given a course in home nursing by the Red Cross.

All of the host families were impressed by how courteous, tactful, and accommodating the Maidens were, without quite knowing the secret of their charm. Some likened it to a highly developed aesthetic sense: Just as the girls would arrange a bouquet in a vase and somehow make everything fall into a perfect order, they fit themselves into their living space with a delicate aesthetic sensitivity. Actually, their ability to "fit" was directly attributable to an attitude that was characteristically Japanese. There is no precise translation of the Japanese word *kigane*, which refers to feelings of reserve and constraint out of respect for another person's feelings. If a girl were tired and wanted to go to bed but her hosts were still up and doing things, kigane would keep her from excusing herself and retiring. If she wanted a cup of tea, even though she knew her hosts would be happy if she would help herself, kigane would keep her seated. The reluctance to express a personal desire for fear of appearing selfish or putting someone out or causing friction was kigane, and it was an attitude that had been ingrained in them since childhood.

However, while kigane made for good family relationships and accounted for the graciousness and adaptibility that made the Maidens such welcome houseguests, it also happened to be a quality which, given their circumstances, made them all the more vulnerable. Coupled with their inferiority complexes, it was one more restraint on their will, keeping them subdued and acquiescent. And when their sharply aware hosts realized that there was another side to this sublime quality, and that what they had previously perceived as a positive was in some respects a negative, they took it upon themselves to provide the dynamic for change. They sat and talked with their girls and encouraged them in the plainest possible manner to be more open and assertive in the expression of their feelings and forthright in their dealings with people, to say yes only when they meant it and no if that was what they felt. By their example they showed them how misunderstandings could be avoided through honesty; and when invitations and situations came up, they insisted the girls make decisions and choices on their own.

The Maidens were unaccustomed to thinking for themselves and speaking their own minds, but in the generally less restrained atmosphere of American society, under the benign influence of their American hosts, they gradually became more outgoing and began to project their personalities more comfortably. In large part they had not felt good about themselves because it was in the sight and judgment of other people that they evaluated themselves, and in Japan the visibly disfigured were looked down upon, as though their handicaps were the consequence of personal failings rather than outside circumstances. Time spent with people who valued them none the less for the way they looked, who saw them as individual people just like everyone else, who genuinely cared about them and were actively adding new experiences that helped them develop healthier attitudes toward their circumstances, was more than liberating or supportive, it was therapeutic.

Each had lived through a time when she welcomed death more than life; but now the whole other side of the girls' emotions —their capacity for joy and laughter, the feelings that made life worth living in the first place—was coming back. And as their early timidity was replaced by a surging confidence they began to want to meet new people. They willingly spoke to community groups about the customs of their native land, and demonstrated the tea ceremony. They became daringly independent about traveling in public. At first their hostesses had felt it necessary to accompany them every time they left the house, but now they were commuting in and out of New York on their own. And in dramatic contrast to Hiroshima, in New York they found their disfigurement opened rather than closed them to human contacts. Strangers took a kindly interest in them, approaching them on the subway or at bus stops and asking if they were a Hiroshima Maiden. The frankness was a welcome change and sometimes led to a rewarding exchange. One girl found herself talking to a woman who had lost a son fighting the Japanese Forces in the Pacific, and the mutual understanding of the pain and sorrow caused by war that came about through their conversation brought her face to face with the fact that people everywhere were basically alike in their humanity.

All of the Maidens had a deep awareness of the extraordinary generosity, untiring efforts, and many sacrifices that were being made on their behalf, but they also expressed a certain bewilderment about its source. After all, they were receiving better treatment all around in America than they had in their very own homeland. Perfect strangers were showing them more magnanimity than their own countrymen. "What I still don't understand," one of the Maidens said to Helen Yokoyama during a home visit, "is why these people are doing all this. Back in Japan I was told they have a guilty feeling about dropping the atomic bomb. Is this the reason?"

Time and again, Helen Yokoyama displayed an instinctive ability to grasp the significance of an occasion and know what was called for to make things work for the Maidens. She had proven to be a pivotal person whose sensitivity and acuity was capable of rescuing an immediate emotional reaction from escalating into an ugly conflict, converting it into a detailed illustration of the diversity among people of different backgrounds and orientations—and in such a way as to bring about a respect for those differences. It was why the Maidens called her *Sensei*, a Japanese term respectfully reserved for master teachers. She had had numerous opportunities to talk with the Americans involved in the project, and it was her conclusion that while their motives were multifaceted and there were probably a few who were making a political statement through their participation in this project, most were simply acting in accordance with a tradition of philanthropy. "Yes, these are people who deplore war," she replied. "But I don't believe this is the only reason for their involvement. I think they volunteered because they are people responsive to human suffering."

The girls were not satisfied. Historically, philanthropy was an alien cultural and philosophical concept in Japan. A traditional reluctance to get involved in the troubles of others, plus the absence of the "Good Samaritan" ethic in Japanese religion, generally explained why there were so few philanthropic foundations or programs in Japan. While the Japanese had a strong sense of obligation in certain situations, such as to Emperor and family, they were largely lacking in feelings of altruism. "But they take me into their homes and treat me as though I belonged to their family. It is not their duty to do this. It is not their duty to give me expensive medical treatment. Why do they want to do all this?" asked one girl.

"Suppose," Helen Yokoyama said, "that some people have a philosophy of life which enables them to regard all human beings as belonging to a single family. Even though they might not know each other, even though they might live thousands of miles apart, they might still believe in their closeness to one another and in their obligations to one another. The same love that members of a family feel for one another can be felt by by these people for all others, especially for those who are terribly in need of help. Is this not possible?"

"You mean that these people are helping me because they love me?"

"I believe they do."

It was a different way of thinking than the girls were used to. At that time in Japan the term *love* was used only to describe relationships between members of the opposite sex and within a family, and never applied to *humanity*. So Helen Yokoyama thought surely the girls would have difficulty absorbing the meaning of the concept of a love for mankind, and suspect some ulterior motive. But to her surprise and delight she found she was wrong about that.

At first she thought maybe the girls were receptive to the idea because they had not been exposed to people and ideas in Japan—ostracized in the community, their schooling interrupted, they had been unable to feel much of anything other than their own misery. But when she visited them in their American homes and saw them sitting by the hearth in cashmere sweaters and tweed skirts, speaking joyfully of their present lives, she knew where the explanation lay. The experience of being cared for and made to feel wanted had brought out a creative growth in their response to life and other people. Being loved had re-established their own capacity for loving.

The transformation of Michiko Sako was a golden example of the regenerative power of human love. She was a country girl, orphaned at the age of eight when her mother died of tuberculosis, the same disease that had claimed her father two years earlier. Their tragic passing was just the latest in a series of premature deaths that had plagued the Sako family history with the constancy of a curse; when a freshman, Michiko wrote an essay about her tragic heritage that was awarded first prize in a high school writing contest. Until that time, few of her classmates knew of her "dark side," and from that day on she felt she walked around school with an aura of difference that was directly tied to the old feudal prejudice against orphans. It was just the beginning of a life of gradual withdrawal and alienation that culminated with the atomic bombing. Michiko Sako was the girl whose scars pulled tautly at the corners of her mouth, making it physically impossible to smile—inspiring her to write the poem "Smile, Please Come Back" that had been made into a hit record. Even if she had been able, there was nothing in the ten years after the war that Michiko would have felt like smiling at. All that changed in America, however, where she found herself taken in by a white-haired, ruddy-faced gentleman who looked like Robert Frost and shared the poet's love of nature and hobby of watching wildlife, and his petite, gray-haired wife, Vesta, who lived up to her namesake, the Greek goddess of the hearth, with her love of cooking. The couple had been unable to have children, but without affectation, as if it was the most natural thing in the world, Michiko Sako became the daughter they had never had, and they the parents she had lost. They took her into their lives completely. The language barrier did not prevent basic understandings; to the contrary, the way blindness makes a person more sensitive to sounds and smells, communicating without words forced them to rely on expressions and vibrations to know what the other was feeling and saying, which often led to finer understandings. Almost physically, Michiko felt other barriers breaking, built up through the years of loneliness and desperation, under the touch of this elderly couple. It was like a second upbringing that opened her mind to new ways of thinking and gave her a different view of herself and the world.

Michiko was in the hospital when Mother's Day came

around, but she made sure that her American mother received a greeting card on that day. It was the first ever for Vesta, and she regarded it as one of her most treasured keepsakes. "When I die, if nothing else is put in my coffin, be sure to put this card in," she told her husband; and when she phoned her Japanese daughter to thank her, she repeated that line. Michiko's reaction was normal enough, but in her case it seemed as though a miracle took place, as the emotions recently released inside her combined with her restored capacity for physical expressiveness to permit a smile.

From time to time it did occur to some of the Maidens that they were looking upon America at its best and only seeing the sunny side of this country. And hearing from the Japanese-Americans who visited them in the hospital what it had been like living in resettlement camps during the war made it all more believable. And there were occasional episodes that let them know Americans were capable of contradicting the ideals they allegedly stood for, of turning their backs on some while opening their arms to others. Two girls who stayed for a period of time with an interracial couple saw racial discrimination in action one evening when they were taken out to dinner and the husband, a black man who worked at the United Nations, was refused service (the irony that there was a stronger bias against black Americans than against foreigners from a former enemy nation was not wasted). Hiroko Tasaka realized she was being given a first-class view of America the evening Dr. Hitzig took her and three other girls to a ritzy New York restaurant where they were served by uniformed waiters who were as attentive to their desires as a circle of admirers. After a sociable drink they were shown menus, and when they expressed concern about the prices and discussed among themselves whether they should limit their orders to an appetizer, Dr. Hitzig told them to order what they wanted, all that mattered was that they enjoy themselves. It was almost midnight when he sent them home in a taxi, and Hiroko sighed happily as she watched the colored lights of the city flow past in a rainbow blur. It had been a delightful evening and she was savoring the memory and the tastes when the cab stopped for a red light and she found herself staring out the window at a gaunt, unshaven man in a brown overcoat who stood rummaging through a trash can. His image remained in her mind, for she could not get over how, immediately after an evening in which she had been so indulged and pampered, she could be watching a derelict scrounge for scraps. She felt too good to let the experience dilute the pleasure of the evening for her and too tired to try to extract some profound meaning from it; but something was stirred inside her that made her feel it was important to remember that even in America poverty and wealth lived side by side, and there seemed to be no justice in its distribution.

And then, as if to disabuse them of the notion that American medicine was infallible, the project took a tragic turn.

The original plan had called for the operations to be finished at the end of one year. The girls were told this, as were the people of Hiroshima. But by early spring it was clear they were far behind schedule. The problem was not the slowness of surgery (the surgeons were working in teams, sometimes performing two operations simultaneously, Dr. Simon or Kahn on the hand, Dr. Barsky on the face); the bottleneck was created because there were only four beds available to them. Since each girl remained in the hospital for as long as a week after her operation, there was a necessary wait until a new patient could be accommodated.

Barsky had appealed to the hospital administration for additional beds but had been told that they could not afford to give away any more space to the Hiroshima Maidens. In order to vacate the beds sooner, he had set up a clinic where treatment that did not specifically require hospitalization (bandages changed, stitches removed) was given, and that had relieved the pressure some. Nevertheless, when Norman Cousins wanted to know how close the girls were to their return, Barsky had to tell him that the whole group would not be ready to go back until the end of the summer at the earliest.

Cousins saw this as a problem. Already a year had passed, the length of time he had originally estimated it could take to complete the surgery, and he felt it was important that they keep their word; people in Japan were waiting. Barsky said he understood, but he felt it would be a mistake to send the girls back with scabs or great discolorations on their faces. "What about sending them back in two groups then?" Cousins suggested. "Those cases that are essentially done can return on schedule, the rest can stay until the end of summer." Barsky had no objection to this, and even thought a staged return could work to their advantage. This way they could observe the impact of the first girls to return on the Japanese people, their families, and the medical profession over there.

In general, there had been less to be done on those girls who were scheduled to return early. But when their names were announced, one of them, Tomoko Nakabayashi, rushed to Dr. Barsky and begged for one more operation. Tomoko had been fourteen and running an errand for her grandmother in the business district of the city when the bomb fell on Hiroshima, and although she suffered no facial disfiguration, her arms were badly burned and her right hand was left bent and twisted. For ten years she had worn long "opera gloves" to conceal her injury, but her year in New York had made that unnecessary. Her entire outlook had brightened, but there remained a long white scar on the inside of her forearm that she said would keep her from wearing short-sleeved blouses, so she wanted a third operation.

"You don't really need it," Dr. Barsky told her.

Tomoko pleaded. "If it is so slight, then certainly the effort on the part of the doctors is not so great. Please."

With a shrug of his shoulders, Barsky said that since it was a minor procedure he would try to slip her into the schedule. Overjoyed, Tomoko danced around the ward, but her celebration was too hasty.

Many years later, Dr. Barsky would set the stage for what went wrong with Tomoko by simply stating, "When there is not eternal vigilance with anesthesia, there is trouble." Indeed, early in his career, in an effort to keep everyone in the operating room aware that there was a patient under general anesthesia, he had developed a crude device for monitoring a patient's pulse. He wanted to rig up a visible signal, like a small light that would throb and click to the beat of a patient's heart. He happened to have a young patient in the hospital at the time who was an electrical engineer, and he talked it over with him and they came up with a device that hung on the wall, was connected to a patient's opposite foot or hand, and flashed and clicked in time with the heartbeat. It looked for a while like they had invented the prototype for a new, inexpensive operating room feature—until the day a nurse unhooked the patient before she unplugged the cord and the light continued to flash and click, flash and click. It seemed all this time they had been picking up the oscillations of the alternating current. Subsequently, a more reliable pulse monitor was developed, but at the time of the Hiroshima Maidens Project the operating surgeon depended on the anesthetist to keep track of life signs. And if he was operating on an extremity he was even more dependent on the anesthetist because the patient's face was usually screened by a sheet, and he would probably be operating under a tourniquet, so he was working in a bloodless field.

The operation on Tomoko Nakabayashi began early on the afternoon of May 24, 1956. After the anesthesia was administered, Dr. Simon tied a tourniquet around her arm and began surgery. The procedure was not complicated, and he was midway through when he noticed the anesthetist frantically pumping the oxygen bag.

"What's going on?" he asked.

"She's too light," the anesthetist answered. Then he said, "She's stopped breathing."

Simon moved swiftly to the other side of the table. He did not hesitate because he sensed what had happened and knew time was of the essence. Within thirty seconds he had Tomoko Nakabayashi's chest cavity open and he was massaging her heart with his hands. He was getting no response so he turned to the help of a defribillator, a device that helped electrically activate the heart. It worked, he was able to get a complete restoration of a heartbeat, but he did not know how much good it would be because according to his calculations she had gone without oxygen for more than ten minutes.

Everything that could be done for Tomoko was done. She was placed in a respirator in the recovery room at Mount Sinai, where a mechanical lung kept her breathing. On top of the long steel-and-glass tube in which the frail, waxen Tomoko lay was a gauge, its black arm swinging inside a narrow range. Underneath the respirator were the bellows. A battery of doctors and nurses kept watch over her.

Norman Cousins was called and he came over to the hospital immediately. Nurses who were scheduled to go off duty at 4 p.m. asked to be allowed to stay. Specialists came and went. Everyone hoped for the best, but it was apparent that these were the last moments of her life.

At 7:30, a priest arrived to administer the last rites. Of the twenty-five girls, Tomoko was the only Catholic.

For another two hours the instruments said she was still alive. Around 9:30, Cousins opened the door to the recovery room and looked in. The bellows were still going and the black hand in the indicator was flickering feebly. Dr. Simon was standing over the respirator. He looked up and shook his head. After another minute the indicator stopped.

It was a newsworthy death. BEAUTY HUNT FATAL—HIROSHIMA MAIDEN DIES IN SURGERY topped a front-page obituary. Various repercussions were expected in Japan, so the New York City coroner asked a Japanese pathologist at Mount Sinai to assist with the postmortem. Their autopsy report concluded Tomoko had died of unexpected cardiac arrest and respiratory failure under anesthesia. The foreign offices of Japanese newspapers in the States seemed dissatisfied with the official releases. Citing medical sources in Japan who claimed female *hibakusha,* or survivors of the atomic bomb, suffered from a syndrome that rendered them periodically sensitive to heart failure, they demanded further details. In response, the medical examiner issued a statement: "There was no evidence of any structural damage to the heart, brain, or other organs attributable to a radiation effect of the atomic bomb explosion in 1945 which resulted in the thermal burns, the complications of which necessitated reconstructive surgery."

The story was kept alive by leftists in Japan who led the charge of treachery, accusing Americans of killing Tomoko twice, and calling for the return of the Maidens before any more died at the hands of American technicians. It was not the majority opinion, but there was concern at Hiroshima City Hall that the pitch and venom of the rhetoric could poison public perceptions of the project. A sad note was added when, a week after Tomoko's death, her final letter arrived at the home of her parents. They found it lying in a stack of letters of condolence sent from people all over Japan. It had been written and mailed the day before her fatal surgery and in it she had sounded excited because the American doctors had agreed to give her one last unscheduled operation to eliminate the traces of the previous surgery.

Meanwhile, in New York the gathering clouds created a crisis atmosphere. Norman Cousins was deeply shaken and felt he was to blame for Tomoko's death. The American doctors were heartsick. At a steering committee meeting the possibility that the entire project would collapse was discussed. Naturally the remaining twenty-four girls were upset, and no one knew what their reaction would be, or what should be done if the girl scheduled next for an operation declined further surgery.

As tragic as Tomoko's death was, Helen Yokoyama consoled herself by remembering that Tomoko had gotten what she wanted and died a happy girl. A lovely light had gone out, but she felt some good must come out of it because she did not want this unfortunate accident to ruin an effort that had been triumphant in every other way. So she went by herself to the ward to have a talk with the other girls.

Next on the schedule was a girl named Misako Kannabe. When they had first arrived at Pendle Hill, Misako sat by herself, separate from the group, watching everyone. Helen had tried to get to know her but the girl had retreated inside a protective shell and allowed her only to scratch the hard surface. All she knew was that the girl was from a country village outside Hiroshima, that no one else in her family or town had been disfigured the way she had, and that she had spent most of the postwar years in a back room making wigs and toupees by lamplight, preoccupied with the question of why she had survived when there was nothing to live for. Helen Yokoyama sensed that if she tried to direct Misako's response she would resist and go the opposite way. So when Helen approached her she used the reverse strategy. "Misako," she said, "you've heard of the sad event. It's odd, but so many girls who are on the list way after you keep calling and saying, 'This is the time when I can really show my gratitude to the doctors and let Mr. Cousins know we still trust him. Can you arrange it so I can come in next?' And I told them to hold the line, I'd have to ask Misako first. Your operation is slight, but still, you're in a position to refuse. What should I say?"

The reaction she got was not what she expected, and more than she could have hoped for. Misako Kannabe yelled at her. "What do you think I am? Do you really think I'm that kind of person? How dare you speak to me like that. Of course I'm going next." And turning her back, she stomped away.

A shadow seemed to pass over the project with Tomoko's death, but afterwards it was possible to see it as a blessing of sorts, for it not only gave the other Maidens an extraordinary opportunity to demonstrate their gratitude and trust by reaffirming their faith in the American doctors (on her own, Misako approached Dr. Kahn and, taking him by the hand, whispered, "Remember, you are going to operate on me tomorrow"), ironically it put suspicions in the cynical Japanese medical community to rest once and for all. From the outset, the we're-as-good-as-they-are attitude of the Japanese doctors chosen to come to America had been a source of embarrassment and aggravation to Helen Yokoyama, who felt responsible for the behavior of all Japanese participants. "Chosen" was not really the appropriate word, for their names were put forward by the Hiroshima Medical Associaton because they were physicians wealthy enough to be able to leave their private practices for months at a time and anxious for the prestige that came from "studying" abroad. After several months of observing the techniques used by Dr. Barsky and his associates, Drs. Ouchi and Harada had been replaced by two other "chosen" Japanese doctors, Dr. Masakazu Fujii, who, like the Reverend Tanimoto, had been profiled in John Hersey's book *Hiroshima,* and Dr. Sadam Takahashi, a young surgeon. Takahashi was an arrogant man, not especially interested in the girls or in gaining knowledge, enthusiastic only when it came to attending the Metropolitan Opera or a New York Yankees baseball game. He was not present at Tomoko's operation, but had come immediately when he heard there was a problem. Pacing the halls, he had muttered, "So, they've finally done it." Helen was infuriated with him. She had watched the American doctors stand under the hot heavy lights for up to four hours at a time. They were working free of charge, which was unheard of among doctors in Japan. Once she had asked Dr. Barsky why he was doing this, and he had said, "My father always told me to provide for the family first, and when you've done that, repay what you owe to society. And Helen, until now I have not been able to do that." Those words rang in her ears as she turned on Dr. Takahashi and snapped, "How dare you talk like that at a time like this." Newsmen were approaching so she lowered her voice to a fierce whisper. "Be careful. If something happens, you are to blame."

But in the six hours it took Tomoko to die, Dr. Takahashi underwent a prodigious change of heart. He witnessed the huge efforts that the doctors and nurses made to save Tomoko, and was moved by the vigil Norman Cousins kept outside the recovery room. He was standing beside Dr. Barsky when he went to the ward and addressed the girls awaiting surgery, saying, "Friendship develops easily in the sunshine of joy and happiness, but the friendship that grows in the darkness of sorrow and tragedy has roots that are firmer and deeper, and blossoms that last much longer." The next day Takahashi apologized to Helen Yokoyama, admitting, "I have been wrong about the project." That was all he said, but when the first group of girls left for Hiroshima several weeks later, Dr. Takahashi escorted them back. He took personal charge of the 9-square-inch wooden box wrapped in white cloth that contained Tomoko Nakabayashi's ashes, as well as a lock of her hair, which he delivered to the Mayor of Hiroshima, who in turn placed the urn in the hands of Tomoko's father. As much as anything else, it was Dr. Takahashi's heartfelt account of the resuscitative measures that had been taken to save Tomoko that put a positive face on the tragedy in the community and was responsible for a change in attitude in the Hiroshima medical circles. All the grief expressed over Tomoko's death finally gave way to a real sympathy for the American doctors and an appreciation, for perhaps the first time, that this was not a public relations stunt.

6

From the beginning the Hiroshima Maidens Project had enjoyed a lucky streak. So many times when things could have fallen through, an incidental act of grace—usually in the form of a gesture of human helpfulness from an unexpected source—had saved the day. Though she did not consider herself a religious person, Helen Yokoyama could not help feeling at times that something greater than humanism or the power of positive thinking kept the project on course.

That said, she thought it would be foolish to count on it to always be there, and the return of the first group of Maidens started her thinking about the situation that awaited the remaining fourteen girls. In a few months the good life would come to an end for them; they would be going back to problems and, in some cases, poverty, and she did not think they had any idea of the difficulties that lay ahead. She had become especially anxious when most of the operations were completed and the girls were thinking only of enjoying themselves. They were showered with garden parties and dinner invitations; and when they were not being entertained they would take the train into New York and, with a giddy sense of freedom, wander the streets, sometimes disappearing for whole days at a time.

Helen Yokoyama's earlier fears about the difficulties facing the girls in America were now reversed. She was afraid they were becoming slightly spoiled, and that when they returned to their own nests they would be restless, dissatisfied, and unable to settle down. Just as she had previously done everything in her power to prepare them for the social and psychological adjustment to America, she now labored to prepare the girls for the return to postwar Japan. There was no book to go by for this sort of thing, but in the belief that conversations with great people would take their minds off the creature comforts and social liberties they were growing accustomed to and remind them of the elevated spiritual qualities they had been exposed to, she tried to arrange a series of meetings with esteemed individuals of international stature. A request for a conference with President Eisenhower was politely refused by his aides without an explanation, and an effort to get together with Helen Keller, who had overcome the triple handicap of blindness, deafness, and dumbness, and who had visited Hiroshima twice, failed because she was in Europe at the time. The girls did share an afternoon with Pearl Buck at an office in the United Nations building, but the most profitable meeting was the time spent with the renowned Zen Buddhist philosopher Daisetz Suzuki, who was lecturing at Columbia University. He cast life-after-America as a Zen problem. "Remember the beauty of not having," was the essence of his message. At the end, when he asked if there were any questions, one girl piped up, "Yes. Soon we are leaving for Japan and the moment we arrive there will be reporters and photographers. I'm afraid. What are we to do?"

Throughout the project, Sensei had done her best to shield the girls from unwanted media exposure, even though it often meant doing battle with Dr. Hitzig, who was continually setting up interviews and making television plans without consulting the committee first. He would show up on the ward and announce, "Helen, I've arranged for us to appear on TV this morning at ten o'clock. Please have two girls ready," in a voice that did not admit discussion. It got to the point where Helen dropped her tact. She knew Dr. Hitzig felt the presence of the girls on TV could raise funds for this and future projects, but she had made up her mind that the girls would not be used to raise money, and if there were no funds or if the money ran out, then they would go back to Japan. "No, Dr. Hitzig, the girls are not going on TV," she would say resolutely. And every time, after an attempt to reason her out of her intransigence failed, he would throw a tantrum, yelling at her for being so uncooperative, mussing his hair, moaning that he had already made a commitment, that if she were to back out it would leave him looking like a fool. At first his temperamental outburts startled her, but once she got used to them she would remain composed and let him rant on. It was all a little extreme, she thought, but if he had spoken with her first he could have avoided the inconvenience and embarrassment; television appearances were simply out of the question. Now, having sheltered the girls so well during their stay in America, she too had lingering doubts about how well they would be able to stand up for themselves and hold their own under pressure from the media upon their return to Japan, and she listened keenly to Suzuki's reply.

"There is no reason to be afraid," he said with a wise and knowing nod. "Just say to yourself, *Inu ga wan-wan hoeyoru wai,*" which translates, "The dogs are barking, woof, woof."

There was only so much she could do, but when she learned that a New Jersey hostess was actively recruiting a nice husband for her girl, inviting eligible foreign college students to the house for dinner, Helen wanted to fly home immediately. To encourage a boy-girl relationship at this time was most inappropriate. If the girl became involved and had a love affair and word got around to the Japanese press, it would be scandalous. Even if a promising relationship had developed she would have insisted the girl go back to Hiroshima and put off making any final decisions. That had been her advice, in fact, to the one girl who did receive a proposal, Hiroko Tasaka.

During their stay at Pendle Hill, a letter came from an

American man who wrote he had seen a photograph in the daily newspaper of the Hiroshima Maidens arriving in America, and he wanted to send a message to the one wearing the mask. Take heart, he had written in a note, and trust the doctors. He said his brother had lost his nose in a bomb explosion while fighting in the Philippines and plastic surgery had made him more handsome than before.

It was the first mail received by any of the girls, and Hiroko was the envy of them all. She drafted a gracious thank-you letter in Japanese, which Helen Yokoyama translated into English and Hiroko signed. To her surprise, she received a box of candy from the man in return.

Hiroko was one of the first girls to enter the hospital, but before surgery could be safely performed on her the doctors felt her physical condition needed strengthening, so she spent a waiting period of several weeks on a supplementary diet. She was still waiting her turn on the operating table when Mrs. Yokoyama came and told her she had a visitor.

Hiroko stared at her, and Mrs. Yokoyama said, "The man who wrote you at Pendle Hill."

It took a moment to register, and another to remember his name—Harry Harris. In a whirl she brushed her hair and tied on her mask. It did not trouble her that she was about to meet someone she did not know—she had done a lot of that lately. Still, she was nervous when she first gazed upon the stolid, ruddy face of the man who stood in the reception room waiting for her with a bouquet of flowers in his hand. Had Helen Yokoyama not been there, Hiroko would not have known how to handle the situation. As it was, she stood silently, bringing the bouquet close to her face now and then, listening to her visitor talk while Mrs. Yokoyama translated.

"He says he lives in Baltimore, where he drives a cab. He says he is a baseball fan and he came up to New York to see the Orioles play the Yankees—I guess that's the name of two teams—and since he was in the neighborhood he thought he would stop in and pay his respects."

She thanked him very much but could not think of anything else to say; apparently he could not either and after awkwardly shaking her hand he wished her well and left.

To date, Hiroko's observations of Western social customs were narrowly based on the way hospital personnel related. From the way doctors held the door open for nurses and men let women exit from the elevators first, she surmised that conventions between the sexes were the reverse of the way things were done in Japan. After the Baltimore cab driver was gone she thought that perhaps his calling on her was part of a cultural courtesy. After all, this entire project was possible because of the generosity of people unknown to her. But when a package arrived in the hospital mail several days later, addressed to her from him, containing a pink bedjacket, even she had to admit that something else might be going on, though she had no idea what that might be.

At last Hiroko was wheeled into the operating room and the first stage of a pedicle flap was constructed. All went well and soon she had taken up residence with an elderly couple who lived in a spacious old frame house at the end of a lane named after them in Peekskill, New York. A month later she returned to the hospital for the second stage of her skin transplant, and at that time the cab driver came back for another visit. On this occasion she was more attentive to the details, noticing the amble to his walk, like a man with seaworthy legs; the way his blunt features had only to shift slightly for a frown to change to a grin. They had a friendly chat through Helen Yokoyama, from which she learned he had spent a lot of time at sea. During the war he had served in the Navy as a Boatswains Mate First Class, and for some years afterward he had worked as a Merchant Marine seaman. Cordial as he was, Harris confused her. He did not pity or patronize Hiroko in the least, but after he was gone she still did not understand why he had come.

The next time she saw him was in early December, and she was pleased that he showed up. The awkwardness of their first meeting had given way to a genuine friendliness. His voice was cheerful and his round eyes and furry brows lively with the holiday spirit. After scattering season's greetings around to the other girls on the ward and the nurses on duty, he took Hiroko aside. Fumbling in his pocket, he came out with a small store-wrapped present. "Merry Christmas," he said in a tone that appeared to try and keep the event low key, as though this was something he had found lying around and thought maybe she could use. But as he watched Hiroko delicately unfold the bright Christmas wrapping, the corners of his mouth curled up slightly.

Inside a case, mounted on a field of black velvet, was a 24-karat-gold-plated Bulova watch. Hiroko stared at it a long time.

"Do you like it?" he asked.

She knew enough English now to say simple things. "Oh, yes, yes. It's beautiful. Thank you."

But it was too much. An expensive piece of jewelery was too personal a gift, and she did not feel right accepting it. But how could she tell her suitor that without insulting him? She looked at him; as if expecting her to protest, he wore a decisively masculine expression that said if he wanted to buy something pretty for a woman that was his right, and his pleasure. She thanked him again.

Then, acting as though he had just remembered something, he reached into another pocket and came up with a second present. "And Happy New Year."

What has come over this man? she wondered, looking totally bewildered.

He sat there literally glowing as he watched her discover a gold bracelet for her other wrist.

All she could do was look at it. Surely the income of a cab driver, even in America, could not allow for such extravagance. Taking a deep breath, she apologized and said he must return the gift.

"I can't," he replied jauntily.

"Please."

"It has your name on it."

Examining the bracelet more closely, she saw that Hiroko was indeed engraved on one side. She sighed. As she turned it over in her hand, something on the inside caught her eye. There, printed in tiny letters, was Earl. It was his middle name, he explained.

At first the Baltimore cab driver had seemed like such an unlikely prince, his hospital courtship of a disfigured Maiden such an implausible romance that it was viewed by the project organizers with more bemusement than alarm. Once it became obvious that it was something more serious, however, Hiroko's guardians found themselves in a dilemma. At a steering committee meeting Dr. Hitzig, who found the whole business utterly incomprehensible, suggested an end be put to the affair. "You have to admit, it's an unusual situation, and it could even be an abnormal situation," he maintained. "Where it's normal for one person to feel sympathy for another, with a disfigured person it could become something else."

No one knew what to do, and since Helen Yokoyama told the group that if they stopped Harris from seeing Hiroko it would certainly affect her mood, nothing was done. But from then on, whenever Harry Harris came to the hospital, Helen made a point of staying close by. Not that there was anything remarkable to observe; often when he came to see Hiroko they would sit together without talking, or stroll together down the hospital halls, and then he would go. Once he brought his sister with him, who burst into tears when she saw Hiroko. "I'm so sorry this happened to you," she said. For the rest of the visit she talked about their brother and how he was getting along. The closest Helen heard Harris come to flirting was a comment he made about how the sunshine seemed to follow Hiroko from room to room. Nothing he said or did made her suspect that his actions were motivated by any unnatural emotion, but finally she felt it was her responsibility as chaperone to determine the nature of his intentions. The next time he came to visit she stopped him on the way from the elevator and asked him to please come with her to the nurse's station. There she asked him point blank what his purpose was in coming to see Hiroko.

The question did not appear to surprise him. "Mrs.

Yokoyama," he said, his voice just above a whisper, "I've seen life on the streets. I've been a military man and a seaman, a gambler and a drinker. I'm not like that anymore, but I've been around enough to know where the beauty in life is, and in Hiroko there is something beautiful."

He was sincere, she could tell, and she was touched because she agreed with him and not many people thought that way. The test, however, came when Hiroko was due for major surgery. A roll of tissue was detached from her abdomen and implanted in her face, and she wrote Harry a letter and asked him not to visit her until the graft was completed. He telephoned Mrs. Yokoyama, upset that they might have had a falling out over a misunderstanding he knew nothing about.

"No," she said. "It's just that Hiroko is entering a difficult stage of surgery now and she doesn't want you to see her like she is."

"But that doesn't matter," he protested.

It meant a lot to hear him say that. "If you truly care about her, then you will respect her wishes."

"Okay," he sighed, and there was something in his voice that made her feel sure that he would stay away, but that as soon as Hiroko was willing to see him again she would find him waiting for her call.

Part of Hiroko's pedicle tube was used on her arms, the rest went to her face, where a major portion of her keloid was excised and replaced with new skin. A total of thirteen operations were performed on her, the largest number of any of the Maidens, earning her the title "Champion Surgery Girl," something she was proud of. When it was done she was still severely disfigured, and her mouth was little more than a slit in a smooth flap of skin with lips drawn in with lipstick; but her inability to straighten her arms would no longer interfere with her ability to work, and she felt presentable enough to appear in public without her mask.

A year and a half had passed since Hiroko had decided to trust the doctors one more time, and for the first time she did not regret the decision. As the project wound down to its final days, she was excited to be going home and seeing her family and finishing her training as a dressmaker; but she was also sad at parting from the people she had become attached to in America. She had spent most of her time with the elderly Peekskill couple and had grown extremely fond of them. It was hard saying good-bye to them, but saying sayonara to her admiring cab driver was even more difficult. He had stayed away, just as she asked, though his letters came frequently. When she was ready to see him again, she asked Helen Yokoyama to call him for her. On the phone he hemmed and hawed. Wondering if he had had a change of heart, Helen asked him, "What is it you want to say?" Well, what he had to say, he said, had come after many hours of mulling it over before finally reaching a decision. "Yes?" she said, beginning to lose patience because she fully expected him to apologize and say he would not be returning to the hospital. "I want to marry Hiroko. Will you ask her for me?"

When Hiroko learned he had asked for her hand in marriage, only the audacity of the suggestion impressed her. "What is he talking about?" she asked Helen Yokoyama. "He must be joking. And if he isn't, he's crazy." She liked him very much, found him amusing, and enjoyed his company; but marriage was ridiculous. She had not come halfway around the world to find a suitor; and she had to get back to Japan to get on with her life.

She rejected the whole idea. "Absolutely not," was her answer. But it was easier delivered to Helen Yokoyama than to Harry in person. Three times he proposed to her. The first time she said, "No, thank you," with the emphasis on no, and looking down in confusion she changed the subject. The second time she tried, gently, to explain the impracticability of his suggestion. He looked serious as he listened, reflected on what she said, and spread his hands as if to say, We don't have a great deal of time for you to change your mind. The third time she let herself think what being married to him would be like. She thought he was a good and sincere man, almost Oriental in his thoughtfulness (whenever he brought her a box of candy, he brought a second box for the other girls), but even more sensitive than a Japanese man (in Japan no man looked twice at her except to stare). She tried to guess what it was he felt toward her. He said it was love, but she thought it was more likely that something in her situation called to something in his nature. "I'm sorry," she said finally. She would be forever grateful that he had put the romance of a proposal into her life, but the answer was no.

Over an eighteen-month period, 138 operations were performed on the twenty-five Hiroshima Maidens. From a strictly surgical point of view, the results were moderate. Compounding the difficulties presented by the tendency for Oriental skin to form keloids when burned and to darken when transplanted, and the unavailability of prime donor tissue, was the fact that most of the girls had been in their growing stage at the time of the bomb, and the contractions had impaired natural development. Bones were bent, muscles and tendons shortened, and joint capsules, nerves, and blood vessels shrunken. When ten years of unrelieved tension was suddenly released, fingers did not click straight, lips snap into place, eyes go back where they belonged.

Plastic surgery, too, has its limitations. If the injuries had been a matter of rearranging tissues—such as when protruding ears are brought back—dramatic results would have been possible. In major deformities such as these, however, where massive amounts of tissue had been lost or destroyed, substitutions could be made but not replacements. One could make it better, but it would never be as good as the original. What was gained was only good in comparison with what was started with.

In at least a dozen cases, there were spectacular successes in liberating hands and fingers from their clawlike contractions, making it possible for the girls to use their limbs normally for the first time in many years. As for their facial appearances, they were markedly improved, though far from perfect. The common reaction from people seeing the Maidens for the first time was, "Gee, I don't think they look so great. They still have scars. The grafts stand out on their faces like a patch on a tire...." One rush hour, a neighbor of Dr. Kahn's saw two Maidens on the New York subway, and his comment was, "You mean to tell me you operated on those girls?" It was less than Drs. Barsky, Kahn, and Simon would liked to have done, but they knew it was all that could be done.

Appropriately enough, a good turn from someone who had no previous involvement with the project took over where the surgery left off. Helen Yokoyama first became aware of Miss Lydia O'Leary through an article in *Reader's Digest.* In some ways her story paralleled that of the Maidens. Miss O'Leary had been born with "a hideous flaming birthmark from chin to forehead," and because of this she spent an unhappy youth evading the cruel, piercing stares of her playmates. Her parents had poured out thousands of dollars on visits to eminent skin specialists, but there was nothing medical science could do for her. After college, when her facial blemish stood in the way of a job, she hid herself away in a back room, making a living by painting place cards. One day she was painting an iris and something spilled that washed over a purple petal, concealing it perfectly. From that she got the idea of "touching up" her birthmark. Experimenting until she found a formula that would not run when wet, rub off, or crack like a mask, she had finally produced a lotion that was waterproof and indistinguishable from skin when applied to most facial disfigurements. Patented under the name Covermark, it was presently being marketed out of Miss O'Leary's office on Fifth Avenue in New York City.

As she read the article, Helen wondered if this simple method would work for the Maidens, as the general contour of their faces was close to normal, but the roughness of the surface skin remained a problem. She decided it was worth a try and made an appointment to visit the O'Leary office, taking along six of the Maidens. The waiting room was crowded with wary individuals who peered at them from behind upturned coat collars and downturned hat brims. Miss O'Leary was out of town that day so her assistant welcomed them and led them into a small room with a sink and mirror. She was a slim woman with pleasant features and a stylish air of sophistication about her that one would expect of an executive with a cosmetics company. While she related her employer's story to the group, she started rubbing makeup off her face, and before their incredulous eyes a dark scarlet birthmark appeared on the woman's cheek. No one could say anything. They had thought she was going to show them how to apply a base, never suspecting she was about to reveal a personal disfigurement.

"You see the possibilities?" she said with a smile.

As she reapplied Covermark to her face, she showed them how it worked and how to make it match the color of their skin. Adding rouge and powder, the stain was invisible in two minutes' time.

When Miss O'Leary returned from her trip, Helen went back for more information. This time she met the inventor of Covermark and found her to be a lovely, auburn-haired woman whose sympathy for those suffering from facial faults was boundless. When she heard about the Hiroshima Maidens, she said she wanted to make a gift to the girls of a lifetime supply of her cream. More than that, she said she had been having trouble finding a Japanese company to handle her line of cosmetics and mentioned the possibility that one of the Maidens might be interested in acting as her Japanese distributor.

While the discovery of a miracle make-up that concealed superficial facial blemishes was a cause for celebration among those primarily concerned with the appearance of the Maidens, the timely offer of employment was in tune with the very thoughts of the Quakers, who were more concerned about the Maidens' ability to provide a livelihood for themselves upon their return. As a matter of fact, the effort to develop or further a skill among the girls had led to an inspired idea of creating an opportunity for one that would, in turn, provide jobs for others. It was Ida Day's personal vision: Since so many of the Maidens were accomplished seamstresses, but it was difficult to make a living sewing in Hiroshima where most women did their own sewing, why not select one girl to remain in New York and study fashion design? Then, after her graduation, she could return to Japan and set up a top-notch establishment which would employ the other Maidens.

When she presented the idea to the steering committee it was approved wholeheartedly, and there was little need for discussion about which girl should be awarded the opportunity to study in America. Hideko Hirata was the oldest Maiden, and in addition to her maturity and talent, she was terrifically compatible with all the girls. The decision to invite her to stay was an easy one. Surprising everyone, however, Hideko graciously declined the offer, saying she did not feel physically strong enough to fulfill what would be expected of her. The slot was unfilled when Ida Day recommended that the invitation be extended to Toyoko Morita.

For ten years Toyoko had clung to the hope that some monumental plan was working out that might be personally painful to her in the present, but would make sense at some future time; over the past year and a half it had all added up. There had been some uncomfortable moments in the hospital but her stay in American homes had been all lyric. (For some reason the doctors at first had trouble administering anesthesia to Toyoko. Most of the girls would count one, two, three, and by six they were unconscious. Each had a slightly different tolerance level, but Toyoko would count in a clear firm voice all the way to twenty, twenty-one before she began to be affected. The doctors were puzzled and after holding a brief conference, questioned her. It was not until she admitted that before coming to America she had been a heavy drinker that the mystery was solved. The same tolerance her system had built up to accommodate alcohol was resisting the anesthesia.) Odd as it sounded, there was something familiar about Toyoko's new circumstances; since leaving Japan she had returned in many ways to the style and standard she had been accustomed to before the bomb. Once again, she was a member of a well-to-do household, enjoying material and intellectual advantages.

Of course, there were differences, too, some of which she came to accept as a matter of course for this part of the world, and some of which opened new lines of thought about her own country. She would always remember the morning her hostess invited the gardener to join them at the breakfast table for a cup of coffee. Her parents had commanded the presence of groundskeepers throughout her childhood and the class lines separating family members and common laborers had been strict. "Oh, my goodness," Toyoko thought to herself, glancing anxiously about as the man stomped into the kitchen and dropped heavily into a chair at the table. She did not know what to make of such overt friendliness with servants at first, but as she sat in uncomfortable silence while her hostess and the gardener chatted, she found herself wondering about a custom she had previously taken for granted. The sharp lines and divisions that defined relationships in Japan had always seemed like connections to her; but for some reason in America making those distinctions meant separating people. By the time the man excused himself and went about his chores, Toyoko felt as though she were approaching an important new insight. Though it was impossible for her say what it meant yet, she could not help but see her hostess's cordiality as part of a unique attitude toward human relations that included her own warm welcome. One thing was certain; she knew she would see Japan with fresh eyes when she returned.

In a very real sense, Toyoko was a community project. After the first period of hospitality she went to live with a different family for a little over a month, and after that her visits averaged around six weeks. Sometimes she thought it was too much moving around, but once she got to know her new family she always liked them and was glad to be there, and soon enough the advantages to multiple arrangements were revealed. Her contact with a wide circle of people provided her with a great range of experiences and, since everyone around her was eager to make her stay in the States as profitable as possible, it led to some significant opportunities. After her hopes for a music career were dashed, she had fixed on the idea of becoming a fashion designer; sewing came naturally to her, and she felt that helping other women make the most of their beauty offered her some recourse against her disfigurement. Toyoko had been midway through her first year in a Tokyo design school when she was offered the chance to come to America for free surgery, and when her hostesses realized she was already pointed toward a career, they took out subscriptions to fashion magazines for her, put a sewing machine at her disposal, and arranged for her to have a personal tour of the famous New York women's clothing store Bergdorf Goodman, where she was taken behind the scenes and shown the many steps required to complete a custom-made dress. The work of designers, patternmakers, alteration experts, and others was explained in detail as she watched them on the job, and when it came time to leave Toyoko felt that if she saw nothing else, that visit was worth the trip to America.

It had been Toyoko's understanding that the project would last approximately one year, and on that basis she had been given time off from school and her place in the class had been reserved. But the surgery was being done slowly, in stages, and when she learned she was not going to be part of the first group of girls going back, she wrote a letter explaining her circumstances and asking for an extension. It came as a shock to her to find she must either return immediately to Japan or lose her standing as a student.

Remembering how she had studied for a year in preparation for the difficult entrance examination; and worked in a dress shop in order to pay expenses, going without sleep every third night to get the orders done on time; and the ecstasy she had felt when she first learned she had been accepted for school; remembering it all she thought over her situation again and again, trying to make things come out her way. And when they didn't, and everything she had put up with while trying to establish herself within the restricted sphere of her life now looked like an exercise in futility, she was devastated.

She happened to be in the hospital at the time the depressing news arrived from Japan, and she was so demoralized she thought of refusing any more operations. One of the girls who knew what she was going through must have said something to the project organizers, because a few days later Mrs. Ida Day called on her. Ida Day was known to have a sensitive appreciation of all the girls' problems, and from the way she asked Toyoko if something was bothering her, it was apparent she already knew what was the matter. So Toyoko bared everything. Her head bowed, she said she did not know what she was going to do now, since all her plans revolved around her finishing design school.

Ida Day remained silent for a while, and then in an almost offhand way she said, "Well then, why don't you stay?"

In her highly emotional state, Toyoko was not listening attentively and she muttered, "If I can't return to school, I don't want to go back."

Ida Day continued. "Maybe we could work it out for you to attend design school in America."

Now Toyoko was listening and she did not know what to say. She had never dreamed of the possibility, and even as she considered the idea she doubted it could happen because her knowledge of English was so limited. Slightly dazed, Toyoko waited for an explanation.

Several weeks later, Ida Day and Toyoko Morita met with the headmistress of the Parsons School of Design in New York City. There was no entrance examination to pass, but she had been told to bring along a sample of her work. Since she had made costumes for a community project at Christmas time, and a variety of clothes for her hostesses and herself, she had a number of garments to chose from. She decided to present a Chinese cocktail dress which must have been a good choice; by the time the meeting was over it was clear that if she wanted it there would be a place for her at Parsons.

Toyoko was a bit overwhelmed. Only one thing stood in her way, her mother, who had objected to her coming to America in the first place. In a long letter she described the wonderful opportunity she had been given, and entreated her mother to understand how much this meant to her. The response was predictable. Japanese mothers liked their daughters to stay close to home.

"No," her mother had written angrily, "you must come home with the others."

Not a flicker of emotion disturbed Toyoko's face as she folded the letter back into the envelope. The authority of the command was diminished by the seven thousand miles that lay between them; for years she had been doing her best to forge a new life for herself, and she refused to turn back now.

No national polls were taken, so it would be next to impossible to say precisely how the Hiroshima Maidens Project affected American attitudes of the day—but for Norman Cousins it had been a far-reaching force for good. He thought it had demonstrated dramatically that it was not always war with its urgent necessities that could pull people together and turn a vision into a practical project. At a time when there were conflicting claims about the nature of atomic age warfare, he felt that the realization that it had taken a year and a half of painstaking, expensive operations just to effect an improvement, not a restoration, on twenty-five individuals gave people a more realistic sense of what to expect in the event of a nuclear attack on an American city. And an anonymous letter with an accompanying donation to the project let him know it had provided an outlet for other Americans who were looking for a way to do something concrete and symbolic for "peace." It read:

> Ordinarily, a request for contributions to another worthy cause would bounce off my charity-hardened conscience—the contribution might be forthcoming, but without a deep feeling of concern for the implications of my act. In this case it is different. This program seems to be a fine example of what Americans as individuals rather than as faceless citizens of a powerful nation, can and should do to further the cause of world peace and international understanding. With the Russian satellites in the sky, with America's deep anxiety

about her position in the world, with citizens like myself wondering what we or anyone can do to prevent a catastrophic war and feeling helplessly at the mercy of the governing Powers That Be in the United States and Russia, a program such as that undertaken by the Hiroshima Peace Center Associates provides at least a glimmer of hope that man can, if he will try, heal himself rather than destroy himself.

If the implications of the project were one kind of success story, the transformation of the Hiroshima Maidens was something close to a Cinderella tale. In many ways, Cousins felt they were no longer the same women who had left Hiroshima. Underscoring the improvement in their facial appearances and the full use of their arms and hands, a life had come back to their eyes. "When you looked at them they no longer seemed to blink back from a half-lit world," Cousins wrote in one of his final reports.

To his way of thinking, personal resurrections had taken place and the Maidens were evidence of the power of life over the power of destruction. Their outlooks had been profoundly enlarged now that they knew they belonged to a wider world. He knew that they would be forced to confront the occasional defeat and constant challenge of unpredictable human response, but he was confident in the belief that they were prepared for the drama of life that awaited them. Indeed, he felt their experiences had given them an increased awareness of their capacity to conquer great difficulties.

Of course, no one knew for sure if the Maidens would be able to sustain their courage among old surroundings and situations, and as optimistic as he was, Norman Cousins attached considerable importance to the maintenance of a working relationship with the girls for a year or two after their return. He thought some form of job placement service could be set up for those qualified to embark on careers, or in the case of girls needing additional study, that some arrangement should be made to pay for the required tuition. His concern about a follow-through accounted, in part, for the very special offer he had extended personally to Shigeko Niimoto.

For most of those who met her, Shigeko was a delight. Her affectionate nature enabled her to make links on personal, even intimate levels. She was always forthcoming with an honest and heartfelt response, and quite capable of flashing out a startlingly intuitive truth. Norman Cousins found the simplicity of her outlook so charming, her pluckiness so endearing, that he singled her out in one of his articles: "If this group had an official cheerleader, [Shigeko] would be instantly elected to the job. She has the bounce and joyous alertness of a character out of Dickens." Her lack of inhibitions and desire to please explain how, in articles about the Maidens, Shigeko's melted doll's face came to stare from the pages of the *Saturday Review*, and a profile of her showed up in *Time* magazine.

But for the project supervisors, Shigeko was a problem. Though she seemed to make friends easily, there was another side to her high-spiritedness. She craved to be the center of attention, and she tended to be uncooperative and lagged behind in any group activity unless there was an observing outsider. Westerners found her cute when she sidled up to them or showed off, but by Japanese standards her behavior was frivolous and obnoxious, and among the girls she earned a reputation as childish and immature.

Shigeko was oblivious to the tensions she created. As a person who took things as they came and reacted instantly on her feelings, she was unmindful of the impression she made or effect she had on people around her. When her assigned roommate no longer wanted to live with her, she was not inclined to analyze the reasons for their incompatibility; it meant she would have the next home to herself.

Because of her affinity with young people, she was placed in families with children; and even though they were often much younger than she, there was genuine interest and affection expressed between them. Her visits averaged three to four weeks, which did not allow enough time to become deeply attached, but she kept a book with everyone's names, addresses, and telephone numbers, their birthdays, and a snapshot of each.

Shigeko was one of the most stubborn surgical cases. Six months into the project a communication from Norman Cousins reporting on the progress of the surgery expressed concern about her. "So far, only one operation out of almost fifty has not been successful: little Shigeko Niimoto, to my mind the sweetest girl of the group. Apparently all of the prime donor area has been used up in previous operations, and the doctors had to do the best they could with less adaptable skin. The result was that while the general configuration of the lower part of her face has been improved, the color and consistency of the skin tissue are poor."

Shigeko could tell that the American doctors were making little headway in her case. Nothing was said, but she could see for herself the improvements in others, while her own gain was minimal. She was not disappointed, however. Just as she did not resent the Japanese doctors who had been unsuccessful because their failures had created the opportunity for her to come to the United States, she did not resent the American doctors because the whole American experience had been good medicine for her. She was accumulating a greater knowledge about the world she lived in, and she loved the sensation of feeling united with many different people.

Nevertheless, if further surgery was not going to make a dramatic difference, then she did not see the point in continuing. One afternoon she went to Norman Cousins's office and made her feelings on the matter known. First, she expressed her gratitude for all he and the doctors had done, and then she implored him to let her forego any additional surgery. She said she felt her time in America could be better spent preparing for a career when she returned to Japan. Ever since she had seen what had happened when there was a shortage of qualified medical personnel she had wanted to become a nurse, she explained, and her experience in an American hospital had reaffirmed that desire. Was there any way, she asked, that she could be enrolled in nursing school for the duration of her stay?

That afternoon Cousins assured Shigeko that he would look into her request, and at the next steering committee meeting he raised it for discussion. Surgery would continue, about that there was no doubt. Even though her face could no longer be helped, there were still improvements to be made that would give her back the use of her hands. But in regard to her desire to study nursing in America, there were reasons for caution. The English language was well beyond her command and she lacked the necessary high school education to qualify for a nursing program. Moreover, there was a question about how well she understood her own limitations. As one of her hostesses who was consulted testified, "Shigeko has a shrewd native intelligence, but not much intellectual interest. She may not be up to advanced study."

The point for Cousins was that Shigeko wanted to better herself and he believed she should have an opportunity to learn for herself what her limitations were. It was his opinion that she should be enrolled in public school as a special student to indicate to her some of the long-term problems involved in her wish, neither crushing her hopes nor giving them unqualified endorsement. And to give her the best possible chance of succeeding, he offered to take her into his own home, and to speak personally with the Superintendent of Schools in New Canaan, Connecticut, where he lived.

She was given the Cousinses' guest room, a spacious, upstairs chamber with flowered wallpaper, dormer windows, and a separate bath. With the help of a local high school principal and a teacher who had lived in Japan and understood the language, a program was mapped out that was flexible enough to be fitted into intervals between operations, visits to the clinic, and a weekly Red Cross class she was also attending. As it happened, going back to school was not as easy as Shigeko thought it would be. She found she had trouble focusing her mind on any one subject long enough to understand and remember without other thoughts entering her head. When she tried to talk to Norman Cousins about it, he suggested she had just been away from school too long and gotten out of the habit of studying. But she thought it more likely it was a peculiarity of her brain; she always got more from listening than reading.

And, too, the domestic life at the Cousinses' proved diverting. His four daughters took to Shigeko, and she to them, like sisters. On a given evening they would put on a fast record and give her a Charleston lesson, and in return she would form them in a line and lead them through a Japanese folk dance about coal miners. It seemed there was always something more interesting or fun to do than *study*.

Shigeko spent a cozy winter in New Canaan, and unabashedly fixed on Norman Cousins the way orphans attach themselves to people who give them special attention. She felt that he was able to see inside her and appreciate her inner worth, and there were moments of epiphany between them when she experienced something like absolute understanding. When he came home from the office she would greet him with a long, warm hug in the American way of greeting. A petite girl, not five feet tall, she would press her ear to his chest until she could hear his heartbeat. If she had had recent surgery or been to the clinic to have a dressing removed, he would check the progress under the light of a living room lamp. There was no reticence on her part, no self-consciousness when he examined her puffy misshapen hands, only an eagerness to please. Sometimes, after he had been away for several days on a trip, when he came home he would stay up late playing the piano. She liked to sit quietly on the stool beside him, watching his hands and listening to the music. The first thing she did when she was able to move her fingers again was figure out a little tune on the piano to surprise him.

The day that Tomoko Nakabayashi died, Shigeko was in the hospital recovering from an operation of her own. The following afternoon Norman Cousins came to take her home and she noticed the tenseness about his face, as if he were fighting against extreme pain. As they were driving through Central Park she guessed (correctly) that he had been up all night and had not been able to eat anything since the tragedy of Tomoko's passing. To get him to stop she told him she was hungry, so he pulled up in front of a cafeteria and they went inside. But he refused to take a tray for himself and, after they had taken a seat at a table, he turned down her offer to share a sandwich, with a sorrowful smile and shake of his head.

Feeling she had to say something, she reminded him, "After winter comes spring. Flowers will bloom in time."

Cousins remained silent, looking steadily at her. Then he stood up and left the table. Shigeko gazed sadly at his retreating figure. He was gone a long time and when he returned his eyes were red as if he had been crying; but apparently it had done him good because he seemed more relaxed, and when she ordered him a bowl of soup he took his first meal in thirty-six hours.

In the time she had lived as a full-fledged member of the Cousins family, Shigeko had become a precious part of Norman Cousins's world. He felt that in some innocently instinctive way she put him in touch with the feelings that provoked his deepest responses. When he looked at her now, he was oblivious to her scars, and it was not because of the surgery, which had been of little help, but due to a suffusion of character and appearance that somehow made the scars invisible once the spirit was known. Sometimes when he came across a picture of Shigeko, he was actually startled by her disfigurement and did not recognize her at first. As he tried to explain it, "Shigeko doesn't feel she is disfigured. If she did, you would see it. The fact that she doesn't think of herself in these terms gets inside you and dominates your own attitude." He thought she gave new meaning to the old saying that a person is responsible for his or her face.

Naturally, as the project drew to a close, he took a personal interest in her plans for the future. One evening he sat her down and asked her what she thought she was going to do when she got home.

Shigeko grew quiet. Even though she knew the dream she had been living would someday come to an end, she could think of no reasons for returning to Japan. She was flourishing here. The openness of American society set her free to be her natural self. Most of all, she was happy living under the Cousinses' roof and had grown accustomed to thinking of herself as a daughter in his family. Even her own mother in Hiroshima had written her letters urging her to try to remain in America. She did not want to go back, there was nothing to go back to. And that was what she told him.

Norman Cousins was smiling. He did not bother to explain the circumstances that made it necessary for her to return with the other girls first; that it was a delicate situation and he did not want it to appear that he was playing favorites; that it was known by some Japanese people that her operations had been the least successful, and if she remained it might set off a rumor that the Americans were hiding their failures. He said there would be many details to be worked out and they would take time. In the meantime, he said, when she got home she should talk it over with her parents to be sure it was agreeable to all concerned parties; and if it was, he too would like for her to come back to America and live as his daughter.

Shigeko felt a quick bound of excitement. Along with her natural father and the Reverend Tanimoto, whom she considered her spiritual father, she had come to think of Norman Cousins as the third father in her life, and it was reassuring to hear his thoughts were the same. But what she ultimately derived from the invitation to come back was something much deeper, as from a faith. She had a renewed sense of her life as being determined by outside influences: One waited and watched for events and people to come along, and when they did, one rose to embrace them. She had no notion of where her personal destiny was heading, but now in one of her self-dramatizing moments she saw herself as the cinder-faced daughter on whose foot the glass slipper had fit.

7

When the day came in late October for the remaining Hiroshima Maidens to say farewell, the airport scene was very different from the way it had been that chilly day in May a year and a half earlier. They had been a sorry sight descending the ramp of the Air Force plane at Mitchell Field, some with faces bandaged to hide unsightly scars, looking as bewildered and frightened as refugees. This time they radiated well-being and a sense of inner ease; they were neatly and attractively dressed; in fact, they looked like a group of women who had just graduated from a finishing school.

On hand to send them off were their Quaker "parents," and there was much hugging and kissing and weeping, generally considered deplorable behavior for Japanese people. The newspaper journalists captioned a photograph of the scene, "Hiroshima Maidens in Tearful Farewell to 'American Mommies.'" As well, there were private moments of silent exchange. On her host's birthday, Michiko Sako had wanted to get him a present but since she had lost her father early in life she did not know what a man would like. Finally, she settled on a necktie because she had noticed he had a rack of them in his closet, and it pleased her no end to see that he was wearing the one she gave him.

The plane bearing the Hiroshima Maidens away rose skyward, as though swept into the air by the profusion of waving hands and blown kisses. They were headed home, but they were taking the scenic route. Several weeks earlier, when their forthcoming return was on everyone's mind, Helen Yokoyama had asked if rather than flying directly to the West Coast and then on to Japan, they might arrange a sightseeing tour across a portion of the American countryside. She did not want them to go home thinking of America as just the East Coast, but wanted to add to their collective impression scenes of the West, and the faces of the people who lived there. There was not time to go cross-country by bus, but the committee had agreed to fly them to Los Angeles via Albuquerque, New Mexico.

After two days in New Mexico, two days in Los Angeles, and a week in San Francisco, where they were warmly received by the Japanese-American community, it was time to go home. On November 4, 1956, the Hiroshima Maidens and an entourage that included Norman Cousins, Drs. Barsky, Simon, and Hitzig, and Ida Day, began the last lap of their trip. Because free air passage for this escort committee had not been part of the original agreement with the Air Force, and officials had refused to authorize any additional passengers, Cousins had worked out a deal with Pan American World Airways. In exchange for promotional considerations (he agreed to mention their name and the fact that this was a "courtesy flight" in all his written accounts of the trip), they had provided one of their Clippers to fly the Maidens and their retinue to Tokyo.

An hour after the coastline of the United States of America dropped away beneath them, an engine conked out; it was a testament to the Maidens' newfound confidence in the future that even when they noticed that one of the propellers had stopped spinning, and when the plane appeared to be hanging motionless in the air and about to drop, no one panicked. Even when the wing dipped as the pilot made a wide, smooth turn and took them back to San Francisco for another plane, it was more a diversion than a scare.

There was a flurry of excitement as the girls approached Japan and the stewardess handed out Japanese immigration forms, which required the girls to consult their passports. Although passport photos had been waived prior to their coming to the United States, upon their return, photos had been taken and this was the first time they had seen pictures of themselves. The squeals of delight reminded Norman Cousins of the exclamations generally reserved for excursions to the attic and the discovery of old photographs. "It is someone else," one girl cried. "They will never let me in again."

The girls were elated by their improvement, but Cousins couldn't help remembering an incident at the Honolulu airport the previous evening when a passerby, seeing the girls for the first time, inquired whether something could be done surgically to help them. The question had made him wonder how the Japanese people in general and the Japanese parents in particular would react to the change in the girls. The response to the first group had been favorable, but, as everyone knew, the Japanese were extremely polite. He had warned everyone not to expect miracles, but was there a true understanding of the limitations of plastic surgery? Or had they expected the girls to be completely restored to their former normal appearances? What were the thoughts of the medical community in Hiroshima with respect to his promise not to forget the eighteen girls who had not been selected? And what would they say when he expressed his determination to see that all those survivors in Hiroshima and Nagasaki who could benefit from the kind of surgical treatment given the Maidens in the United States were given *their* chance? A good deal of the opposition to the Maidens Project had focused on its selective nature. Why were only scarred single females taken? Why were no men included in the group? The answer, of course, had been they had to start somewhere, and it seemed the young women had experienced the worst of the disaster. But he had come to think of the Hiroshima Maidens Project as the "pilot project" in a grand effort—assuming, of course, that the Japanese reaction to the results of the surgery on the twenty-five was approving.

Cousins knew that for the project to have a satisfying resolution there were numerous questions that needed to be answered. But any worries he might have had about the Maidens' ability to stand up for themselves were dispelled during their one-night stopover in Tokyo, when they were the honored guests at a luncheon meeting of the Japan-America Society, one of the most influential and cosmopolitan groups in Japan. Several hundred people attended, among them foreign correspondents and leaders in government, education, industry, and labor. Instead of huddling together as a group, as they would have done a year earlier, the girls circulated among the various tables, putting the guests at ease by taking part in table discussions. Following the lunch came formal speeches, and after Norman Cousins complimented them on their "dignity, courage, patience, and tact," and Dr. Barsky expressed the hope "that our project, like the proverbial pebble falling into the stream, may steer the course of the stream of international relations for the better just a little bit," one of the Hiroshima Maidens spoke.

Michiyo Zomen had been designated to make the appropriate acknowledgments, and when she was called up to the head table, she carefully threaded her way through the crowded tables and jutting chairs. Behind her, two huge flags covered the wall— the stars and stripes, and a red sun in the center of a white field —and in front of her a bouquet of microphones were arranged. Helen, who was standing beside her, could see the girl was trembling and she whispered, "You don't have to make a speech. You can just say thank you."

Michiyo's voice was nervous and halting when she started to speak. Then she stopped, and after a painful hesitation, in spectacular fashion her left arm suddenly shot high into the air. "I hold out my arm to you," she said in an entirely different tone of voice. "This is not a simple thing. It means much to me to be able to do this. For years my arm was bent tight like this." She folded it at the elbow. "But in America they gave my arm back to me." Again she thrust her arm open to the group. "What you do not see is the heart that is so full. If the heart could speak, it would tell about this feeling that we girls all now know."

Four hours later they were flying over Hiroshima in a military staff plane that had been placed at their disposal by the commander of the Far East Forces. It was dark by the time they began their descent to the Iwakuni Airport, and the girls gazed through the windows at the blinking lights of the city below. There was no way of knowing what they were thinking, or if any of them compared in their minds the missions of the two U.S. Air Force planes of 1945 and 1956; but when the plane taxied to a stop and the hatch door swung open, their moment of truth arrived. Enormous search lights illuminated the runway. Reporters, photographers, and newsreel cameramen were perched on a scaffolding at the foot of the stairs of the plane. Beyond them was a cheering throng. Some of the girls spotted their relatives and were eager to get off. And yet they hesitated when the time came to actually brave the onslaught of their homecoming reception. No one wanted to go first. The Maidens searched each others' faces, paralyzed by the reawakened fear of public attention.

And then, from way at the back, Shigeko's voice sang out: "*Inu ga wan-wan hoeyoru wai*—The dogs are barking, woof, woof." In a chain reaction of mirth, the girls began to laugh, and turning to the crowd, they tripped merrily down the ramp.

The pictures that filled the front pages of the next day's newspapers and blazed across theater screens throughout Japan were a testament to how much the Hiroshima Maidens had changed. They had come home laughing.

HOME

8

There was no end to the favorable reviews given the Hiroshima Maidens Project in the press. It was touted as a victory for people-to-people diplomacy. Hands of friendship had stretched across the ocean and former enemies had established and expressed their love for one another, making the public aware of a relationship between human beings that could only further the cause of peace and goodwill on an international level. Interracial and intercultural understanding between East and West could only continue to grow stronger with the Hiroshima Maidens serving in the capacity of beneficent ambassadors for both sides of the world.

As for the radiant return of the Maidens, it had all the elements of a storybook ending. Their ordeal as A-bomb survivors had become a saga of uplift, their trip to America the vehicle of physical rehabilitation and personal growth. They were on their way, predicted Norman Cousins, "to becoming great ladies." *Time* magazine even provided an appropriate fade-out image:

Under graphic before-and-after photographs of a Maiden, the caption read "From Horror to Triumph."

But it did not end there. When the Maidens stepped down from the plane, they not only were public figures; they were heavily vested symbols, and interest in their experiences and reactions ran high in the Japanese media. Radio interviews were broadcast and television appearances staged. No newspaper or magazine was complete, it seemed, without a number of column inches devoted to the Hiroshima Maidens. Reflecting the feeling that their city possessed a special distinction, and this imposed on its citizens the need to act on behalf of world peace, virtually every "peace event" sponsored by city officials required their presence.

When publicity became a fact of their homecoming life, they accepted it at first as a responsibility that flowed from the privilege of going to America. All had been moved to feelings of peace and humanity, and each retained a sense of obligation to somehow convey to others the new sense of the world that was opened to them. Speaking through the media seemed like the perfect outlet because it enabled them to feel they were giving to many others, after having received so much from so many themselves. So they talked about how they had been deeply impressed by the genuinely humane way of life and thought in America; how they had been encouraged to believe in themselves; and how they had come to feel that, in spite of their tragedies, life could emerge with a new vitality. Their knowledge of world affairs may not have been sophisticated. They did not understand the intricacies of international politics or the exigencies of the Cold War. But their experience had been a person-to-person kind of international consciousness-raising, and inherently they were making a case for the power of harmonious relations among the people of the world.

In time, a relatively short period of time, the satisfactions gained from communicating through the media turned sour. The Maidens tired of going over the same ground again and again, and began to feel overexposed. Moreover, they were rarely pleased with the outcome. All too often they found their stories changed for dramatic effect, and riddled with inaccuracies. Frequently the nature of the questioning during an interview was disturbing. Reporters did not ask only about America, but about the bomb —the memory of that terrible day, and the horror that lay behind the relentless years of grief—assuming they would want their most troubling, agonizing moments redeemed in public awareness. Some of the questions were absurd: Was there a boost in *Saturday Review* sales while you were there? Weren't you, in a sense, guinea pigs for American surgeons? The presumptions underlying these questions were so far from what they had in fact experienced it seemed impossible to put things right. No, they replied, not at all, they were treated like daughters; but for some reason the heartwarming extension of the human spirit they hoped to communicate rarely came through in the articles that were printed. Disappointed, frustrated, they began to decline interviews, only to find that reporters refused to take no for an answer and would show up outside their doors, uninvited, sometimes as early as six in the morning.

The enormity of what was thrust on them was complicated further by the great expectations of the Reverend Tanimoto. He had high-minded hopes that when they came back they would continue to meet regularly at his church and participate in various "peace activities." Feeling as he did that since they had had the benefit of getting to know people concerned with international relations they would want to do their share in making an appeal for world peace from Hiroshima, he tried to arrange for them to make public appearances at demonstrations and rallies, summoned them to press conferences, and announced plans for the publication of a magazine featuring articles, stories, and poems written by the Maidens. He thought there were any number of things they could and should do, and he was prepared to promote them all.

This put them in a most difficult position. All acknowledged that the Reverend was the one who had started the project, for which they would always be appreciative. And they knew what atomic bombs did and that a way must be found to prevent their future use. But they were no longer comfortable with the role the

Reverend wanted them to play. Standing on a platform before a crowd to display their scars and describe their suffering was not their idea of a suitable expression of their desire for a peaceful world; it was his, and they had begun to feel a little like an advertisement for his programs.

Besides, in their present states of mind they were not thinking of themselves as messengers of peace; they had begun for the first time in all those years to think of themselves as ordinary Japanese women, entitled to a normal life, for whom transcending the past meant not letting the bomb get the best of them. They were anxious to make up for lost time by getting on with their lives. The most pressing and consuming concern was finding the right place for themselves in Japanese society.

While a number came back to congenial family circumstances and comfortable homes that showed little evidence of the destitution that had been everyone's common plight ten years earlier, the majority returned to far more humble settings with a minimum of worldly goods. One girl returned to a dingy, windowless shack built of rough planks and insulated with straw.

Parental responses to their experience were extreme in their range. Their mothers expressed dismay upon observing that they had picked up mannerisms and expressions which were unmistakably American—sitting crosslegged instead of the Japanese kneel, calling other girls in the group by their first names, and dropping the polite—*san*. A dramatic conversion took place in Michiko Yamaoka's mother. After the war she had been so bitter she would throw stones at passing American soldiers and run out of the house when American planes flew overhead, shaking her fists at the sky and crying, "Give me back my daughter." Now, each morning upon rising, she would bow in the direction of America and voice a prayer of thanks. Keiko Kawasaki's father was less gracious in his appreciation. When his daughter came home with a sizable monetary gift from her hostess on top of her own allowance savings, she suddenly became the hen who could lay golden eggs and was hammered at to take advantage of her American connections and ask for more. But it was Takako Harada's father who displayed the least amount of gratitude for what was done for his daughter. A hard, overbearing man who seemed to take pleasure in crushing Takako's sweet, gentle spirit, permitting her to go to America had been his way of saying, "Here, see what you did." While in the States this retiring, self-effacing girl had developed a precious degree of self-confidence, only to lose it in the first few days she was home, as her father went to contemptible lengths to make his feelings known that the A-bomb Maidens ought to be sacrificed to the cause of peace by being put on exhibit.

Then there was the unpublicized consequence of all the publicity. It created a charged and distorted kind of celebrity status that none of them felt good about: They were known for their faces but not their beauty; they were heralded as victims. Not only did the publicity cause them a certain mental strain, it generated an inadvertent and unfortunate set of negative side effects in the community. Rather than serving as examples that might encourage other bomb victims to take a more positive approach to life, the girls found themselves the objects of envy. It was not the changed attitude and brightened expressions that caught the public eye so much as the new clothes, stylish haircuts, and make-up the Maidens wore. When they made presents of some of the souvenirs they brought back, such as ballpoint pens and stockings, they were said to be showing off, as though they were trying to give the impression they had so much they could afford to give some of it away. Some had felt a singing inside that made them want to let all their friends and neighbors know about what they had seen and learned, but they encountered what seemed like the feigned indifference of those who resent anyone who has enjoyed himself while they have struggled. Put on the defensive by sarcastic comments about how lucky they were to receive an all-expense-paid trip to America, they found themselves flashing back with the rejoinder that they did not go as tourists.

But their total experiences in America *had* given them an increased awareness of their capacity to conquer great difficulties.

It was reassuring to know that there were friends in America who cared deeply about what happened to them. What's more, the Friends Meetings which had sponsored them had let it be known that they considered their job only half-done if the girls simply returned home to lead the same sort of lives their injuries had committed them to before, and they would not rest content until all were well on their way to making good.

In most cases they were now able to mix openly, they had the full use of their arms and hands, and they felt capable of managing challenging positions. Nevertheless, their prospects on the whole were still limited. Some needed to finish their interrupted schooling before they could qualify for the job of their choice, others required additional study in an area of special training, and a few who wanted to start businesses of their own lacked the start-up funds. When it became apparent that the only thing holding them back was money, the American families who had hosted the Maidens, working through Helen Yokoyama, put up the funds necessary to finance these efforts; and this continued concern for their welfare provided the solid base from which many of the Maidens, step by step, pursued their individual lines of interest.

A look at how they were faring a year after their return showed that, all in all, they were doing quite well. Save for a few girls who had been unable to take advantage of the opportunities offered them because it had been necessary for them to help their families and so had become tied down at home by nursing and housekeeping responsibilities, the rest were either gainfully employed or attending classes. Less the five of them, that is, who had married.

For ten years the Maidens had been led to believe that they were sentenced to spinsterhood by the ugliness of their scars, and that even if their looks were improved by surgery, they carried the curse of the atomic bomb in a more insidious way, for they were doomed to bear deformed children. But prior to their return they had been disabused of the "common knowledge" that hibakusha necessarily carried within their bodies hidden mutants caused by exposure to radiation. Helen Yokoyama, reminding them she had worked at the Atomic Bomb Casualty Commission, told them that the research facility had so far been unable to establish a higher incidence of genetic mutations in the offspring of survivors. Support had come from the Japanese doctors, who had said the odds of their giving birth to normal, healthy children were as good as any woman's. Unenlightened attitudes persisted (matrimonial bureaus, which arranged marriages throughout Japan, had informed applicants from Hiroshima and Nagasaki that survivors were not acceptable as brides and grooms), but the girls' fears were enough allayed that many had returned with marriage on their minds.

Of the five weddings announced within the first year back, not one was arranged in the formal sense. Some began with an introduction by a matchmaking friend or a meeting set up by a family member, others came about as a result of a chance encounter; but all evolved out of a satisfying personal relationship with a man who gave every indication that he and his wife-to-be had come together on the closer level of feeling that two people in love have for each other.

Not that all the weddings were easily achieved. Michiko Sako's relationship with a National Railway worker nearly ended in tragedy. When they announced their engagement, his family opposed it on the grounds that the damage she had suffered would surely show up in their children, and they threatened to disown him if he went through with it. Michiko was brought to the point of utter despair when she discovered she was already carrying his child, and one morning when she could stand it no longer she boarded a train she thought was headed toward a famous shrine where she intended to take her life. But in her confusion she had taken the wrong train, and by the time she realized her mistake she was approaching a station close to the house where Helen Yokoyama was staying. The very day Helen found Michiko sobbing on the doorstep, she marched straight to the home of the girl's fiancé and had it out with his family. Either they changed their minds or she would go to the newspapers with the story, which would look wonderful in the headlines: SUITOR CASTS OFF PREGNANT HIROSHIMA MAIDEN. Shortly afterward, grudging approval was received, and the couple was properly married.

Nor did it all end happily ever after. When she returned, Atsuko Yamamoto took a position as a switchboard operator at the New Hiroshima Hotel, where she found herself courted by the assistant manager. He was handsome, athletic, university-educated, and she was flattered that he showed so much interest in her when there were so many other pretty women walking about town. There was a cunning streak in him that made her slightly wary, but that was characteristic of many "après-guerre" Japanese men, and it was also exciting to be around. He spoke relatively good English, and after they married he took charge of their American correspondence, writing long letters to her hostesses full of rhapsodic passages about Japanese traditions (plagiarized from English guidebooks to Japan) and profuse thank yous for the regular checks they sent that allowed Atsuko to purchase new clothes seasonally and him to join the Hiroshima Lawn and Tennis Club. It was shortly after Atsuko gave birth to a daughter (they named her Toshiko, meaning "fourteen," the number of years after the bombing that she was born) that his letters began to include references to his personal frustrations as a "featureless hotel-man." He wrote that he had come to realize the opportunities for advancement belonged to those with an education in hotel administration. The best had studied abroad, which brought him to the point: to help him actualize a longstanding dream, and to improve his position as provider for his wife and daughter, he wanted to come to the United States and attend an American university. The only hitch was that he could not afford to pay his own way. Would they be willing to sponsor him? Sensing they might be dealing with an opportunist, Atsuko's hostess wrote back they were not in a position to finance his ambitions, and not long after that the marriage began to fray. Atsuko's husband became surly with her and talked about his family responsibilities as a burden. He said he refused to sacrifice his future for the sake of a child, and eventually he found consolation in the company of another woman. Toshiko was three when her father left; Atsuko has not remarried.

For many, the transforming success of the surgery and the tangible evidence of the Hiroshima Maidens' ability to rise above their circumstances would be found in the final tally of marriages and number of robust babies they produced. Eventually, twelve would marry, exactly half, and nineteen healthy children would be born to them.

While it was generally assumed that they all had their hearts set on becoming brides and mothers, in fact the desire for a traditional future was not the same for everyone. For several girls the yearning for intimate relations with a member of the opposite sex had passed; at some point they had given up imagining it was possible, and now they no longer contemplated men in that way. For a few the right marital partner never came along. All were exquisitely sensitive to the impression they would compromise their tastes and standards in men just because they were disfigured. The very thought of accepting a proposal from a man who was motivated by pity was enough to raise their sights to a level that parents and friends sometimes called unrealistic.

At least one girl, however, was liberated from the notion that the only means of achieving a meaningful sense of self-completion was through marriage. Masako Wada's interest in social work was directly tied to the atomic bomb; while recovering from her injuries she had realized that she would someday probably end up in the care of a social welfare organization, and she decided that until that day came she would like to work with the people who would eventually look after her. That was how she had come to be one of the Maidens hired on staff at the Reverend Tanimoto's Blind Children's Home, and why her American hostesses arranged for her to visit various institutions for the handicapped, and receive lessons on a braille typewriter at the Lighthouse in New York City. At the time there were no such things in Japan, but when Masako returned there were five: four bought for her by the Quakers, and one donated by the Lighthouse. She fully intended to resume her job at the Home, but conditions in the workplace had changed. Although Norman Cousins had made an earnest effort to extend some symbol of American friendship to the other eighteen Maidens by making certain they were given a chance to receive free surgery in Hiroshima, and facilitating an exchange of letters and gifts with a group of Bucks County, Pennsylvania, Quakers, they still felt left out, and resented it. Her co-workers who had not been chosen to go to America made life so difficult with their petty jealousies that, to her bitter disappointment, Masako was forced to quit. But she did not give up. It was a setback of sorts, but in a good way, for upon hearing that she had lost her job, her Friends Meeting offered to finance her education—the two years of high school she had left, and four years at a university—and give her the means to answer the higher calling of becoming a social worker. The opportunity to receive academic training, and the special perspective her personal experiences gave her, came together with the force of a new mission in life, and she went on to become a highly respected caseworker at a home for solitary, aged A-bomb survivors in Hiroshima. She never married, but there were no regrets. When asked about it, she insisted it was not a matter of the atomic bomb closing down that option. Rather, she felt, it was the case that whatever situation she was put in it was her nature to try to make the best of it. Through her ordeals she developed certain strengths that led her in a particular direction, and they happened to be job-oriented.

It would be hard to weigh all the private benefits and personal gains the experience of living with an American family and taking part in American community life gave the Maidens. Certainly their particular outlook on life was different from those of people who had never been out of the country; the chance to experience two entirely different ways of living in one lifetime broadened their thinking; and a new world of opportunities was opened to them at home. (Suzue Hiyama did become the Japanese distributor for Covermark.) But what they actually did with it, and how it helped them through the years ahead was expressed differently for every girl.

In a literal sense, Masako Wada owed the opportunity to become a social worker to her host families for they had provided her with the scholarship that allowed her to complete her education. But as a caseworker, it was her overall experience while in America that she drew on as a source of wisdom, for it provided her with a model she tried to repeat in her practice. Just as she had never met any of her host families before entering their homes, the elderly patients who entered the nursing home where she worked came in as strangers; and just as the healing qualities of family life had helped her to become involved in the world positively, so she saw it as her role to help them learn how to live out the last of their lives actively and happily within a supportive community of friends.

For Tazuko Shibata, there were things she could do now which she had not been able to do before, and would never have done if it were not for that experience. While in the States she lived with relatively wealthy families, including several company presidents who conducted much of their business out of their homes, assisted by personal secretaries. Her observation of these crisply efficient and businesslike women, so different from the obsequious "office girls" in Japan whose main job was keeping their boss's teacups full, motivated her to want to become a "professional secretary." When the Hiroshima Chamber of Commerce arranged for a series of job interviews for the Maidens with local businesses, Tazuko was hired by a firm that manufactured electrical switches, and although at first it seemed like a public relations move, in short order her attitude and abilities were noticed and she was promoted to an executive position. Eventually she became a chief of a project team, and she always credited her success to the exposure she had had to the American secretaries.

Throughout her life, Yoshie Harada would carry her memories of America like a cross to ward off evil tidings. She was the first Maiden to marry, but her life was beset with difficulties thereafter. With two babies in the fold, her husband lost his job and remained unemployed for six years, forcing her to support the family on the meager income from a physically punishing job on an assembly line at a seaweed factory. There were times when she felt she almost could not go on, but then she discovered a secret source of strength. When faced with hardships that might otherwise have broken her spiritually and physically—the pain that came from working under sweltering conditions day after day, the despair she felt when her husband told her he was in love with another woman—she would retreat into reveries, remembering the surprise birthday party her American hostess threw for her, living in two worlds at once.

It most definitely continued to inspire Hideko Hirata. More than any other girl, she seemed to grasp the essence of the project —that the tangible benefits of surgery were really secondary to the spiritual regeneration. She was the oldest Maiden and probably the most introspective: As the flash of the atomic explosion cut across the sky it had seared her retinas so badly she had permanent "blind spots" in each eye, and ever after she wondered if her limited vision was the direct consequence of her blind hatred toward the enemy during the war. There were not any outstanding incidents about her while she was in America, but she seemed to come to new depths of human feeling that prompted her, upon her return, to devote herself to another group of unfortunate people. She could have gone into business for herself, or worked for pay, but instead she decided to do volunteer social work with an outcast group known as the *burakumin*. These were the people engaged in such lowly tasks as the slaughter of animals, the tanning of leather, and the removal and disposal of refuse; and centuries of social and economic discrimination had kept them living in wretched slums. Equipped with a new electric sewing machine that had been sent to her by the Friends Meeting that sponsored her, Hideko opened a sewing class for the ostracized and impoverished burakumin women. It was deeply rewarding work for it filled her life with purpose, but it was done without her parents' consent or comprehension. When Hideko talked about a personal Golden Rule—to do for others what had been done for her—her parents wondered if living abroad she had been exposed to and caught some Western habit.

Hideko Hirata became a shining example of the girls' new-found ability to empathize with the pain and suffering of others, and the desire to carry on the spirit of the project in some way, which was why she had been the initial choice of the project organizers to stay and study at Parsons. But the physical weakness she had cited in turning down the offer was more than an excuse. Never one to bring her problems to others, she never mentioned that with each passing day a pain deep inside her was getting worse. She continued to teach, adding a night class for women who worked at day jobs, even as her health weakened. By the time she went for an examination, cancer had infiltrated her stomach wall. A total gastrectomy was carried out at the Hiroshima University Hospital; twenty-eight days after surgery, on April 8, 1958, Hideko Hirata died. There was suggestive evidence linking exposure to high levels of radiation to stomach cancer, so her name was duly added to the toll of human lives taken by the atomic bomb.

There was another side to the story, naturally. For an anthology of the lives of the Hiroshima Maidens to be complete it would have to include not only themes of transformation, resurrection, and reclamation, but tales of disillusionment, dashed hopes, and defeat. The America they experienced in 1955 was an open, wildly optimistic country, and pleasantly seduced by the American habit of thinking that they could do whatever they set out to do, at least one Maiden found that this conceit eventually brought even more heartache to what she had already endured. The spirit moved in Michiko Yamaoka was of the highest order—in her dreams she saw herself as a nurse in a hospital like the ones she had been in and out of for years—but she came back to a life of adversity almost beyond comprehension. She never knew her father, her mother worked in the amusement quarter of Hiroshima as a solicitor for prostitutes luring men into seedy hotels, and while Michiko was in America her mother's dissipated life finally caught up with her. Too diseased to work any more, the pitiful old woman had sold all the furnishings in their home and borrowed money to cover her living expenses, so Michiko returned to an empty house and a list of debts. Forced to take menial work so they could be sure where their next meal would come from, Michiko continued to harbor the hope of someday becoming a nurse, and her Friends Meeting wanted to help her make it happen. But there were bills to pay off; one setback (a burglary) followed another (a fire); and then there was her mother's natural genius for using guilt and ill health to control her daughter's devotion. She talked incessantly about what a burden she was and how things would be easier if she were not around. Eking out a sparse existence doing free-lance sewing so she could be at home to take care of her mother, Michiko came to wonder if the way things turned out would not have been easier to accept if she had never known the difference. Imagining the life she might have led if only she had been able to take advantage of the support offered by her hostesses was as depressing as thinking about how it would have been if she had not been in Hiroshima on that day.

And the way things worked out for some girls was undercut by the vision of something better they had seen in America. Suzue Hiyama had stayed for quite some time with an elderly Connecticut couple who had what she considered the ideal marriage. Her hostess was a lovely white-haired woman, very elegant, who took great pleasure in doing things for and with her adoring husband. She would change her clothes and pretty-up for him before he came home from work each day; and on weekends she would accompany him when he went trout fishing in upstate streams, even though she had no interest in fishing herself and got carsick on long rides. In subtle, tender ways, full of the kind of restrained emotion that one associated with the Japanese, her husband would let her know how much he appreciated her thoughtfulness and company; Suzue thought it was a beautiful relationship, and she wanted the same for herself when her time came. But a traditional marriage in the East left little time for romance or leisure or companionship. She married a businessman, and in order to get along with his associates and get orders from clients he was obliged to go out in the evenings, while she stayed at home. Their lack of time together became a source of family dispute, but by custom the Company came first, so in the best tradition of Japanese womanhood she settled for the satisfactions found in children.

Once the initial euphoria passed and the people of Hiroshima had a chance to assess the overall results more objectively, community attitudes toward the Maidens Project also took a cool turn. For one thing, the surgery had not been as effective as most people had expected. Even though Norman Cousins had been pointed in saying the girls' features would not be perfectly reconstructed, people were still of the opinion that a cosmetic miracle would take place, and the Maidens would come back as if they had never seen the bomb. When it did not happen (they looked much better, but in a number of cases the disfiguring marks were still bad enough to attract attention), there was a general letdown. For another, even judged by their actions after they got back, they did not live up to many people's expectations. A lot of survivors, including a few of the "other eighteen," were playing an active role in the movement to link the Hiroshima experience to the wider movement against nuclear weapons. When none of the Maidens showed an interest in political activism, and collectively they did nothing to enlarge the project beyond twenty-four individual experiences, people began to say they must have been spoiled during their year abroad. There was speculation that they had become self-centered, that once the good things other people desired had come to them they had lost their social conscience. Ironically, their new independence of spirit and their self-direction became the basis of a new criticism; not knowing what else to make of this, people accused them of becoming, in a word, "Americanized." This impression intensified the feeling of some local citizens who had been critical of the enormous effort that was expended for such a small group from the beginning.

Then they had called it a publicity stunt designed to win over the people of Hiroshima by showering a vulnerable few with special attention; now they claimed that much more could have been done if the money and resources directed toward the Maidens had been brought to Hiroshima.

It was not all groundless criticism; nor was it entirely fair. First of all, an effort *was* made to provide all atomic bomb survivors with the same kind of surgery given the Maidens. After obtaining an estimate of the number of cases that could benefit (hundreds at the least, perhaps thousands, he was told), Norman Cousins had proceeded with a second phase to the Hiroshima Maidens Project, which involved sending a distinguished senior surgeon from the West to Japan to treat the more difficult cases by way of illustration. Several months after escorting the Maidens home, while on a trip to Lambarene in French Equatorial Africa to meet with Dr. Albert Schweitzer, he had heard about a South African plastic surgeon who had reportedly had amazing results repairing the ravages of leprosy. He called on Dr. Jack Penn in his Johannesburg office, and before he left had recruited him to go to Hiroshima.

Up to this point, Norman Cousins had been a very lucky man; but Dr. Penn's visit was wrong from the start. Inadequate efforts were made beforehand to solicit approval and formal invitation by "the right people" in Hiroshima, so consequently Dr. Penn was snubbed when he first arrived. To make matters worse, he came on the scene with a heartiness that ignored the niceties which were an essential part of professional protocol in the East. Without consulting anyone, he announced his intention of operating on several hundred cases over the next two weeks, and called for "the local boys" to fill the hospitals up from one end so that he could pass them through the theater and out the other end. His arrival was a fiasco. The Japanese were a proud people, the medical profession especially so. Coming to Hiroshima to treat A-bomb patients was not the same as going into the African jungle and lining up the natives. It took an emergency meeting of the Medical Association, at which the Japanese doctors who had accompanied the Maidens to America reminded everyone of Norman Cousins's humanitarian intentions, before any cooperation was forthcoming.

In surgical and public relations terms, the second phase was certainly not the triumph the first phase was. Fewer than one hundred patients were treated and the results were mixed. The secret to Dr. Penn's reputed success was the use of a special anesthesia which lowered blood pressure during the operation so there was less bleeding, but in several transplants the grafts burst when pressure returned to normal. Seen in the larger context, however, the net accomplishment was all good. Norman Cousins had fulfilled his vow to provide every A-bomb survivor with the opportunity to undergo plastic surgery free of charge. Not only that, his chain of projects ignited a reaction in the Japanese medical community that led directly to the development of plastic surgery as a medical specialty there; an Association of Plastic Surgeons was organized, with Dr. Arthur Barsky nominated as its first honorary member, and medical schools throughout Japan were beginning to include courses in plastic surgery. Perhaps the most significant by-product of Cousins's efforts on behalf of the Hiroshima survivors was that they so dramatically testified to the failure of the Japanese Government to help hibakusha on their own that, embarrassed by the successive one-sided humanitarian gestures from Americans, the authorities finally saw fit, twelve years after the bombing, to enact an A-bomb Victims Medical Care Law that provided free medical examinations and care to persons certified as having A-bomb-caused health problems. The issue had been building and a relief law would have come in time anyway, but in a tribute to all he had done to publicize the need for one, the measure was proposed in the Japanese Diet as the "Norman Cousins Bill."

As for the Maidens not doing their fair share for society, it was a matter of interpretation. While it was true that none of them emerged as a visible spokesperson for peace, the organized peace movement in Japan at that time was fraught with dissension and dispute; a swirl of political manueverings surrounded all so-called "peace activities"; and though everyone said they wanted peace, different groups were at such ideological odds they were unable to put the interests of their respective parties aside long enough to unite on a strategy for the common goal. The Maidens' complex relationship to the peace movement was captured in the dilemma they faced when a Quaker who had hosted them decided to protest the continued testing of hydrogen bombs in the South Pacific by sailing a boat into the restricted area. It was big news in Japan and reporters were eager for comments from the Maidens. At heart they, too, objected to further testing, and yet they had to be careful that anything they said could not be twisted into an expression of anti-American sentiments, so they refused comment.

At times like this they turned to the one person they could count on for sound advice, Sensei. Helen Yokoyama had had every intention of separating herself from the project after their return to Japan, only to find herself inexorably drawn back into the lives of the Maidens because they had come to depend on her whenever they had a problem. Recalling the old Chinese saying, "The tree, the tree / it wishes to stand silent / but the wind will not allow," she remained their confidante and counselor. She thought it was extremely unfair for anyone to burden these girls, who had been through so much, with ongoing obligations. The beauty of the project, in her estimation, had been the selfless display of people giving without wanting anything in return. If the Maidens wished to pass on the benefit of their experience to others, she thought it should be their decision, and the expression should be made in terms of what was right for them as individuals. That was why she told them, "Not all of us are born into this world to become leaders, and if we reach beyond our abilities we are apt to make mistakes. But those of you who feel you have a message to deliver can pass it along in your own quiet, personal way, through every association and every contact, and it will ripple like a pebble tossed in a pond, whose fall starts widening, concentric waves."

Each in her own way had followed that advice, taking no stands but talking about her experience when the situation called for it, and stirring people to new awarenesses of war and peace by their example. Misako Kannabe, for instance, went on to become a hairdresser in Canada, catering to a Japanese-Canadian clientele; from time to time she would be asked about her scars. People expected to hear about a car accident or house fire, and when she told them she had been in Hiroshima it often elicited an admission on their part that they could never forgive America for dropping the bomb. Of course they fully expected her to agree, but she would patiently explain it was not as simple as that.

Emiko Takemoto, who succeeded in becoming a respected member of the faculty at Hiroshima's most prestigious design school, never lectured her students about the bomb. It was a matter of their being able to see for themselves by the irregularities of her face and hands what it had done to her; her presence at the front of the classroom was proof enough that she had refused to allow her injuries to disfigure her life. At a certain level she believed this registered as a kind of "peace education."

With the passing of time, as their daily activities became centered around the home and children and work, the Maidens gradually withdrew into their private lives. Things were not entirely easy for any of them. Though they rarely talked about themselves, now and then one of the women would break her silence and grant an interview, or the newspapers would decide to carry a retrospective of the project and call around to find out whether they were married, or what they did for a living. For the most part they were ready to put behind those details of their lives that were precisely what made them interesting to the press, toward which they remained suspiciously hostile. Because to choose of one's own volition not to marry was an unconventional position to take in Japan, it was interpreted in light of their status as "A-bomb Maidens," and for years to come those who remained single would have to contend with the image of themselves as love-starved old maids whom no man would have as his wife. At some point, when they could no longer give a gracious set of replies to the reporters' loaded questions, they simply stopped talking.

In the following years, their activities as a group were limited to infrequent get-togethers. Once a group of girls held a pleasant reunion at a restaurant, at which time they made believe they were part of a *This Is Your Life* television program twenty years down the road for Norman Cousins, whom they pictured as an old man and themselves as homey middle-aged women flying over the Pacific to meet him again. Annually they would meet for a picture-taking session that produced a mass-mailed Christmas card to all their host families. They continued to think of their American friends, and many maintained a private correspondence with the "American mommy" they had grown particularly close to. But without the link from abroad—the visit of a Quaker couple, the nostalgic return of Norman Cousins at five-year intervals—the group of women became scattered. No ill intentions, just a human story of people whose interests took them in different directions. A strong feeling of connection to America remained, but it was usually expressed on the personal level, such as when Yoshie Harada heard her hostess was ill in the hospital. If she could have afforded it she would have flown to the States and nursed her back to health personally; as it was, she placed her faith in the old folk tale that said if one thousand paper cranes were folded in the name of a sick person it became a talisman and they would recover. Late at night, when everyone else in her household was sleeping, Yoshie would sit in the dark and fold cranes until she had two thousand, one for insurance, which she strung together and sent to America as an eloquent example that the bond of continued caring was mutual and alive.

For the rest of the world the story of the Hiroshima Maidens appeared to have come to an end, save for the three girls who found their futures in America: Shigeko Niimoto, Toyoko Morita, and Hiroko Tasaka.

If she had had any doubts, six months back in Japan was time enough to convince Shigeko Niimoto that she would be better off living in the United States. Though some said she had been spoiled by her stay in the land of plenty and simply was unable to readjust, she maintained that, given her situation, America was a more hospitable society for her kind. Six months was also the length of time it took Norman Cousins to feel he had adequately assured the other girls that he was not playing favorites—bringing Shigeko back was actually a symbol of his concern for all of them —and to complete the transportation arrangements for her return trip.

Early that summer, Shigeko moved into the Cousinses' stately New Canaan home. Contrary to press reports stating she was formally adopted, she was not, but in virtually every other sense she became a legitimate family member. One evening the cousinses' oldest daughter explained Shigeko's presence to a dinner guest this way: "Shigeko was supposed to be born into this family, but she was born in Japan and Daddy finally found her and brought her back home."

Above everything else, Shigeko prized her relationship with Norman Cousins. He, in turn, felt she was a special human being, gifted in an almost magical way with an ability to connect to people, and he was determined to provide her with the opportunity she needed to make a go of it in this country. Just as he had taken care of the necessary paperwork allowing her to return to the States, he made the necessary preparations for her education. Privately she concluded he must have made some kind of deal to get her admitted into nursing school because in June he delivered the graduation day speech at the Waterbury School of Nursing, and shortly afterward she was notified of her acceptance into the fall class.

Taking care of people came naturally to her, but the sincerity of her motives did not make the reality of her chosen career any easier to attain. Even though a special curriculum was designed in view of her language limitations, she had difficulty completing an assignment if it meant concentration and discipline for any sustained period of time; and her initial enthusiasm began to fade as it became increasingly evident she did not have what it took to make it through nursing school.

The method of learning that seemed to best suit her temperament was education based on the accumulation of experiences, the kind of schooling that took place as a fringe benefit of living in the same house with a man as diverse in his interests as Norman Cousins. It seemed there was always some interesting guest dropping by to discuss politics, literature, or world affairs from whom she learned by listening. But her true mentor was Cousins, who in addition to his magazine interests had become a national spokesman for such organizations as the Committee for a Sane Nuclear Policy and the World Federalists. Although Shigeko was naive about the historical and economic tensions that made wars, the sense of world-mindedness she gained from Norman Cousins, plus her own experience of feeling at one with so many people, prompted her participation in a public demonstration on August 6, 1958, at the United Nations Plaza.

"Marchers Honor A-bomb Survivor," ran the caption under a photo of the mass gathering that appeared in the *New York Times.* The accompanying article read:

> A group of Americans carried flowers yesterday to a young Japanese woman on the anniversary of the day in 1945 on which the atomic bomb brought her and her townsmen great suffering. . . . Smiling and gracious, the petite Miss Niimoto accepted their tribute and . . . told the well-wishers . . . "People ask me, 'Aren't you confused to belong to two families?' And I answer, I am not confused. I feel enough love for both. I was born in Japan and I have love for Japan. Now I belong to an American family and have love for the United States. But I think this is not enough. It is not enough to love only two countries. Now I want to become a citizen of the world and many times I have thought all people must belong to each other. Maybe they will feel happy and free only when they all become citizens of the world."

After giving up her nursing studies, Shigeko took a room at the home of a Nisei couple in New York City, and a job as a nurse's aide at St. Luke's Hospital. It was a menial position, her duties consisted primarily of serving meals to patients and emptying bedpans, but at least she could say she was living on her own. In contrast to Japan, where a young woman had very little opportunity to meet young men socially, in New York Shigeko received numerous invitations. A highlight for her was the annual dance given by the organization of Japanese-Americans who had fought on the side of the United States during the war; in 1959 they selected Shigeko as Queen of the 442nd. But the social event that would stand out most in her mind that year was the party for foreign students held at Rockefeller Plaza, where she met her first romantic interest.

Actually, she met him an hour beforehand while shopping. He was working as a sales clerk in a store, and she noticed him no less for his self-confident suaveness than for the fact that he was Japanese. They had a brief exchange at the cash register, and when she met him again at the international party they talked all evening. As it turned out, he was far more than a clerk; his father was the equivalent of an American senator in the Japanese Diet, and he was a music student working part-time for reasons that had to do with his visa. His instrument was the piano, as was Norman Cousins's.

There was no pretending that Shigeko's looks were those of a normal young woman. Although surgery allowed her to open and close her mouth properly and turn her head without having to twist her upper body, the lower half of her face, even when caked with make-up, had a coarse, distended texture; her hands were stubbily misshapen; and her body was so patched with scars left behind by the skin transplants that she thought she looked like a world map. But this did not seem to make any difference to Mr. Sasamori, who appeared to be captivated by her vibrant personality.

Something very exciting began to happen in her life. Always before, her relationships with men had been platonic friendships; now, for the first time she was going out on dates to restaurants, movies, and concert halls. It was new and different for her, but she had a charmingly coquettish way of acting and talking that gave the impression she was more experienced than she was, and because of this she was partly to blame for what happened.

Shigeko would call what followed "a love story," though the turns in the plot would make it an unconventional romance at best. Her amorous initiation into womanhood was enhanced by the validation of her worth as a female, for so long obscured by her scars. But when she found herself pregnant and then she was spurned by her lover, she was devastated. Near panic, she went to Norman Cousins, who had assumed responsibility for her as if she were an adopted daughter. When she confessed the trouble she had gotten herself into, his first reaction was that he should go to Japan, confront Sasamori's parents, present the problem from one father to another, and appeal to the family tradition, which he knew was strong in Japan. But after considering the potential damage to all parties involved, he decided not to try to pressure the young man into accepting responsibility for his actions. Instead, he bought Shigeko a ticket to Los Angeles, where his sister lived and where the one person whose judgment in matters regarding the Maidens he was willing to defer to had recently taken up residence.

When Helen Yokoyama answered the phone, she heard a shuddery breath on the other end of the line, and Shigeko's voice whisper, "Sensei? I need to see you right away." Without asking any questions, Helen gave her the name and address of a coffee shop where they could meet.

The instant she saw Shigeko's face—pale with eyes swollen red at the rims from crying—she figured the story out. There was nothing new in one sense, she thought; Shigeko's happy-go-lucky attitude had finally caught up with her. But as she looked at Shigeko sitting with her head bowed in a new helplessness, Helen's maternal instincts welled up spontaneously and she felt in a way that it would be cruel to speak to her now about her lack of responsibility. The girl was floundering; there were moments, she confessed, when killing herself seemed the only way out. After a moment of silence Helen advised Shigeko not to despair, and she went on to tell her about a classic Japanese novel she had read with a somewhat common storyline. It was about a country girl who fell in love with a member of a traveling troop of entertainers when they passed through her village. They had a brief, passionate affair, and then he moved on. When she found herself pregnant she did not know what to do because it was considered a disgrace to bear a child out of wedlock; but after searching her heart as well as her conscience, she decided to take a defiant stand and bear a "love child."

The story had not had a neat and happy ending. The man had come back and had a reunion with the woman and child, and then he had gone off again. It finished with the characters' futures left up in the air, the way so many Japanese books ended. But at the end of the telling, when Shigeko looked up, her gaze was brimming with a feeling of such intensity it appeared as though a spirit had taken possession of her. It helped to know that she was not the first woman to find herself trapped like this; but it romanticized her predicament for her to be given a heroine she could identify with.

On September 21, 1962, at 9:30 a.m. in a hospital in Santa Monica, California, Shigeko gave birth to a plump baby boy. Despite the scientific conclusion that A-bomb survivors were not bearing a disproportionate number of abnormal offspring, she had nursed a tiny terror that other expectant mothers did not share. Her first words upon hearing his cries were, "How is my baby? Is he all right?" "Perfect," a voice assured her. "Thank God," she sighed.

Lying with her baby in the hospital bed, the miracle of birth was magnified in Shigeko's mind by the circumstances of its conception as well as the uncertainties attending its delivery. *This is going to be a very special child,* she thought to herself, *who will someday grow up to be an important man.* She christened the baby Norman Cousins Sasamori.

The boy was six months old when Shigeko moved back to Connecticut; shortly after that, Cousins found her a position as a live-in nurse with his friend and neighbor, the celebrated photographer Margaret Bourke-White, who had been stricken with

Parkinson's Disease. Shigeko had no previous knowledge of Mrs. Bourke-White, so it was difficult for her to know how remarkable a person she had been before her illness. The woman she shopped and cooked for, exercised and bathed, was an invalid whose speech was impaired and coordination so poor she had difficulty writing or walking. Once a week, therapists came to work with her. Following the instructions of the physical therapist, Shigeko would walk Mrs. Bourke-White back and forth across the room and move her arms up, down, and around. After the speech therapist left, she would lead her through vocal exercises, first the vowels and then the consonants. It was a basic English lesson for Shigeko as well.

She got to know who her ward had been by sharing her favorite pasttime of looking over her old photographs of the Nazi concentration camps, Moscow under siege, Gandhi before his assassination. There was nothing to pity in this activity; the woman seemed proud of her accomplishments, and confident she would take more great pictures. Shigeko and little Norman were the subjects of numerous character studies, though unfortunately most of the photos were blurred because Bourke-White's hands were so palsied she could not hold the camera steady. One time she asked for Shigeko's help because she could not remember how to change lenses. Shigeko had never owned a camera, never even taken a picture, so she did not think there would be anything she could tell the famous *Life* magazine photographer that would help. Luckily, however, it was a Nikon camera with directions in Japanese, so she was able to oblige.

Shigeko was Margaret Bourke-White's home-care nurse for just over a year before the regular nurse returned and she found herself out of a job. Over the next three years she tossed about, trying different positions. She went back to Japan to learn a trade from her brother, who had branched out of the family oyster business and opened a restaurant. But she was unable to serve a serious apprenticeship because of her duties as a mother, and when she wrote that she was ready to come back to the States to stay, Norman Cousins brought her back and set her up in an apartment in New York City and helped her find work at Mount Sinai Hospital as a nurse's aide. She managed fairly well for a while, but was not able to spend the time with her son she thought a mother should, and eventually resigned.

When Shigeko originally returned to America after the project, the plan had been for her to learn English, enroll in a training course, then get a job and take care of herself. Eight years had passed now, she was no closer to picking up a trade, and a child had been added. There were those who felt she had overstayed her welcome, but Norman Cousins continued to think of her as a free spirit he liked having around, and so he moved her back into his New Canaan home, this time as a working member of the household, doing the chores of a domestic servant. It was also true that she was an intimate part of the family circle, and over the next two years she did her best to repay the family for what they had done for her.

At last she decided the time had come, for the sake of the Cousinses as well as herself, to strike out on her own, and she decided to move to Boston. After staying with friends until she got to know the area, Shigeko rented a second floor apartment in a Victorian mansion in the quiet suburb of Newton, Massachusetts, where she mounted various efforts to establish herself as a "healer." Some proved more successful than others. The period of time she was employed as a nurse's aide at a hospital found her changing sheets and emptying bedpans again. When she decided she needed a practical education of some sort, she took a course in *shiatsu*, a massage technique applied to acupressure points; but when she placed an ad in a local paper offering individually customized massages, she found herself on the receiving end of strange phone calls from men who thought she was running an Oriental massage parlor.

By far the most rewarding was her free-lance work as a home-care therapist with the physically handicapped. The majority of her patients were victims of accidents or strokes who found it impossible not to respond positively to this charming and lovable woman who used her own past—often in quite unexpected ways—as a touchstone for understanding the healing possibilities within oneself. The simple, direct way she had of combining a traditional regimen of rehabilitation with an exalted belief that people were not necessarily limited by their circumstances worked medical wonders.

As a single mother, she was unable to work on a full-time basis, however, which would have made things extremely difficult if she had not been subsidized all this time. The new Maverick she drove, the regular allowance and the credit cards, were supplied by Norman Cousins, who had fully understood her need to go her own way, to the point that he was still willing to underwrite it.

Throughout the 1970s, Shigeko continued to practice home-care nursing and to raise her son. From time to time, she was interviewed by the press and would candidly voice her opinion on a range of subjects. When asked if she ever brooded about the past she replied, "I'm too busy." Did she ever think of returning to Japan to live? Only to visit, she said, for she intended to die and be buried in the soil of the country which had given meaning to her life.

Then in the early 1980s, after more than a decade during which the idea of nuclear war was all but dismissed by the public, the possibility was again on people's minds. This burgeoning awareness of the nuclear threat produced the largest antinuclear demonstrations since the early 1960s. What had happened in Hiroshima paled in comparison to what would happen if there were a nuclear war now—by this time there were at least 50,000 nuclear warheads in existence, and their megatonnage was equivalent to more than one million Hiroshima-sized bombs—but Hiroshima was indicative of the gruesome reality of an atomic bombing, and a new premium was placed on the survivors as they were called upon to relate their firsthand experiences. Shigeko became a sort of professional witness, giving testimony to groups and gatherings all over the United States, and telling them that the way out lay in loving one another.

Back in Hiroshima there were those who were critical of her performances for peace, which they found too theatrical, and she was accused of trying to aggrandize herself. Certainly she did enjoy her new feelings of importance, of being cast as a star in the great drama of her time. But she felt deeply that at last the events that moved her life along were building to something more dynamic than her own concerns, and were vitally relevant. When she spoke she often was heard to say she was representing others —all the innocent people who died in Hiroshima and will have died in vain if there is another nuclear war; the children who would be killed if more bombs are dropped, or will have to live their lives like her, with burns and scars. And she was thinking of them and their silent support when she titled her autobiography, published in Japan in 1983, "Go on, Shigeko."

Under normal circumstances, Toyoko Morita would not have received serious consideration as an applicant at Parsons School of Design. Her qualifications did not meet the standard admission requirements, her drawing ability was as awkward as a child's, and her appearance was still not altogether presentable. Upon meeting her, Anne Keagy, who was Chairman of the Fashion Design Department at the time, doubted she would be able to fit into the art school scene, knowing as she did that the students there tended to be not only more appearance-conscious than the average person on the street, but more outspoken. On the strength of Toyoko's determination and Norman Cousins's appeal, Ms. Keagy agreed to take Toyoko on, however, more or less as a charitable extension of the Hiroshima Maidens Project.

For her entire stay, she lived with Ida Day and her husband in Forest Hills, Queens, a convenient commute by subway to midtown Manhattan where Parsons was located; and she devoted herself to her studies with a passion that impressed those who were familiar with the Japanese as a people who traditionally took their education very seriously. Occasionally she took advantage of the leisure activities offered by the Days—for a change of pace she would sometimes attend a concert at Carnegie Hall where they were season-ticket-holders or spend a Sunday in their sailboat

—but her work was of paramount importance and Toyoko filled most of her free time reviewing her notes, sketching, or paging slowly through fashion magazines. It was true that Toyoko was highly motivated from within, but the pressure of knowing that a lot of people in both Japan and the United States were watching and counting on her added to the already burdensome weight of doing advanced studies in a foreign country.

Over the course of that first year it became evident that, despite certain liabilities, Toyoko had a number of things going for her. She was a quick study, as demonstrated by the phenomenal progress she made in her drawing ability. Where at the start of school her best sketches looked like everyone else's rough drafts, by spring, when the class took a trip to the Bronx Zoo to pencil animals, her tigers veritably leaped off the page. It was also clear that she had a natural sense of design. There were those who could take classes, visit museums, fabric houses, and department stores, and expose themselves to all manner of learning and influence and still never know what colors and materials went together. Others, like Toyoko, could take one look and usually get it right.

At the end of the first year (when her classmates went home for Christmas and Easter to relax and celebrate the holidays, she returned to Mount Sinai where Dr. Barsky put the finishing touches on her surgery), she was happy when she read her end-of-the-year evaluation report. Her instructors wrote that she had undeniable talent, she was a conscientious worker, and she showed abundant potential. School administrators expressed such a high opinion of the work she had done that the President of Bergdorf Goodman, the exclusive Fifth Avenue store known for its exquisite jewelry, fashions, and furs as well as being something of a laboratory for promising design students, hired her on a part-time basis over the summer vacation. She only worked one day a week, on Saturdays, as a seamstress in the alterations department tucking shoulders and waists and shortening hems, but the experience enabled her to become better acquainted with the construction of Western clothes.

The true confirmation that she was on her way to becoming an established designer came, however, when Toyoko was notified that she had been awarded one of the name scholarships set up at Parsons to cover the tuition of a second-year student. It was important for her to know if it was given to her on merit or was simply an extension of the largesse that had paid her way until now, so she went directly to the Chairman, Anne Keagy, and begged to be told the truth. She was assured, "You won, Toyoko, because you deserved to."

She came into her own during her second year. The stage had passed where she felt she had to prove that her presence at Parsons was not just a matter of connections and charity; and over the summer she had taken an English class at Columbia University, so she was able to participate more fully in class. Though at no time had her fellow students made her feel like a "special case" (in fact the entire student body seemed to her to be composed of highly idiosyncratic individuals who were more apt to see the poetical implications of walking around disfigured than the practical limitations), now there were those who wanted to sit near her in hopes of picking up pointers from the way she did things. Years later, a classmate who went on to become a Seventh Avenue designer would recall her work habits ("so precisely ordered it was like having a tea ceremony going on next to you"), her technical virtuosity ("distinguished by the meticulous attention to detail and superior quality of craftsmanship that have become a trademark of Orientals"), and her creativity ("Clothes at Parsons were designed as one-of-a-kinds, *haute couture*, and Orientals, while they made excellent copyists, were traditionally weak on the artistic part . . . but Toyo, she could make a piece of fabric look like a rose").

Capping the successful completion of her second year at Parsons, Toyoko's scholarship was extended to cover her third and final year; and that summer, as part of a special Parsons study group, she spent some sixteen weeks in Europe receiving seminar instruction from European couturiers and visiting museums.

A $400 grant from Parsons paid the tuition costs, but her

travel and living expenses were provided for by private monies raised by the Ridgewood Society of Friends, who had sponsored her during the Maidens Project, "to make sure that Toyo [does] not have to walk from Paris to Rome and then swim home without her supper," as the fund-raising letter read. The truth of the matter, however, was that most of her supporters were looking beyond Toyoko as an individual and thinking that the better the training she received—to which this trip would add greatly—the better the position she would be in to provide for others when she returned to Japan.

Ida Day was the architect behind this undertaking; she had a glorious vision of an exclusive custom-design dress business that would be operated by and employ only women injured in the bombing of Hiroshima. As she imagined the "Hiroshima Shop," Toyoko would design the clothes which, in turn, would be made by other Hiroshima Maidens skilled with needle and thread, and the opportunities did not stop there. Such an establishment conceivably could open up other possibilities: Two girls who had been making ends meet with a small knitting business could depend on it as a new marketing outlet; some of the eighteen women who had not been chosen to go to the United States for surgery and had been unable to find decent work would now be able to learn a respectable trade.

All through Toyoko's last year at Parsons, Ida Day continued to make plans for setting up a "Hiroshima Shop." Since it was her opinion that the customers who could support such a business were in Tokyo, not Hiroshima, and the staff would need a place to live while they worked, she placed a priority on finding a place in downtown Tokyo that could double as a home and a business. When an exchange of letters with Helen Yokoyama resulted in the discovery of a small two-story house that sounded suitable ("In location it is ideal, for it is in a district where many Americans live," Helen wrote. "It is near a market known for its clean vegetables [no night soil for fertilizer] . . . [and] it is on a corner and cars can be parked on two sides"), she turned her attention to raising the money to get the venture off to a running start. In a guest editorial printed in both the *Friends Journal* and the *Saturday Review,* she made the appeal: "If [anyone] would now like to share in this final phase of rehabilitation, financial contributions to furnish the house, buy sewing machines, or pay the first few months rent for Toyoko's shop would show the people of Hiroshima that the friendship of American friends did not conclude with the girls' return."

It all sounded good to Toyoko, who was content to let her benefactor undertake the necessary arrangements and attend to the details while she continued to apply herself to her studies in the belief that getting top grades would be the best preparation for the days to come; and her dedication was duly rewarded when she was one of only three students in the school to graduate with honors. At the annual May fashion show, when several of her designs were displayed, they evoked such enthusiasm from fashion editors that the *New York Times* printed a feature article about her that was highlighted by a tribute from the Chairman of the Fashion Design Department at Parsons. "In the time [Toyo] has been here she has improved more and worked harder than any other student," Anne Keagy was quoted as saying. "Now she has exceptional scope as a designer."

She spent most of the month of June measuring women for clothes, as she had already established a clientele of about fifty American customers whose orders (mostly cocktail and evening dresses to be made of Japanese silk) assured her an initial run of business after she opened her shop. In July, her four-year sojourn in the United States came to a close and she flew home to Japan. By August, she had moved into "Hiroshima House," and in September, Ida Day arrived. Mrs. Day had arranged to inaugurate the grand opening of the "Hiroshima Shop" to coincide with the height of the Tokyo showings of the latest Italian and French fashions, and announced that the internationally trained designer Toyoko Morita would make her debut with a fashion show-luncheon at the fabulous Imperial Hotel on October 7. She promptly set about promoting the event, making the rounds of the newspapers, contacting members of the American community living in Tokyo, making up posters, and sending out invitations.

Toyoko, quite naturally, was thrilled. The only reservation she had concerned the name of the shop. She did not think "Hiroshima Shop" had a smart sound to it. She thought there were associations that would turn customers away. And she had come to the point where she wanted to separate her career from her past. For Ida Day, who had felt all along that a personal triumph for Toyoko would symbolically manifest a triumph for the Hiroshima Maidens in general, it was a plausible line of thought; it would even make the shop more promotable. So together they settled on a new name: *Toyo, Haute Couture.*

The several weeks preceding the opening were frenetic with activity. With Toyoko to launch the enterprise were two Maidens, including Hiroko Tasaka, and two of "the eighteen"; but several other girls from the group also came up from Hiroshima to help her get ready. It was a hectic time and the "work force" had to stay up all night on several occasions to make last-minute adjustments; but there was a gaiety to the preparations, too, that came from a communal effort to complete a major task.

Long before the doors of the Phoenix Room at the Imperial Hotel were scheduled to open, a crowd had begun to gather. At noon, when the doors were finally opened, more people poured in than there were seats to accommodate them, so by the time the show began the walls at the back of the room were lined with standing spectators. Understandably, Toyoko was apprehensive about how her designs would be received, and throughout the show her eyes shifted from the models—[three Japanese and one American model]—parading through the room to the fashion editors scribbling in their notebooks. As her collection of nineteen pieces, ranging from trim career-girl ensembles to lavish ball gowns, was presented, the audience would burst into applause; but she was not convinced that they were not just being polite until the end, when she walked out on stage and was presented with a bouquet of flowers by the wife of the Mayor of Hiroshima, and heard an ovation that would be described in the next day's papers as "thunderous."

The press loved the story and played it up big, acclaiming Toyoko as a brilliant new discovery in the fashion world, a truly original Japanese designer who was capable of felicitously blending the simplicity of the East with the modernity of the West into an elegant style of her own. The *New York Times* reported: "Experienced fashion observers . . . declared that the Hiroshima Maiden surpassed current collections from Paris in the smartness of her designs."

As for Toyoko, a headline in one of the American papers pretty much summed up how she was feeling: "HIROSHIMA MAIDEN" FINDS A DESIGN FOR LIVING. She still bore the scars that not even the most skilled American surgeons could erase after two years of trying, but she had been searching for and now felt she had found that deep inner certitude of self, which came from doing the work that gave her the kind of fulfillment that she sought in life. In interviews, when she was asked about America or the bomb, she would answer that questions about either came together in her mind with a single reply: The best way to repay those Americans who had given her a future, the best way to forget the nightmare of her past, was to devote herself wholeheartedly to her work.

For the first year or so that *Toyo, Haute Couture* was open for business, all went splendidly. Responding to the reviews that predicted Toyoko's designs would set a new style for Japanese women, an immediate and increasing stream of customers filed into the shop to be outfitted. Her fashions were the rage that fall, and not just among a Japanese clientele; she also developed a large following of embassy people: French, Australians, and a number of Americans, including Ambassador Reischauer's wife. The volume of work they were getting was so great that Toyoko felt the need to expand, and taking a loan from Ida Day to cover moving costs and the initial increase in rent, she relocated in a much bigger house adjacent to the popular Ginza District and spacious enough to allow her to take on three additional seamstresses.

For the first time since her home had been scattered across the scorched earth of Hiroshima and she had lost everything but her life, Toyoko felt she was living as she was meant to. She felt at home in Tokyo. In four years abroad she had had the opportunity to develop her intellectual tastes to a higher level of sophistication. She had become cosmopolitan in her outlook, and so independent and street-smart that her classmates joked that more than turning into a woman of the Western world, she had been made over into a New Yorker. Living in Tokyo made her feel like she belonged to the world. She was in constant contact with foreigners. She got together frequently with people interested in the arts who could discuss new trends, many of whom had been exposed to different cultures and progressive social ideas, such as the problems a woman faced earning her own way in a society dominated by men.

But all was not as it seemed. Despite a deluge of orders, the eager anticipation felt by the "work force" when Toyoko returned from America had melted into disillusionment. Where at first laughter, singing, and the constant chatter of gay conversation had filled the upstairs room, where the Maidens were sewing, like sunlight, now the atmosphere was gloomy; there was fussing and arguing; and *Toyo, Haute Couture* seemed haunted with hushed voices that stopped whenever Toyoko entered the room.

Trying to ascertain what went wrong and why is difficult. Some said the seeds of conflict were sown when the name of the shop was changed; that after that Toyoko seemed to lose sight of the original vision and be more concerned about making a name for herself; and they would cite as proof the fashion show, where she accepted all the credit and never once acknowledged the efforts or contributions of those who assisted her or mentioned their role in the undertaking. Some said that success turned her head; that after her spectacular debut she treated her assistants like maids, not Maidens, and instituted working conditions that were as austere as the apprenticeship system of feudal days. (As more and more orders came in, Toyoko expected them to put in longer hours, until they were working from early morning to late evening, seven days a week; on top of that she gave herself a high salary—25,000 yen a month—but put everyone else on a 1,500-

yen-a-month draw against commission, according to the finished piece.) Others maintained that nothing essential in her character changed; that as well as being talented and creative she had drive and ambition, which came into play more and more and eventually took over.

Toyoko saw it very differently, of course. While she knew that many people were counting on the shop to provide ongoing employment to other Maidens, she did not take that to mean that a cooperative venture should necessarily provide uniformly for everyone. To her way of thinking, *Toyo, Haute Couture* was *her* salon, the fruit of *her* personal achievements. That was not to say that those who were assisting her were not an important part of its success or failure, just that she felt what was in her best interest would ultimately serve their interests. And while she would admit that perhaps she was more authoritarian than need be, Toyoko thought it appropriate to maintain strict control over the internal affairs of the shop, at least until the debts were paid off and profits assured. As for her salary, she felt she had worked hard against long odds to attain a higher position for herself, and she deserved a larger share.

There were other dynamics at work: In certain respects, Toyoko was a liberated woman caught between the pull of the Western ideal of personal fulfillment and self-expression and the traditional Japanese values of loyalty and harmony within the group, who found herself siding with the former. In the end she proved simply not to be a leader who was able to inspire a spirit of sacrifice in those around her, and one by one, beginning with Hiroko, the girls who had embarked on this venture with her exited with an alibi.

Throughout this period, Toyoko did her best to put a good face on what was happening, and managed to keep Ida Day from learning about the divisions, quarrels, and departures. Unable to interest any other Maidens in joining her and faced with a shortage of seamstresses, she worked out an arrangement with a design school in Hiroshima to send four of their promising students to live and work for her on a kind of internship program. The whole business dismayed her greatly when she let herself feel the weight of all the responsibilities that were hers alone, and when it got to be too much to bear, with no one to turn to, she started drinking again.

Then, in 1968, an intermediary approached her in the traditional Japanese manner on behalf of a widower from Hiroshima. Even though she felt strongly that women were entitled to personal and professional aspirations beyond those of a traditional housewife, she had never given up hope that someday a good man would come along, and believed she was capable of combining her career with a relationship. The official go-between was quite enthusiastic about the match, and plans were being made when Toyoko entered Tokyo University Hospital for treatment of a digestive irregularity, only to have it diagnosed as rectal cancer.

It was not a cancer that had been statistically linked to radiation exposure, though the doctors said one never knew for sure about these things, but it was a serious condition and they recommended a colostomy, a surgical procedure in which an artificial anus was created through an incision in her side that opened into the colon. It was too drastic a decision for her to make on such short notice, and the thought of presenting herself to her prospective husband in that way was too embarrassing to consider. Instead, she agreed to undergo what she deemed to be a less radical procedure: the surgical removal of the cancerous tissue, followed by a series of radiation treatments. The results were extremely painful and required her to wear diapers thereafter, but in her mind that was preferable to the alternative.

The marriage proposal was put on hold during her illness and eventually withdrawn, which was just as well, she told herself, all things considered. After that, she made several return trips to the United States, proceeding on to Paris to observe the new directions that American and European couturiers were taking. It was all a part of keeping up-to-date, and what was eminently apparent was that *haute couture* was on the way out, and ready-to-wear clothes were coming in. Women just did not have the time to stand for hours of fittings; they wanted to be able to go to a single store and find everything they were looking for immediately. Changing with the times, Toyoko closed her shop and accepted a position with an Osaka clothing manufacturer designing a line of dresses that were then mass-produced. She also found the time to teach design at one of Tokyo's better fashion institutes. She was shuttling between Tokyo and Osaka, making occasional trips to the States, until 1974, when the cancer came out of remission. This time there was no deliberation; it was a matter of life or death, and a permanent colostomy was performed.

When she went to Hiroshima to recover, she decided to remain so she would have family nearby in case of future complications. For years after that she continued to teach, design ready-made clothes and make custom suits for faithful clients. The fate of *Toyo, Haute Couture* would remain a sensitive topic. Though it eventually became a modestly successful enterprise, whenever it came up in conversation, she would bristle at the suggestion that it was a real might-have-been-that-never-was because of any fault or foible of hers. Her way of answering questions about what happened would be to admit that perhaps she had high expectations of others which could cause trouble when they went unfulfilled, but that the passing of *haute couture* from vogue accounted for the demise of the shop. However, when she attempted to interest others in the original group in starting up another custom dress business based in Hiroshima, it was clear that much trust had been lost in Tokyo.

Toyoko never married. There were relationships with men, and several more inquiries from intermediaries, but she remained a career woman, first, last, and always. Sometimes she would wonder if her dedication to the pursuit of one goal in life had denied her something important, but just when she would begin to yearn for a companion, or worry about growing old alone, or think about what her life would have been like if she had taken a different course, she would find herself listening to one of the Maidens who had devoted herself to motherhood talk about the compromises that had to be made living with another, and how lucky she was that she did not have family obligations, was free to travel, and had an occupation that gave her feelings of accomplishment.

Today, Toyoko lives in a modern apartment on the outskirts of Hiroshima. She removes her shoes at the door, but inside the furniture is Western and the paintings and prints on the walls are views of the world outside Japan. Her work remains the center of her life, but she also makes time for some of the traditional arts such as oil painting and writing haiku. She shows little interest in politics and shuns publicity except when it pertains to business. While she has a reputation as a successful designer in Tokyo, she is better known in her hometown as one of the Hiroshima Maidens.

Toyoko has not forgotten how she suffered during those awful years after the war, and there are bitter disappointments that still torment her. But when she reflects upon the life she has led as a whole, she is able to say, without irony, that what she has done with her life in many ways fulfills the dreams she had for herself as a younger woman. Her work has been a kind of salvation, giving her the status and satisfaction that she feels would have been hers if there had been no such thing as an atomic bomb. In the sense that she has realized her ambitions, she is able to say she has prevailed over her destiny.

As a dressmaker who knew how difficult it was to mend a hole or tear in a fabric, Hiroko Tasaka had no illusions that it would be any easier to repair skin. Her facial scars still held a frightening attraction for strangers, but after twenty-seven operations—fourteen in Japan, thirteen in the United States—she was reconciled to the fact that the best that was humanly possible had been done, and she was prepared to face life with realism and a cool courage.

Nevertheless, just in case she forgot that as a handicapped person she would have to put up with attitudes that did not equal her own in maturity and objectivity, after a year of preparation and a passing grade on her entrance examination, she was almost rejected by the graduate school of her choice on the basis of an admissions bias that favored physically attractive applicants. It took the beneficent intervention of Helen Yokoyama, who spoke personally to the principal and pointed out the public relations benefits the institution that accepted a Hiroshima Maiden would accrue, to open to her a place in the Tokyo Design School that she deserved on her own merits.

Harry Harris proved as relentless in the continuation of his courtship as she was intent on completing her training. His letters came with faithful regularity, sometimes two or three a week, and although they were usually short on sentiment and long on the mundane details that made up his existence, there was never any doubt that the object was still matrimony. She enjoyed hearing from him, but just before classes started she wrote that she did not want to divide her attention. The next two years of her life would be devoted exclusively to her studies, and this would be her last letter. Not one to be discouraged, he wrote in reply, "Do what you have to. I'll wait."

As she had it planned, when she graduated she would go back to Hiroshima where she had been promised a teaching position at her old sewing school. Before that could happen, however, Toyoko Morita returned to Tokyo and asked for her help. It was not what Hiroko wanted to do, but knowing that Americans had put up the money and were counting on this venture to create opportunities for other girls hurt by the bomb, it was what she felt she ought to do.

Many of the diverse problems and complications that arose were of a type too petty to enumerate; the issue for Hiroko was simply that she expected to be working *with* Toyo, not *for* her. Nor were the tensions of the situation eased by the fact that Toyo paid herself a high salary, while Hiroko received a commission based on the completed work, which was barely enough for her to live on.

A year was her limit. She was a designer in her own right, and she was anxious to open her own shop. Making as tactful an exit as she could under the circumstances, she took an apartment in Hiroshima and went about looking for the right business opportunity. She found a shop easily; on her way to the grocery store one day she made a wrong turn that took her past a row of storefronts, one of which was empty. When she went into the shop next door to find out if it was still vacant, she found herself talking to the owner, who rented it to her on the spot.

She named the shop *Dress Room Miyuki,* after the temple where she went to pray for a sign that coming back to Hiroshima had been the right decision. At first she depended on orders through family and friends, but when word got around that her work was superior and her rates reasonable, she began to add new customers. Business expanded so rapidly that at one point she had six seamstresses working for her full-time.

Five years had passed since her return, and Hiroko was doing what she thought she had always wanted to do. She was even teaching sewing classes during the evenings and on weekends, her lifetime ambition. Yet, there was an unresolved feeling inside. She had noticed it when she first returned from America and was living at home with her mother. Something was missing that she had grown used to when she was part of an American family: the sense of completion brought about by having a man around the house. It was a feeling that had left her home when her father died; and it was a feeling aroused by the letters that kept coming from Harry Harris.

She had made the sensible decision to return to Japan, but his marriage proposal had never lost its grip on her imagination, and now she felt his steadfast devotion pulling on her emotions. Inwardly, she reasoned that if she were Miss Japan it would have made some sense for him to wait and hope for her to change her mind, but since beauty was not a factor, the man must truly love her. And knowing that someone felt that strongly about her after five years apart, with thousands of miles separating them, created a force she found increasingly difficult to resist.

If she had still been in her twenties, it would have been an easier decision to head off, by herself; as it was, she was thirty-three, and it seemed the older she got the more reasons she could think of for not making a major change. She did not really know this man; they had never even been together outside the hospital.

He was not very well educated; that was evident from his letters that were as full of misspellings and grammatical errors as her own were when she wrote him back. And marrying a foreigner entailed more risks than marrying a fellow countryman, which itself offered no guarantees of happiness. She felt it would be foolish, too, to abandon a career just when it was beginning to provide her with a secure livelihood.

But a sweet decency radiated from Harris's letters that made her feel a good heart was more important than an educated mind, and against the protestations of family and friends, Hiroko wrote Harry a letter accepting his proposal. No one knew how it would come out, but as she rationalized it to herself, even if the marriage failed, the regrets would not be as great as those that would linger if she never took the chance.

There were complications and delays. At that time, U.S. Immigration laws made it difficult for a single Japanese woman to travel to the States. Consequently, there was almost a two-year wait before Hiroko was able to depart for America—on the pretext of visiting Norman Cousins.

When the plane landed in New York, she walked down the ramp with the rest of the passengers, not quite sure where she was to meet Harry. As she entered the large terminal, there seemed to be people everywhere. Then she saw his familiar round face looking nervously out of the crowd. When he saw her he waved, strode forward, and when they were at arm's length, after a moment of indecision, he extended his hand. Her heart went cold. Coming from a land where arranged marriages were a custom had made it somewhat easier to conceive of agreeing to marry a man with whom matters of a personal nature were left undiscussed; but just how little she knew about this man was suddenly, stunningly, evident when she saw that both his forearms were branded with black tattoos.

There was no way she could have known. When he had visited her in the hospital he had worn long-sleeved shirts. Unable to conceal her chagrin, tears began to flow.

"What happened?" he asked, confused, looking back and

forth from her to the crowd as though he thought someone had struck her.

"Your mother never said anything to you?" she managed to say, glancing fearfully at an ink-drawn heart with an arrow shot through it and the word LOVE scratched underneath.

"About what?"

She was too upset to answer. Only later, after they had walked together through the crowds to the baggage wheel and waited stiffly for her small suitcases to appear, after he had loaded them into the car trunk and they were driving away from the airport, was she able to explain. In Japan, only criminals and gangsters had tattoos.

From there, things only got worse. After a quiet wedding ceremony at a Methodist church in Baltimore the newlyweds moved into a low-rent high-rise, and Harry went back to work driving a cab. With nothing to do and nobody to talk to, Hiroko found herself sitting around the apartment counting the hours until he got off work. Once, just to get out, she decided to walk to the post office and mail a letter; she forgot the way back, however, and no one could understand her when she asked directions. Her difficulty with the English language not only kept her home-bound after that, it was also a block in her relationship with her husband. The pidgin English that had been mutually intelligible in letters did not hold up well in everyday conversation. Harry spoke too fast and his sentences ran on, so that much of what he said sounded like gibberish to her. In order to communicate on the most basic level, they resorted to sitting down at the kitchen table and writing each other letters again, which they were able to translate with the help of an English-to-Japanese dictionary.

But the most troublesome aspect of their difficulties was too delicate even to broach: To her dismay, her mother-in-law turned out to be a domineering, insensitive woman. At the wedding she paced around, wringing her hands and letting the guests know she neither approved nor comprehended her son's actions in this matter. Afterward, she expected them to visit her every day, and if they did not she would call on the phone and ask what was wrong. When she was alone with Hiroko, her behavior ranged from chilly to nasty. It was almost second nature for a Japanese woman to tolerate all kinds of discomfort; and by custom she was wedded into her husband's family, not just to the husband himself, so Hiroko did everything possible to be a good daughter-in-law. But she knew it was going to be an onerous task when she offered to do the woman's alterations and mending and the next time they got together she was handed three suitcases full of clothes, containing not only her mother-in-law's garments, but a collection she had taken up from her friends.

The year was 1965, and the contrast to her experience in America in 1955 could not have been more dramatic. The land of paradise had become a world of pitfalls. Only now did she realize how sheltered they had been by the Quakers. In her mind she likened her first trip to living in a greenhouse that let only sunlight in; now all it did was rain.

Weather permitting, she would take walks to a park two blocks away where she would sit on a bench and try to study her English lessons book. But she was unable to concentrate, and spent most of her time making friends with the squirrels and worrying about what she should do next. It gave her a sick feeling to think she had given up her career and come all the way back to the States just to learn she should have been content where she was. Sometimes she scolded herself for trading a life as an active businesswoman for that of a bored housewife, and sometimes she felt sorry for herself; but whenever she let herself imagine how the newspapers would play up her return (she did not even have to close her eyes to see the headline: AMERICAN SAILOR JILTS HIRO-SHIMA MAIDEN), her eyes would open wide as though to dispel a nightmare, and she knew that whatever the sacrifice, running back home was not an alternative.

It helped to have a husband who understood the pressures weighing on her, and considered it his duty to shoulder them where he could. By turns tough and tender, a man who could be outwardly coarse but who turned out to have a noble spirit, Harry never forgot what she had given up to be at his side. When he saw how unhappy she was, he changed his job so his hours were regular and he could be home more, and then he went out and found them a nicer apartment with air-conditioning.

She could not have asked for more from him, and when she realized the rest was up to her, she decided it was time for her to go to work. One morning she sat down with the Yellow Pages and diligently telephoned every tailor in the Baltimore area, asking them, "Do you need a seamstress or fitter?" The question became so polished with repetition that by the end of the day she could ask it without the trace of an accent. All said no except one, who told her the owner was out and suggested she call back later. When she phoned that evening, a woman whose voice sounded more foreign than her own invited her to come in for an interview.

She took along several dresses of her own design and making, and a picture of her Hiroshima shop; and she was hired by a jolly German lady whose employment policy favored immigrants like herself. Her pay was only a dollar an hour, however, so she continued to look for a better position, and when she heard about an opening in a French tailor shop she made a move. Six months was all she could take: the money was good, but the bosses could not get along, her co-workers were constantly arguing, and everyone thought she was dumb because she could not understand what all the yelling was about. Back she went to the German lady's shop, but not for long. Feeling the frustration of a talented woman operating in an environment that did not use her full capacities, she would scan the Help Wanted ads in the daily newspaper, and one day she noticed that the Hecht Company, a nationwide department store chain, was looking for a qualified woman with management potential in the alteration department of Ladies Apparel. "I'm very experienced, and I promise my work will give satisfaction," she told the interviewer. Apparently she was believed, for she got the job; within two years she was promoted to supervisor.

Hiroko and Harry settled into the comfortable routines of a typical working-class couple. He worked the night shift, she held a day job, so they saw each other for breakfast and dinner, relaxed on the weekends, and saved for vacations. They had a pet myna bird named Norman and taught it to speak both Japanese and English. Although appearances suggested Hiroko's adjustment to American life-styles had become complete, in fact she remained resolutely Japanese, returning regularly to visit her mother in Japan. Proudly she took along her husband, who basked in the attention traditionally accorded the master of a house. Surrounded by nieces and waited upon by his doting mother-in-law, he was in serious danger of becoming spoiled, and would talk as if he never wanted to return to the States.

As a couple they were especially popular with the Japanese press, who found the built-in irony of their relationship a source of unending fascination and delighted in varying the marriage-made-in-Heaven theme with a love-born-by-the-A-bomb twist. But often the journalistic gush got things wrong and caused bad feelings. When a Japanese newspaper quoted Harry as saying his feelings for Hiroko were an effort to compensate for the crime of the atomic bomb, the letters she scribbled to friends denying those were his words were smudged from the tears that fell on the ink as she wrote.

From time to time, people she worked with would comment that she seemed to be healing. It was not so, she knew; they were just getting used to her appearance. Even she had grown accustomed to her face; after all, it had been with her longer than not. Sometimes her disfigurement was so far from her mind that she would be standing in front of the mirror putting on make-up and suddenly be struck by the extent of the damage. But it was not in a self-pitying way, rather as if she had noticed something outside herself that was broken and it was a shame. When she thought about her scars it was usually because someone else reminded her. She noticed, for example, that when she first met people they had difficulty remembering her name or understanding what she said, and she had to repeat herself. The problem was not her English; it was just that they were looking, not listening. Sometimes people came right out and asked her what had happened, and usually she was comfortable telling them.

Only once was the curiosity unacceptable. While waiting to meet a friend at the airport, she and Harry had gone into the cafeteria for a snack. As they approached the register, the cashier's eyes widened when she saw Hiroko, and she ducked into the kitchen to tell the cooks and waitresses to come and look. Hiroko saw it all and, turning her back on the help gawking from the kitchen, she busied herself opening a bag of potato chips. When, out of the corner of her eye, she saw the cashier slowly approach her, watching and waiting for her to turn around, she decided to walk away. Halfway to the door, she realized the girl was following her out in hopes of a last look, and for the first time in her life she lost her temper over public reaction to her scars. Wheeling around, she said, "Do you want to see my face? Is that what you want?" The girl was too flustered to come up with anything better than a stammered, "What? No. I was, uh, looking for, uh, the clock." Hiroko glared. "You work here and you don't know where the clock is? You're not looking for a clock. You came to see me. Well here I am. Why don't you ask me what's wrong with my face?" The girl began backing away, passing Harry, who was so dumbfounded he fled through the cafeteria doors. "Well, I'll tell you anyway. It was ruined by the atomic bomb." On the verge of tears, the girl said she did not understand, so Hiroko spelled it out for her: "A-T-O-M-I-C B-O-M-B."

It was an uncharacteristic outburst for this slim, small, normally reserved lady, but sometimes the rudeness of people made her so angry she forgot herself. She understood the interest in her life experiences and she was not unwilling to talk about them because she had always considered it her obligation to remind others of "the hell of that day." And she was convinced that the power that had prevented the further use of atomic weapons came out of a knowledge of the immediate and continuing effects of the atomic bomb on the lives of the Hiroshima survivors. But there were times when she found herself wondering why she should continue to put up with insensitivity and distortions when the personal returns of sharing her past were so minimal and her own peace of mind so much more immediately relevant to her well-being, and she would say to herself, *Let them learn the way I did.*

More than once she swore off the whole business of giving evidence in the case against nuclear war. But when the *Baltimore Sun* wanted to run her account of August 6, 1945, side by side with the recollections of a native Baltimorean who had been the radar officer on the *Enola Gay,* she agreed to do so because it had always bothered her that in the American version the bomb was dropped, the war was over, and that was it, while for her and so many others that was just the beginning. And when an independent film company sought her cooperation in the making of a documentary about how a typical American family faced the nuclear war issue, she had dinner with the family and answered their questions on camera because it seemed to simulate in many ways her first experience in America. When she was asked to testify at Congressional hearings held by Senators Edward Kennedy and Mark Hatfield prior to their "nuclear freeze" resolution, out of respect for their goals she told them what she had seen and experienced thirty-seven years before when she was a thirteen-year-old junior high school student.

Although America was no longer a foreign setting for Hiroko, her family was still in Japan and she had it in her mind that when Harry, who was ten years her senior, turned sixty and retired, they would move back. She thought of it as his turn to cross the ocean and bridge a culture for her, which suited him fine. What more could an old sailor ask for than to live out his retirement years on an island, tending orange groves and tutoring his nieces? And so it came about that in 1983, eighteen years after she had returned to America to become a bride, Hiroko went home again.

With her free time she thought she might write a memoir telling her story in her own words, for looking back she saw that an odyssey that had begun in personal devastation appeared to be drawing to a deeply satisfying conclusion. Most of the so-called A-bomb literature consisted of depressing accounts of survivors who had been unable to live naturally; there were few reports of people who had endured hard times but recovered their health and now lived like everyone else. Hers would be an account in which the positive aspects of her life would predominate, however, for life in many ways had made up to her. She had done everything she wanted to do, and along the way had accumulated experiences and friendships that had allowed her to develop an affirmative attitude toward her circumstances. While stopping far short of appreciation, she nevertheless realized that if it were not for the bomb, much that was memorable in her life would have been otherwise, and who was to say her whether life would have been better, or worse. At the very least she felt she had a strength and resilience, a sense of integrity and of her own worth now that would enable her to handle any adversity that came her way.

But most of all, she prized what she had learned about the healing possibilities of the human heart: One day before they left for Japan, Harry, with no warning, checked into a hospital to have his tattoos surgically removed.

AFTERWORD

In the spring of 1984, I returned to Hiroshima. As this book had been five years in the writing, the purpose of my trip was to update my information; but by then I felt less like a journalist making sure his facts were current than like the keeper of the archives. Since my previous visit, no fewer than a dozen people on both sides of the Pacific had died, and age was eroding the memories of the surviving principals. More and more, I found I had to set the stage and supply the names before a scene could be recalled with relative clarity. Even then, the passage of time seemed to throw a halo around the Hiroshima Maidens Project so events were remembered in the soft focus of the heart rather than the sharp relief of the mind.

The first time we met, I'd found the Maidens almost blithe in their willingness to assume a cooperative role in this undertaking. Of course, it was easier for them to say yes as part of a group than to reveal themselves individually to an interpreter, tape recorder, and a smiling *gaijin*. While my personal connection to the project may have been a ticket in the door, it certainly was not a pass to automatic trust. As I came to learn, on several occasions in the past one of the girls had been disappointed to find their confidence abused by publication. A girl who had poured out her heart in letters to a hostess after her return felt utterly betrayed when the letters turned up in an anthology of essays about and correspondences from the hibakusha of Hiroshima.

It took time and repeated visits to establish the kind of rapport that allowed me to address in detail a past that had been shattered by a disaster so dreadful others have found it "unthinkable." Sometimes I felt like a provocateur of pain, for the Maidens did not simply recite their A-bomb story for me, they relived August 6, 1945, and went through ten long years of struggle and sacrifice again. I was told that most survivors of Hiroshima deliver their testimony in this manner because the atomic bomb remains a terrible mysterious dynamic in their lives, and because they know no better way to let others know just how awful it was than to take them through it step by step. Make of it what you will, it was apparent that an account of an atomic attack is transmitted on a far more complex frequency than a conventional war story.

If the atomic bomb was evil in remembrance, their American experience took on aspects of a hiatus in heaven. The pictures in their scrapbooks, the messages and signatures in the autograph books, were dream artifacts that seemed to possess a magical ability to transport them back to another land in an earlier time. Those memories are still dear to them, and they seemed to enjoy the opportunity to reminisce.

Although they initially agreed to be interviewed out of a lingering debt to American friends, a few resisted when it became apparent that my desire was to understand all the forces that had shaped them up to this point. For some of the Maidens, an in-depth discussion meant probing areas they would not discuss even with someone they knew well. Others had closed the book on certain chapters of their lives for good; and there were those who saw themselves as ordinary women leading ordinary lives, who genuinely did not believe that anything they had done merited examination or documentation, and who preferred to keep it that way.

But to an extent that sometimes surprised me, the overwhelming majority rose to the occasion in a spirit of participation. And to my gratification, many of those who took time out to think about their lives, and made an effort to muse over the meanings of their experiences, found themselves rewarded with insights and resolutions in the end. That, at least, is what certain Maidens told me before my first visit to Hiroshima came to a close.

The second time around I found their attitudes toward the press remained hostile. If anything, they were more cynical and mistrustful than before. I soon learned why. A recent event had aggravated matters: the release of a thin book, hastily written to capitalize on the annual August sixth interest in Hiroshima, that characterized the Hiroshima Maidens as a neurotically preoccupied group, obsessed with their lost youth and stolen beauty. In the writer's crude estimation (he was otherwise employed as a sportswriter for a Tokyo daily newspaper), they were primarily motivated by an effort to compensate for their psychological inferiority, and reflexively blamed the bomb for all their problems, setbacks, and woes. The evidence he put forth in support of this analysis was based less on his direct interviews, for he admitted that fewer than a third of the living Maidens had agreed to talk with him, than on his personal frustration at not being able to obtain the cooperation of the others. But no matter, there could be no other explanation for their reclusive ways, he had concluded, than that they had reverted to their former insecure selves. Incredibly, in a closing note, he recommended "that some sort of psychotherapy is what these women really need."

To the extent that the Maidens have had to put up with gross and oversimplified characterizations, I suppose this could be considered as reflecting another dimension of the bomb. But it is also inexcusable when journalists who say they have come to Hiroshima to learn what nuclear warfare does to the people who live through it, by their coverage end up creating a fallout that in some ways is as harmful to the survivors as the radiation from the bomb itself.

This time I distinctly sensed a more acute concern about health. On my previous visit I had been continually impressed by how outwardly philosophical the Maidens seemed to be about the delayed effects of radiation. It might have been Oriental fatalism that stopped them from dwelling on events over which they had no control; or perhaps they had drawn comfort from the fact that after Keiko Kawasaki died of statistically related A-bomb causes back in 1959, they were all still alive. Whatever explained it, at that time they were not preoccupied with thoughts about when the atomic bomb would strike them down. The sentiments of most were summed up in the following exchange. Asked by a friend, "Aren't you concerned that the bomb could kill you at any time?" a Maiden replied, "Do you think that because you weren't in Hiroshima you are promised a long life?"

But the curse of an atomic weapon is that once damaged by it one can never be sure he has recovered or escaped the consequences. Even though the Maidens did not consciously indulge their doubts, the fear that the bomb would catch up with them has always been there in an unconscious way, producing a low-grade tension that could rise to the surface at any given time. Indeed, I was told this time that there has never been an end to the anxiety that the slightest irregularity signals an oncoming cancer. Of late, that fear has become more pronounced, due in large part to the hideous secrets of radiation that have come out carcinogenically among aging survivors. Cancer has an incubation period, as the accelerating number of cancer patients admitted to the A-bomb Hospital in Hiroshima, and Michiko Yamaoka, who had a radical mastectomy for breast cancer last year, can attest.

In addition to those symptoms of radiation, numerous physical aches and pains remind the women of the different ways they were hurt by the bomb. For instance, sporadic numbness in Atsuko Yamamoto's hands was revealed, under X-rays, to stem from an injury sustained when the blast bounced her along the street like a windblown newspaper. And nerve damage to Yoshie Yanagibashi's legs and back keeps her on regular medication.

Of course, it is sometimes difficult to tell who is suffering from A-bomb effects and who from the natural process of aging. And, as if to remind them just how precarious their well-being is, three months before I arrived Suzue Hiyama, who had stayed with my family, died. Her death followed the demise of her husband a year earlier from liver complications, and the premature death of her oldest daughter from a mysterious illness that remains undiagnosed because her superstitious in-laws refused to permit an autopsy. The cause of Suzue's death, according to the doctors, was cirrhosis of the liver, but those close to the family called it drowning in alcohol to overcome her grief.

Looking at their wounds today they cannot help but notice the changes that have come with time. There seems to be an unevenness to the way the different skins on their face are aging. Where the natural skin has begun to web with wrinkles, the grafts remain smooth and fair; and as though it is a property of abdominal skin to fatten as one grows older, they have also become puffy. Nor is the quality of transplanted skin as good: It is sensitive to the sun, cuts easily, is quick to infect, and slow to heal. Ironically, over time, their keloids have softened and faded, leading some to think there might have been advantages in later life to leaving things the way they were. But at the same time that the women acknowledge that the very procedures that made them more presentable as younger women have become like another affliction with time, they feel guilty for noticing. It is something they observe on their own and sometimes discuss among one another, but they would not want anyone to get the idea they would go back and change things if they could.

My reading of the Maidens' children also changed on this visit. It had been my previous impression that few offspring had any special feeling for what it meant that their mothers were Hiroshima Maidens. In general, they seemed to hold Americans in slightly greater thrall than the average Japanese youth tended to do, and a few dreamed of going to the United States sometimes themselves. But they did not appear to feel they were the beneficiaries of a unique heritage, and in fact, they seemed to be to be singularly lacking in interest or commitment outside their immediate personal concerns.

After talking with their mothers I better understood why this was so. At the time of their marriages, each had made private vows that, should they ever bear children, they would do everything in their power to shelter them from the hardships and humiliations that had been their lot in life. One of the reasons they shun publicity is out of concern that anything written about them will have repercussions for their children. (The effects of radiation are a mystery that retain something of their inscrutability even as they foster new forms of revelation. The fact that investigations carried out on children conceived by survivors after exposure did not detect statistically verifiable evidence of genetic effects does not give assurance that mutations induced are not of a recessive character and might only manifest themselves in the second, third, or even later generations. The first question a go-between asks when she knows a prospective partner is from Hiroshima is whether the parents were victims of the A-bomb; they are especially concerned about the mother.) Wanting only to foster an untroubled existence, they had regulated their sons' and daughters' upbringings in such a way as to distance them from the past and all events surrounding the bomb.

This had made perfect sense; but in conversations with them five years later—now that most of their children are happily married—I sensed they were beginning to have misgivings about raising them without a historical consciousness. When they look around and see a generation of young people whose central concerns are personal comfort and economic security, who grew up in the prosperous years of postwar Japan and have little sense of the war that came before, it makes them wonder if they have not unwittingly contributed to a dangerously naive mentality. The youth of Japan seem to believe in the battlefield myth that says a man is safe if he crawls in the hole sunk by a previously exploded artillery shell because no two shells will land in exactly the same place. Their faith in the future appears to be based on the belief that since the bomb has already exploded over Japan, it won't come again. And so, as parents the Maidens think they probably did the right thing, but as survivors they worry that perhaps they should have done more.

It's difficult to say what the future holds for the Hiroshima Maidens, because at the same time that they are struggling to resolve this inner conflict, their personal dramas continue to take unexpected twists. (Though his loyalty to Hiroko is intense and unflagging, life on the island was altogether different than Harry Harris had anticipated. He had put on too much weight to be of help in the orchards. The only friend he made was an old man who fished off the same dock, and even though they seemed to enjoy each other's company they were unable to carry on a conversation. He could not watch television because it was all in Japanese. Six months after their arrival, Harry said he could not take it anymore, he was losing his voice, he wanted to go back. Now they split their time between the two countries.) It would be a mistake to think the women have entirely overcome their particular tragedies. Granted, the surgery and the spirit of human oneness they received in America helped them deal with the stresses that followed, but that only marginally compensated for the years of rejection and withdrawal that had gone before, and did not offset the reality that they have been maimed for more years of their lives than not. Twice a day, in the morning when they put their make-up on and in the evening when they wipe it off, they are confronted with a sight that leaves them only half at peace. In their imaginations, they each carry an alternative life in comparison.

Perhaps it really is asking too much from these middle-aged women (the youngest is almost fifty now) to heed the call to become torchbearers. At the moment they are a peculiarly fractious group, divided as much by sisterly bickerings as fundamental differences in outlook. "We are like floating moss," was the way one Maiden put it. "The tide moves us around. Sometimes we float in a cluster, other times we go our own way." Considering the ten-year difference in age between the youngest and oldest, and their different situations and personalities, it could not be otherwise.

And yet, certain individuals have come to terms with the fresh emotional challenge of sharing their accumulated knowledge in experienced detail; and there are those among them who look forward to an occasion that will allow them to set aside their differences and unite behind a common theme or aim. They point out that the Hiroshima Maidens Project already has a distinguished humanitarian legacy: Norman Cousins, working with the same group of American volunteers who organized the Maidens Project and using the money that was left over from it, went on to bring another group of war-scarred women to America for medical treatment (Polish women subjected to purposeless and pseudoscientific medical experiments by Nazi doctors in the Ravensbruck concentration camps); and Dr. Arthur Barsky set up a plastic surgery hospital in South Vietnam during the sixties to treat war-injured children, where he met Dr. Tomin Harada on a similar mission of mercy. They say they have points to make that are worth thinking about; after all, who knows better the imperatives of peace and the folly of fighting than those who learned to love others once thought to be the enemy?

The time is certainly right. The climate for hibakusha in Japan has changed considerably; once thought to be ungodly, today they enjoy the eminence of holy people who have experienced a prophetic vision. The eighties have seen the rise of a countervailing peace movement; four decades have passed and there have been no more Hiroshimas, but there are fifty thousand more nuclear weapons in existence and the end of the world as we know it is potentially only minutes away. Meanwhile, the number of Maidens is diminishing; there are only twenty-one left.

Even Helen Yokoyama, an elderly woman now but one of enormous moral strength, has recently emerged from private life to rock the Maidens' complacency. For years, she had hoped that they would turn of their own accord in their own time to putting their experiences down on paper (for publication, for the historical record, or just for their children); since so few have, and she cannot bear to think that stories so rich in intrinsic human values might end without having been written, she has come forward to make a personal appeal. Indeed, at times I sensed something of a pact between us, as if she hoped that their participation in the process of researching this book would rouse them to do something that shows the spirit of the project lives on.

They have never liked being called "A-bomb Maidens" or "Hiroshima Maidens." It was a form of address invented by the press; its associations with the bomb always seemed a little too pointed, and when half of the women married it was no longer appropriate. Often, when they were written about, superficial characteristics that some women appeared to have in common were collected and presented in a way that made it seem they were shared in equal measure. Individual words or deeds were frequently interpreted as representing the group. One woman told me that no matter how troubled she became, suicide was not an option because she knew it would not be accepted as a personal decision, rather it would be reported that one of the Maidens killed herself.

But while they reject the public identity that has been assigned to them, the women are aware that they form a society of their own. The bond of loyalty they feel for one another, forged in the sharing of uncommon experiences, and the pride that comes from knowing there is no other group like them in the world, led them, at one of their regular get-togethers, to come up with a more artful term that everyone agreed captured the image they have of themselves. Today they do not refer to one another as Hiroshima Maidens, but as members of *Satsukikai*. *Kai* is Japanese for "association"; *satsuki* is the word for "azalea." It's the way they view their lives: like a gathering of flowers that bloom in May, the month they arrived in America.

NOTES

The source material I have used in the preparation of this book consists primarily of extensive interviews which I conducted personally in the United States and in Japan between the years 1979 and 1984 with participants in the events described, and of documentary evidence from both countries. Most of the interviews were tape-recorded and most of the written material was copied or given to me in its original form. Apart from the intrinsic importance of each of these two primary sources, I have used them as a means of providing checks and balances, one against the other, to enable me to present the story as authentically and accurately as possible.

In the United States, I met with numerous host families for their recollections. Many had kept scrapbooks during the project, which turned out to be a rich source of newspaper clippings, magazine articles, and letters. When I visited Ida Day, she cooperated with me to the extent of providing me with all the "records" of the project which she had kept on an informal basis. After several sessions with Norman Cousins, he gave me open access to all his private papers that are stored at Brooklyn College and the personal files he kept at the old

Saturday Review offices in New York. I interviewed and corresponded with Dr. Sidney Kahn before his death in 1980, with Dr. Bernard Simon, and on four separate occasions with Dr. Arthur Barsky before he passed away in 1983. Also, I twice interviewed the Reverend Marvin Green, who had been the treasurer of the Hiroshima Peace Center Associates, and before his death in 1982 he turned all the reports and newsletters he had retained over to me. After two requests filed under the Freedom of Information Act, State department documents originally classified were released to me. For background information on Hiroshima, I consulted with Dr. Robert Lifton, the author/psychiatrist who was the first to write about the psychological and social effects of the atomic bomb in his book *Death in Life;* Mr. Aboul Foutouhi, a retired Foreign Service man who was stationed at the American Culture Center in Hiroshima for most of the 1950s; Ms. Barbara Reynolds, a peace activist who lived for many years in Hiroshima; and Dr. Robert Miller, a radiation research specialist who was employed at the Atomic Bomb Casualty Commission in the midfifties. Miscellaneous materials supplementing these interviews were gathered from the Hiroshima/Nagasaki Memorial Collection of the Wilmington College Peace Resource Center. For clarification and elaboration on a variety of issues and details, I spoke with many other individuals to whom I am indebted, but probably do not need to cite by name.

In Japan, I met with eighteen of the twenty-two Hiroshima Maidens. After repeated get-togethers I came to know most of them on a deeply personal basis, so they felt comfortable enough to relate the story of their lives to me in detail. Some spoke English well enough to permit a direct conversation, but most required the services of translators whom I selected for their command of both languages, their ability to communicate a sense of trust, and their skill in asking delicate questions in an inoffensive way. Some of the Maidens had written personal essays or kept diaries and letters, which they gave to me and I had translated. In Hiroshima, both the Reverend Kiyoshi Tanimoto and Helen Yokoyama cooperated completely with my research objectives, giving me time for interviews and responding to my follow-up queries. Drs. Tomin Harada and Goro Ouchi, the two living Japanese physicians who accompanied the Maidens to America, also provided a thorough account of their experience, as did Mr. Kiyoshi Togasaki in Tokyo and Mr. Kaoru Ogura, a public official in Hiroshima. Finally, editors at the *Chugoku Shinbun*, the major daily newspaper in Hiroshima, generously supplied me with copies of all the articles they have published about the Hiroshima Maidens over the years. In Japan there were also numerous individual contributions which added insight and understanding to the work, but need not be individually listed.

Detailed source notes on a chapter-by-chapter basis follow.

Prelude: This Is Your Life

Material for the prelude is drawn directly from a viewing of and the transcript of the *This Is Your Life* program which aired on NBC-TV on May 11, 1955. Further informing this section are comments made by the Reverend Tanimoto and the Reverend Marvin Green during personal interviews.

1

The historical perspective in this chapter is drawn from information obtained from the archives of the Hiroshima Castle, various booklets published over the years by the Hiroshima Peace Culture Foundation, and a personal interview with the retired director of the Hiroshima City Library. The Hiroko Tasaka section is based on extensive and repeated personal interviews conducted at her home in Baltimore, Maryland, and in Japan. The Shigeko Niimoto section is based on personal interviews conducted with her at her home in Newton, Massachusetts, and on visits to Washington, D.C.; a conversation with her mother in Hiroshima; two essays she wrote about her atomic bomb experience, one of which was published in a book entitled *The Life of the Flower Is Very Short*, an anthology of essays by various female survivors, and various newspaper and magazine articles written about her, both in the United States and Japan. The Toyoko Morita section is based on a series of interviews held with her at her apartment in

Hiroshima, and an essay published in *The Life of the Flower Is Very Short.* Corroborating and supplemental testimony was provided by the Reverend Tanimoto.

2

In addition to the sources cited for Chapter One, corroborating and supplemental testimony was provided by the Reverend Tanimoto, Atsuko Yamamoto, Michiko Yamaoka.

3

The author interviews that form the crux of the material contained in this chapter were held with the Reverend Kiyoshi Tanimoto, Norman Cousins, Dr. Arthur Barsky, the Reverend Marvin Green, John Hersey, Kiyoshi Togasaki, Aboul Foutouhi, Dr. Robert Miller, and Helen Yokoyama. The written source materials were: the Reverend Tanimoto's personal diary and letters to the Reverend Marvin Green, Norman Cousins, and the author; assorted documents collected in Norman Cousins's private papers; Norman Cousins's articles in the *Saturday Review* concerning the Reverend Tanimoto and the Hiroshima Maidens, and the chapter addressing the Maidens in his book *Present Tense;* records and newsletters of the Hiroshima Peace Center Associates; declassified State Department documents; and translated articles from the Hiroshima newspaper *Chugoku Shinbun.*

4

In addition to interviews with the previously mentioned principals (Cousins, Tanimoto, Barsky, Yokoyama, Green), the following individuals testified to the information contained in this chapter: Mr. Kiyokai Murata (a *Japan Times* reporter who accompanied the Maidens on their flight to America); Dr. Tomin Harada and Dr. Goro Ouchi; eighteen Hiroshima Maidens (Michiko Yamaoka, Michiko Sako, Yoshiko Yanagibashi, Takako Harada, Suzue Hiyama, Tadako Emori, Terue Kawamura, Tazuko Takeya, Emiko Takemoto, Michiyo Zomen, Hideko Sumimura, Masako Wada, Toyoko Morita, Atsuko Yamamoto, Hiroko Tasaka, Shigeko Niimoto, Misako Kannabe,

Notes

Sayoko Komatsu); Dr. Bernard Simon and Dr. Sidney Kahn; Mr. Glenn Everett (a Washington-based journalist working with the Hiroshima Peace Center Associates); Ida Day; Janet Freeman (head nurse on the female ward at Mount Sinai Hospital in 1955); and some of the Quaker families: Bishop, Barker, Robbins, Sharpless, Valentine. Contributing newspaper sources were: *New York Times, New York Herald Tribune, New York Post, New York World Telegram & Sun, Daily Worker, Japan Times, Chugoku Shinbun.* Magazines: *Time, US News & World Report, Saturday Review, Redbook, Collier's, Christian Herald, Look, Friends Journal.* Documents: State Department memorandums; minutes of HPCA executive committee meetings; reports from host families to Ida Day; assorted communications to Norman Cousins.

5

Virtually the same sources are used in this chapter as in the preceding, with the addition of interviews with Bill and Mary Kochiyama (Japanese-Americans living in New York who befriended the Maidens and visited them in the hospital) and Dr. Takahashi (wife of Dr. Sadam Takahashi, who passed away in the 1970s). Supplemental written material was provided through an unpublished essay, "The Hiroshima Maidens and American Benevolence in the 1950s," written by Michael Yavendetti, Professor of History, Alma College.

6 and 7

References in this chapter are also those for chapters 4 and 5, with the addition of *Reader's Digest* and its article about Lydia O'Leary.

8

The same sources are drawn on in this chapter as in the preceding three, with the addition of personal interviews with Harry Harris; Bernice and Susan Hall (close friends and neighbors of the Cousinses'); Dr. Pietr Hitzig (son of Dr. William Hitzig); Ms. Anne Keagy; and Donald Simonelli (a former classmate of Toyoko Morita's).

BIBLIOGRAPHY

Amrine, Michael. *The Great Decision.* New York: G.P. Putnam's Sons, 1959.

Baker, Paul, ed. *The Atomic Bomb.* New York: Holt, Rinehart and Winston, 1968.

Brinton, Howard. *The Pendle Hill Idea.* Wallingford, Pennsylvania: Pendle Hill Pamphlet 55, 1950.

Cousins, Norman. *Present Tense.* New York: McGraw-Hill, 1967.

Hachiya, Michiko. *Hiroshima Diary.* Translated by W. Wells. 1955. Reprinted. Chapel Hill: University of North Carolina Press, 1969.

Hane, Mikiso. *Peasants, Rebels & Outcastes: The Underside of Modern Japan.* New York: Pantheon Books, 1973.

Harada, Tomin. *Hiroshima Surgeon.* Translated by Alice and Robert Ramseyer. Reprinted. Newton, Kansas: Faith and Life Press, 1983.

Hersey, John. *Hiroshima.* New York: Bantam Books, 1948.

Hiroshima City. Hiroshima City Hall, 1971.

Ibuse, Masujii. *Black Rain.* Tokyo: Kodansha International, 1969.

Jungk, Robert. *Children of the Ashes.* New York: Harcourt, Brace and World, 1961.

Kawasaki, Soichiro. *A Call from Hibakusha of Hiroshima and Nagasaki.* Tokyo: Asahi Evening News, 1978.

Kosaki, Yoshitera, comp. *A-bomb: A City Tells Its Story.* Hiroshima Peace Culture Center, 1972.

Lebra, Joyce, Paulson, Joy, and Powers, Elizabeth, eds. *Women in Changing Japan.* Stanford, California: Stanford University Press, 1976.

Lifton, Robert. *Death in Life.* New York: Random House, 1967.

Livingston, Jon, ed. *Postwar Japan: 1945 to the Present.* New York: Pantheon Books, 1973.

The Meaning of Survival. Chugoku Shinbun, 1983.

Moore, Charles. *The Japanese Mind.* Honolulu: The University Press of Hawaii, 1967.

Naeve, Virginia, ed. *Friends of the Hibakusha.* Denver: Alan Swallow, 1964.

Oe, Kenzaburo. *Hiroshima Notes.* Tokyo: YMCA Press, 1981.

Okada, S., ed. *A Review of Thirty Years Study of Hiroshima and Nagasaki Atomic Bomb Survivors.* Chiba, Japan: The Japan Radiation Research Society, 1975.

Osata, Dr. Arata, comp. *Children of Hiroshima.* Cambridge, Mass.: Oelgeschlager, Gunn & Hain Inc., 1982.

Takayama, Hitoshi, ed. *Hiroshima in Memorium and Today.* Hiroshima Peace Culture Center, 1973.

Kojima, Jun. *Hana no inochi wa mijikakute* [The Life of the Flower Is Very Short]. Tokyo: Kyodo Shuppansha, 1953.

Yoshiteru, Kosakai. *Hiroshima Peace Reader.* Hiroshima Peace Culture Foundation, 1980.

Youth Division of Soka Gakkai, comp. *Cries for Peace.* Tokyo: The Japan Times, 1978.

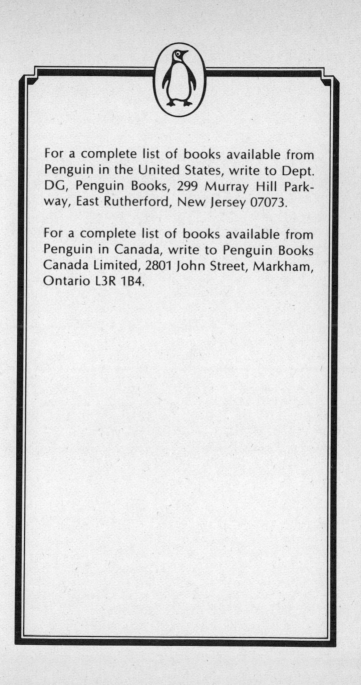

For a complete list of books available from Penguin in the United States, write to Dept. DG, Penguin Books, 299 Murray Hill Parkway, East Rutherford, New Jersey 07073.

For a complete list of books available from Penguin in Canada, write to Penguin Books Canada Limited, 2801 John Street, Markham, Ontario L3R 1B4.